D1273036

turn left at the black cow

turn left at the black cow

ONE FAMILY'S JOURNEY FROM BEVERLY HILLS TO IRELAND

richard mckenzie

foreword by betty white

ROBERTS RINEHART PUBLISHERS
BOULDER, COLORADO
DUBLIN, IRELAND

Published by Roberts Rinehart Publishers
6309 Monarch Park Place
Niwot, Colorado 80503

Distributed to the trade by Publishers Group West

Published in Ireland and the U.K. by
Roberts Rinehart Publishers
Trinity House, Charleston Road
Dublin 6, Ireland

Design: Ann W. Douden

Library of Congress Cataloging-in-Publication Data
McKenzie, Richard.
Turn left at the black cow : one family's journey from Beverly Hills to Ireland / by Richard McKenzie ; forward by Betty White.
p. cm.
Includes index.
ISBN 1-57098-205-8 (hardcover)
1. McKenzie, Richard. 2. McKenzie, Ava Astaire. 3. Astaire, Fred—Family. 4. Astaire family. 5. Actors—United States-Biography. I. Title.
PN2287.M546A3 1998
791.43'028'092—dc21
[B] 97-52321
CIP

10 9 8 7 6 5 4 3 2 1

Manufactured in the United States of America

FRONT COVER PHOTOGRAPHS: The McKenzie family in Ireland, 1970s; Fred Astaire and daughter Ava in Ireland, 1950s
BACK COVER PHOTOGRAPH: top, Fred Astaire, Ava Astaire McKenzie, and Gene Kelly, 1976; below, Fred Astaire in Ireland, 1970s
TITLE PAGE PHOTOGRAPH: The McKenzie family in Ireland, 1970s

ONE FAMILY'S JOURNEY FROM BEVERLY HILLS TO IRELAND

In memory of Mom
and F. A.

ONE FAMILY'S JOURNEY FROM BEVERLY HILLS TO IRELAND

Contents

ONE FAMILY'S JOURNEY FROM BEVERLY HILLS TO IRELAND

Foreword

The same universal bank of words is available to us all, to mix and match as we see fit. There are, however, individuals who manage to weave those same words together in a way that lends a slight glow to even the most mundane events. Of course, a generous lacing of humor does no harm. And, too, I am convinced that it helps to be Irish.

My late husband, Allen Ludden, and I shared some glorious times with the McKenzies. We met them a very few months, perhaps only weeks, before they moved to London en route to Ireland—exactly the time this book commences.

It began as a chance cocktail party conversation at the home of mutual friends; this led us out to dinner—lasting until dawn, which took us all by surprise. By that time we were back at the Ludden house because, having discovered that he and I were both Oz freaks, Richard had to see my complete collection of those wonderful books. That conversation has never stopped through the years despite lapses of time and geographical separation. Invariably, we pick up as though finishing an interrupted sentence—except that now our company has dwindled to three.

As you will discover in this delightful journal, Ava Astaire McKenzie is a unique piece of work. She is a talented and beautiful creature from some lovely friendly planet, not necessarily our own. And, despite the author's attempt to sound like the voice of reason surrounded by a sea of eccentricity, don't fall for it—the two of them are a matched set. All I know is I'm so glad I know them, and I continue to find their adventures great fun to follow.

So will you.

—*Betty White*

With Betty White in Carmel, California.

ONE FAMILY'S JOURNEY FROM BEVERLY HILLS TO IRELAND

Acknowledgments

My boundless gratitude to Pat Golbitz, an editor of talent and endurance who, through a series of serendipitous events, read my journal and scared the bejaysus out of me with her belief that there would be a greater audience than just my family for whom it was kept.

Pat waded through fifteen years' worth of a bewildered husband and father's observations. She browbeat, directed, culled, and chopped and sorted the chaff. She even broke the scribbling down into chapters like a real book.

Pat tells me I have written a love story. She is right about that part. I hope I've rewarded her faith about the rest. Fear and trembling not withstanding, when Ms. Golbitz handed me the toughest job I've ever had, it also came with a lot of fun and a brand new friend. Who can say fairer than that?

And to Frankie Ross and my daughter-in-law, Annie, who, between them, patiently transcribed the years of scribblings—my sincerest thanks.

With Ava in Ireland, 1997.

Introduction

Nobody Asked—But

I was proud to be the son-in-law of Fred Astaire. Prouder still to be his friend and it never mattered very much when his daughter and I opted for a different lifestyle away from Beverly Hills, that my own small place in the southern California sun would be lost in the shadows of Astaire's fame throughout the world. I was able to continue painting and earning a livelihood from work which I still sold where I was known, I'd had my fifteen minutes mini-fame and the ego wasn't bruised until after Fred's death when an Englishman, named Satchell, rushed out a pot-boiler entitled *Astaire, The Biography,* in which he paid a surprising amount of attention to the two of us and which, like most of his other "facts," was almost totally erroneous. According to him Ava was twenty-six when she met me, a Hemingway type with a fierce beard; a widower of one year trying to rebuild his life by running a small art gallery, hoping for commissions; and the first her dad heard of me was when Ava presented him with one of my paintings. After we married, my wife supposedly took me away from all that. "With money her father gave her," Ava moved us to Ireland so I "could paint full time."

I loved the imagery of the beard but I've seldom even had five o'clock shadow and have been un-Hemingway slender all my life. My gallery was large and popular—Lucy Ball was an investor—and I was not unknown about town. I'd always painted full time. My business partner ran the gallery part which represented artists from all over the world. The McKenzies moved abroad without Astaire financial assistance and we lived in London three years prior to Ireland.

Probably, I should simply ignore the man's writing for the fantasy it is, but anyway, my observations were originally recorded solely for the amusement and information of my family, the only ones who will care—and if some of it still reads like fiction, at least they'll know the accounts come from the horse's mouth—not a horse's ass quasi "biographer."

Ava and I met on a rainy afternoon in Beverly Hills when she was nineteen and working in Raymond Burr's beautiful art gallery on Rodeo Drive. I was thirty-three. Ray had just invited me to be one of his artists and Ava was standing near the window with a hand mirror and tweezers, plucking at her chin, when I walked in. She smiled as she held up the offending hair for me to see. She was blonde and plump and lovely and this was my first encounter with her disarming ingenuousness.

With Raymond Burr at his gallery in Beverly Hills, where I met Ava Astaire.

GLOBE PHOTO

At the time, I lived in what is now the city of West Hollywood on a street whose residents once might have been best described as "Bohemian." My apartment sat back on a wide lawn, the top half of a two-dwelling building. The actress Jane Dulo lived downstairs, and during an exceptionally wet winter when she was filming and couldn't get through the mud slides from her house at the beach to MGM, Martha Raye stayed with Jane. I hung a valentine on their door to cheer us all and never missed a year after that, even when Maggie (Martha) was in Vietnam.

I owe so many people for their kindness and faith and help. Oddly, my first supporters were comics (maybe not so odd): Jane, who all but lassoed friends to make them view my work and browbeat them into purchasing as she had; Dick Van Dyke, who brought me to the attention of Raymond Burr; and Maggie Raye, who allowed herself to be browbeaten and kept coming back for more.

With Martha Raye (Page Cavenaugh and Trio in background) at the opening of the McKenzie Gallery in Los Angeles in 1964.

My neighbors were Alan and Dorothy (Parker) Campbell and the playwright Hagar Wilde; Carleton Carpenter, who rented a place behind his house to Wyatt Cooper before he married Gloria Vanderbilt; Dorothy Dandridge, Ann B. Davis, Jon Dall, Tuesday Weld, Nina Foch and the wonderfully dotty Estelle Winwood—all made up the gaggle of performers living within shouting distance. We all called out our windows to each other, and the street was so narrow, little was truly private.

Given the group on that stretch of block alone, plus various other members of the movie community housed within the area, we at one point found ourselves included on the commercial sight-seeing bus tour. And there were sights worth seeing. Jane's

With Lucille Ball, who was a backer of the McKenzie Gallery.

friend Buster Keaton loved to garden and occasionally came over to give us advice and putter about the small garden we shared between us. Marilyn Monroe lived near and sometimes would drop by. Judy Garland fell asleep in the shrubbery across the street after singing at a friend's apartment all night long, and no matter how out of image it may be, I've seen Dorothy Parker, clad in sailcloth yachting togs, take my four-year-old son by the hand and lead him past Nina's large, friendly sheepdog that Kevin feared was a bear. Conversely, he didn't mind the South American kinkajou another neighbor carried on her shoulder when she went to the Laundromat, nor was he skittish about the big iguana lizard on a leash who took the air with his owner on a summer's afternoon.

I was not a widower. I was divorced, amiably. Marie and I simply married too soon. I hadn't known her true age, sixteen, until we became engaged and then proposed we wait for a couple of years until I was out of school and established. She would have none of it. We loved each other but I should have been just one of many romances. Instead, I was her adolescent fantasy got out of hand and neither of us could really overcome Germanic dominance and interference from her father. After the divorce our two boys, Kevin and Tyler, lived with their mother though I spent time with them on weekends and holidays and whenever else I could.

5

About half a year after we met, Ava and I sort of drifted together and began dating exclusively. I already knew Fred Astaire; he, not his daughter, bought a painting of mine before I joined Burr's gallery. We went together for two years; then one evening while I waited in Ava's private sitting room in the house Fred built for the two of them, their housekeeper came in to ask what "Miss Ava" required for wake-up fruit juice the next morning, and it suddenly became clear I was out of my element, involved with someone younger than my children's mother, and that Ava was a privileged part of a celebrated, wealthy family to whom I could offer little. Feeling out of my league, I began to back off. I needed time to accomplish. To prove. And so I did. But my girl married somebody else while I was doing it.

About a month after Carl and Ava married, I saw Fred in Beverly Hills crossing the street towards me. I waited. He didn't step on the pavement when he got there; he stood in the gutter looking up at me, asking what in hell happened between me and his daughter. I assured him it was just one of those things, and though I saw him after that and received his Christmas card, he never broached the subject again. He realized our age difference. He knew my financial instability. He also knew his daughter and I belonged together.

From time to time after she married Carl, Ava and I would see each other. As a rule, we didn't frequent the same gatherings but I would run into her at a premiere or opening night. Or at the supermarket. It was always painful. Sometimes Ava would pop in the studio, "Joy," the scent I always consider her personal property, preceding her. Those years I thought I was out enjoying the town and pleased for her wedded bliss, but I still kept her handkerchief. During their marriage Ava never gave me the least encouragement, any idea that we both might have made a mistake, but one night she came early to a gallery party. Carl was to meet her there. When we danced, we knew it was still on between us. Neither of us mentioned it. I was unaware she had already decided the marriage couldn't continue. And not because of me.

A few months later, my boys lost their mother. They came to live with me and changed my life overnight. I became cook, launderer, lunchbox packer, carpool driver. Most of all protector. Sorrowful though I was for their mother's tragic, early death, I loved having my children with me.

I had painted Shirley Jones' children, David, Shaun, and Patrick Cassidy, as well as Pat Carroll and her brood, and I am forever grateful to those two caring women for their help and inclusion of my boys until I could get us settled into our own family routine.

Ava and Carl remained together and my sons and I went our own way until Ava finally took an apartment with no hope of resuming her marriage. It was the summer I sent the boys to visit their grandparents in Baden-Baden so I might use the time to prepare for a necessary one-man show. And that was that. Ava instigated divorce proceedings. Carl didn't want the split but he understood the need, posed no objections.

It had taken most of their marriage for Fred to actually accept Carl in that position; Ava felt guilty at having put her dad through her divorce and she worried about telling him she planned to marry again so soon. They dined together the night she decided to drop the bombshell, while I waited at home to hear how he took the news. Ava fidgeted, she told me, unable to eat, until she finally decided to just spill it out, but before she could Fred quietly said, "You are going to marry Dick, aren't you," as if it were a statement, not a question.

While the boys were still in Germany, I took a two-level apartment in Beverly Hills, the school at one end of the block, Los Angeles at the other. A hundred kids lived on that short street. Before Kevin and Tyler returned from their grandparents, I both telephoned and wrote them explaining that Ava and I were seeing each other and possibly would marry, but that we would do nothing without discussing it in person with them first. Although their grandmother pressed for an extended stay, they wanted to come home. They were eight and eleven years old. They said they were homesick for us.

Ava professes she is not good with children, but because of her, over a hundred of them crossed my threshold in one day. My fiancée, it turned out, had ordered seahorses from a mail order company in Florida. Enceinte seahorses. One anyway—the male. I expect that is what piqued the lady's interest in the first place. A week before the creatures arrived, the company sent a saline solution to be waiting in preparation, measurement instructions included. Ava misread them. The seahorses hadn't a hope, but they gave valiant effort. Under scrutiny of two hundred-plus wide eyes, the little stallion did indeed undulate in labor during the course of the day. A minute offspring, delivered late afternoon, ended the performance and the tiny family of three packed it all in before dinner—floating to the top of the water container. Victims of a wrong recipe, and causing more concern in the perpetrator than the children for whom the gift was intended.

When we left the street to take up residence in a family house, Ava was included in the sweet send-off from the kids of the block. They brought us a big sign reading, "Goodbye Kevin, Tyler, Ava. And Mr. McKenzie." I like to regard that as special billing.

We were married less than a year later, having applied for the marriage license within an hour after the decree was granted. Fred wouldn't miss our wedding, but he was on the blue ribbon panel of judges for the Emmies that Sunday and was so conscientious he drove like a bat to get there and back to his duties.

Before a gathering of twenty friends and F. A., Episcopalian Ava and I, lapsed Catholic, were married in the home of a minister's daughter and a writer of horror stories, by a Jewish judge during Lent. Twelve-year-old Kevin was my best man, and her boss, Paul Hauge, stood up with Ava. Portending the long chuckle it has been ever since, our married life began on the right foot when Ava put the ring on the wrong hand. Slapping away the proffered left hand, she placed the ring on my right one and laughed so vigorously at my astonishment we had to start over. Later in the car when I demanded an explanation, she realized the confusion had been on her part and was not due to her husband's inability to distinguish left from right. My new bride said she'd been so sure I would make that mistake, she took it for fact.

Fred thought Ava and I knew the world and he often expressed a desire to meet someone, asking us to arrange a dinner party at our house. Even if we didn't know them well (or at all), most people would jump at the chance to spend a quiet evening with Astaire. That, of course, never occurred to him. Finally one day he told us he had declined an invitation on our behalf because we knew too many people already.

Because of her rarefied childhood, Ava was never exposed to the normal kid's diseases. Before Kevin and Tyler were through their bouts of chicken pox in her second season of stepmotherhood though, Ava came down with so violent an attack we thought she would never be the same again. And she wasn't. Somehow it altered her metabolism. She went from a size twelve to an eight, gradually but steadily over a period of a few months and has remained there without dieting ever since. She in fact eats more that she used to (which was never very much). Her figure now matches that knock-out face.

In spite of all the fun, the feeling of complete family, we began to feel restless. Our life as a pair has been blissful from day one, but our spring honeymoon in Canada, and a trip to England and visiting Ava's Aunt Adele at Lismore Castle in Ireland the following summer, awakened a discontent with the hometown and its ways that had been fitfully sleeping in Ava's psyche for years. The return to Europe stirred dormant longings in me, too. A year later the lease on our house came due for renewal. We didn't pick it up. One beautiful California evening at the end of May, we changed our lives completely.

We moved away.

Chapter One

Settling In

We ran out of petrol fifteen miles southwest of the airport. Who thinks to check the gauge on a just hired car? We must keep in mind this is Ireland, casual about such things. Ava thought that a lady in distress would gather sympathy more easily than a grouch who should have had sense enough to read his fuel level, and she prepared to hitchhike to the nearest station while I remained to guard the car, the cats, the cases, and the kid. But almost immediately a teenaged boy offered a lift and a gentleman with his five offspring in tow backtracked two miles out of his way to return my wife along with the fuel.

Ava drove us to our new home. I am uncertain of left and right under any condition and it would be suicidal to reverse thirty years' ingrained reflexes to a chauvinistic need to take the wheel. I shall master the machine at a later date, when no one is looking.

We've been in the cottage less than twelve hours; it is Tyler's initial visit to Ireland and at the moment he is visible only because we know he is one of the two dark specks above that yellow bit bobbing in the harbor where he and a boy he just met have gone to drop lobster pots. When we watched them put out, the yellow boat seemed durable enough, but I have second thoughts as I see it on the horizon. They probably aren't very far away. We can hear the motor and I imagine this light distorts perspective. Ava reminds me a much younger Ty fished from a boat off an island in Sweden, so I guess I'm not to worry.

Ava and I are about to investigate our headland on this amazing day. I can't reconcile the time: ten-thirty p.m. is hardly considered day, but we can't think of this as evening. Ireland nearly parallels the Nordic countries, which would account for the brightness at this hour, but I also believe the quality of light is uniquely Irish. Reflected in the water, it belies description. In its stillness the cool, silver glow is strangely more akin to a frozen winter lake than the Atlantic Ocean on a mild Irish midsummer evening.

Kevin plods across Iron Curtain countries in quest of the Istanbul Hilton; his brother pursues crustacea beneath the late Irish sun. I must turn to other thoughts.

~ ~ ~

Ty corrected my terminology. He and his new friend were "shooting" lobster pots, not dropping them, for gosh sakes. Although both Ava and Tyler assured me that the language is English, I haven't understood a word since we landed in West Cork.

It was a long, difficult day because furniture had to be exchanged from the original mover's van to a smaller vehicle in order to negotiate the narrow lane to our house. I did learn one new word used by the tall men sweating sofas through the low front door. *Boreen*. In Irish it is somewhat less than a road, yet more than a path. Our place sits between a boreen and whatever that little walkway towards the sea at the end of the house might be called.

Ava quickly learned the best-used shops and byroads. Though the local wine merchant, she tells me, does not have chilled wine, one can get it and just about anything else at the post office. The post office in a neighboring village five miles away stocks more unusual cheeses and delicatessen than does ours, but not the Costa Rican coffee beans offered at the post office fifteen miles in the other direction. Rural American small towns still combine postal services with general store supplies, I suppose, but it's a delightful new experience for us in our own village where often the weight of letters or parcels is judged on a butcher's scale. We have no pharmacist, but Band-Aids are readily achieved at the hardware shop. Living here, one comes to realize how much English, as it is spoken in America, germinated in Ireland. In London, we grew accustomed to saying "ironmonger" and "torch." Here, they are "hardware" and "flashlight" again, but a cooker—not a stove—is still what you cook on. A stove is something that heats the room.

Nigel-Wynn and Phyllis-Doris, our two black cats, weathered the long flight from Los Angeles without incident. They endured the six months' quarantine incarceration and the added frustration of confinement to a flat in London for three years, and they rose above the silly names Ava gave them from a Welsh television series. Following the vet's suggestion, they have been briefly allowed outside on leashes all week before they have their breakfast in the house, and this morning, after suffering the final indignity of having their paws buttered, they were let out unrestrained. Under the delusion that the cats wouldn't move until they cleaned their feet and therefore familiarized themselves to their surroundings while gazing about during the process, we learned that a terrace can be covered with greasy paw prints in scant seconds, while blotting up the damage can occupy the better part of a morning. N.-W. and P.-D. sleep soundly inside again, eager to stay close after they bolted through a fuchsia hedge and found a field of cows behind it. Serves them right. We might never get the slates clean.

For years she has purchased fish from the used furniture dealer, declared Aunt Dellie, who found nothing unusual regarding our eclectic post office service. I must tell Adele about the supermarket we discovered that features a cheery range of party crepe papers for sale at the meat counter and that the dairy, which also sells cement and petrol, displays a roadside warning, DANGER—

CREAMERY!

All phone calls go through the post office where the telephone switchboard is situated. It cannot be easy for the operator with people searching around her for razor blades, film or such, and with the hand-crank phones ringing for her attention, but I have never known her to be less than sweet-tempered. One day, I expect, upon completing a call, her soft reminder that I not forget to crank-off will seem ordinary and unnecessary. Now it makes my eyes blink. After we accepted that private phone conversation simply does not exist in rural Ireland, we came to appreciate its fine service. Often, if the person one is calling happens to be out, one is informed where said person has gone, why, and an estimated hour of return, or if there is a telephone at the callee's whereabouts, the operator may well ring through on general principle.

For us, especially now, the system is a blessing. Kevin should be headed in this direction, yet we can go out for the day or overnight to visit Adele at Lismore, confident of receiving the message if he calls. Even collect, which is redundant.

Actually, we have heard from him once already, a panic plea for cash (also redundant) after a Turkish bus driver abandoned all passengers at a rest stop in Austria and returned to the safety of his own borders with paid-in-advance fares as well as the belongings of some people who, unlike Kevin, were not carrying their possessions strapped on their backs. K. thumbed to Holland, which was his destination, and where we wired the money. I think we sent enough to see him in Ireland.

I hoped he saved enough.

Ava and Tyler already seem to have met most of the local citizenry, but only a moment ago did it become clear that few recognize me on sight, including the postman who delivers to our very door. As his squat orange van pulled up to the stone wall enclosing our front yard, I went down to save him the bother of getting out.

"Ye aren't Mr. McKenzie?"

I nodded.

"Then who is the gent with the beard?"

Wife and child plead innocent, but the neighbor who has been helping Ava pull this place together informs us that a fellow who visited the Ellisons last year had a mustache. . . . We'll let it go with that.

~ ~ ~

Some months before moving across the sea to Ireland, Ava and I came over to finalize details and seek advice. Seven years back the Ellisons arrived here, untried city folk themselves. We hoped for a hint or two and I prepared an itemized list regarding power failures, where to batten out the weather, how to test the well and such, but Ava first asked Diana Ellison how she washed her hair.

And her second question pertained to Violet, framed by the window—an old mare wearing her mane like a shawl against the wind. That led to a third question: who to ring if Violet needed medical attention. Diana said that due to her health and thirty-three years, Violet wasn't capable of returning to England with the family. She would be put down. "Violet will continue to live here with us," Ava said, almost whispering as if trying to convince herself. Then my ordinarily stair-wary wife careered downstairs and all but vaulted the pasture gate to weep upon the neck of a startled, frail, little black horse.

Sure of her audience, Violet now canters across the high meadow in front of our house. Although the lady spends each night avoiding her stable in the lower field docilely enough, daytime, no matter how wild the weather, she demands this upper portion of land with its exposure to the sea. She, I'm convinced, is as conscious of her effect on any and all watching from the sitting room windows as she is unaware of her years.

Haughty as a filly, she can be downright bitchy towards Ava, sometimes runs away or stands defiant if Tyler attempts bringing her to stable earlier than she deems reasonable, while I, knowing nothing of horses, am allowed to lead her by a token tug of forelock and usually get nuzzled for the effort. But I have an uncomfortable conviction that Violet considers me as more her contemporary.

~ ∽ ~

Our first reaction upon approaching this house was what a pity it had been built with only the top half appearing above meadowland leading to the sea. Protection gained by nestling the building in this fashion was obvious. But we were delighted to discover that what once was grain loft-storage, with its ruggedly beautiful panorama, had been designed by John and Diana into their main living quarters—one large L-shaped living room, a bedroom and bath.

Clonlea, on the southwest coast of Ireland, in 1975.

PHOTO: DICK DE NEUT

We need only open a window to smell the ocean, glance out a window to see it, walk a short distance to feel it, but the protective, varying ground levels mute sounds to such a degree we don't hear it. A disappointment. Through the growing years I was often lulled to sleep by that music, and had visions of doing so again. Mistakenly, I remarked upon this curious condition to my wife who, too patiently, explained that my remembered sounds were caused by surging waters. We are situated within a cove, a natural breakwater, with scarcely any waves at all.

Snotty kid.

Having had to make do with a swimming pool, her own miniature roller coaster, two horses and a pony, Ava understandably reacts with envy towards my childhood of surf, sand, and sunburn. I can forgive her that. But not the roller coaster.

I didn't even have a swing.

On occasion breakers do explode over Dick's Island, the largest of the scattered small islands between our headland and the peninsula village across the bay. The story goes that the family of cantankerous Richard O'Mahoney built a shelter on the island, provided him with a goat, and abandoned the two of them there where they eventually ended their days. Presumably, they were not left to starve and were checked out from time to time. We haven't a clue what the old coot could have done to warrant exile, but believe it was most likely accumulated orneriness, of which his folk had had enough.

Nothing remains but the name (naturally pleasing), and I choose not to investigate further for fear of a more mundane explanation. I've been told I can be put in touch with the owner, should I be interested in purchasing the property but I doubt it would be a wise acquisition. Since they tell me I grow more surly by the hour, my own family might entertain similar notions and they need not alter the name.

Although we'd been assured by Diana Ellison that we could turn to our neighbors for any assistance and that she would ask them to keep an eye on us, too, we still didn't quite know how to instigate a meeting with them. No one is exactly in the next-door category so we were certain there wouldn't be a welcome wagon or a neighbor offering a seven-bean salad over the backyard patio hedge. Almost though. This morning we found a large bag of potatoes leaning against the front door, and this evening our benefactor came knocking on it: Timothy O'Regan. There is a face to paint.

Tim declined an invitation to come in, but we talked for quite a while outside, leaning on the stone fence he built for the Ellisons. Since my ear hasn't yet sorted out the West Cork patois, we didn't exactly have a conversation, but surprisingly more than I thought filtered through, and I'm sure Mr. O'Regan worked pretty hard on my mid-Atlantic Californianese as well. And we didn't lean on the wall for long or stay in one spot either because Tim's conversational stance is somewhat choreographed. You have to join the dance or lose the thread. We began by talking across the wall, facing each other dead-on until he lit a cigarette and continued speaking, standing sideways with his chin cupped in his hand. Then without missing a verbal beat he abruptly reversed away from me and braced his back and elbows against the wall. I expect on about the count of three he adjusted his cap and turned to the other side. Rather than wait for the full circle, I thought it best just to join Tim on the boreen, where for a few bars we stood side by side and contemplated Violet looking down at us from the upper field. Conversation picked up, providing music for the next step, a stiff, fully upward position, facing each other

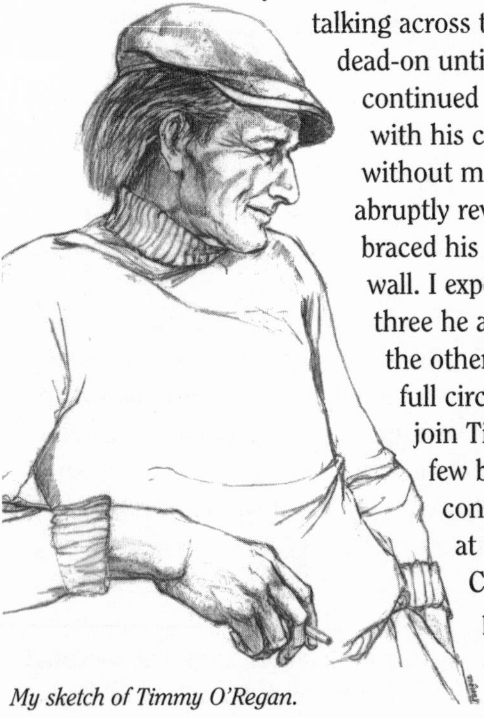

My sketch of Timmy O'Regan.

again, but with averted profiles rather like a tango. A knee bends, an ankle is crossed, and we return to the slow pirouette before sliding down into sort of a half crouch against the stones once more.

Shortly after meeting our neighbor, Ava sensed that Tim was uneasy around a female stranger and she left us alone to become better acquainted; but no one is ever uneasy around Ava for very long and I know that soon enough they'll be having a *scraiocht* of their own. Tim gave me that word after I'd impressed him by saying boreen. I think it means having a good chat. Maybe it means his dance. Anyway I advised Ava to observe him closely when they actually are on more familiar grounds. If she wants to gain information about planting vegetables from the seasoned Mr. O'Regan, she had better learn the Timmy Waltz.

In an odd way, Tim is handsome. I couldn't put an age to him. His is a much used face from hard work in hard weather. Drink, too, I suppose. But he is not overly wrinkled. His hands are huge, his eyes clear and blue, smiling in that Irish crafty way, and he has the sort of long crooked nose that so often accompanies such a lean, high-cheek-boned face. I could only see a few teeth, and since he never removed his cap, I don't know if the sandy hair touching his turtleneck in the back was as full on top or not. We like him a lot. And given our ignorance in country matters, I'm certain we'll soon be indebted to Tim and all the other O'Regans whom we're most anxious to meet.

Fresh milk, illegally purchased from a dear old lady who lives over the hill, is fetched home in gin bottles because we must have containers by which to determine the true measure. I enjoy these treks to the farm; filling my lungs with pure air and chatting in the kitchen while the personification of everybody's dream grandmother ladles up the milk. Completely undoing any benefits the uphill walk has on my waistline, fresh-baked soda bread or free-range eggs are often found resting, still warm, in the basket next to the milk.

My canny old girlfriend only recently advised me how to deal with the problems of cleansing empty bottles. A diced raw potato, shaken vigorously with water, removes residue from bottles like magic, she says. It does, too.

Regarding magic, she also whispered that though the fairies caused the Ellisons some rough going, she feels they are pleased with us. Curiously, according to friends and neighbors, John and Diana did encounter more than a normal spate of misfortune during their seven years at Clonlea, and Timmy says their troubles began soon after Diana had entered a fairy ring, in this case shrubbery growing unplanned in a large circle on a friend's property some distance from here. Some fairy rings are formed of stone, or even of mushrooms, but they always mysteriously appear in circles and, under the circumstances, we're pleased there aren't any nearby. Diana announced in her trained actress voice that the ring would be an ideal place to graze Violet and shortly thereafter, before the Ellisons began having little "accidents" of their own, an unexplained fire blackened the field everywhere except for the fairy ring, which it completely skirted.

This is Ireland. We consider every possibility. Please God, should we accidentally tread upon tiny toes, let them belong to the cats.

~ ~ ~

Locally termed a "borehole," our well descends seventy feet: impressive, we thought, when Diana informed us of the depth, but neither of us is capable of judging dimensions without physically pacing off. So what did we know?

In retrospect, when Diana laughed that she bathed in the same water as John, and bailed even that out to water the garden in summertime, I suppose we should have caught a glimmer of doubt instead of chalking up yet another instance to British oddity. Saturday night, when the taps refused a trickle, we realized Diana's information had come by way of warning.

The water supply is insufficient, and if we buy this house, another deeper well must be a major consideration. From that midsummer night on the point we felt we were home, but we couldn't guess that our first real problem living by the ocean in misty Ireland would be a shortage of water.

Nor, could we conjure a plumber who would drive ten miles on a Sunday morning to the rescue of strangers—foreign strangers—and dismiss any talk of remuneration with, "Ach . . . there'll be time for that later."

Such is the amazing Christy. We shall have much need of this gentleman in the future and although I haven't a hint what he charges, just knowing someone out there cares is worth every penny. He also owns a pub.

~ ~ ~

The electric water pump lives in the tack room, a sort of catchall behind the kitchen. We can hear it running from any room in the house—upstairs included. It isn't all that noisy. My always good hearing seems to have sharpened since we came to Ireland and Ava is convinced that now I can hear the cats purring from any room, too. But the outside walls are as thick as the inner partitions are thin. Country families require shelter from the storm, not from each other, and I probably should take no notice of N.-W. padding the stairs if he didn't shake the living room floor so.

At this stage, the only sound I find unsettling is the not unpleasant humming of the pump, which evokes varying degrees of panic depending upon the length of time it hums. Day and night my ears are geared to that damned murmuring machine. Especially the nights. Ideally, the motor switches on, works until the water drawn is replaced in the tank, and shuts off. If, within a short period, it doesn't stop automatically, the level is too low, or the pump is searching for nonexistent water, it must be turned off manually before it burns out and costs the earth to replace (in the event parts for such mature models are available anymore).

The fairies may like us, but somewhere lurks a gnome who starts the pump in dead of night while I rigidly count the minutes until silence resumes and slumber does not. Actually, our well is a pretty thing. Encircled by stones and situated near the garden, it rather invites wishing. Tossing of coins. I must suggest that to guests.

~ ~ ~

Gene and Helen Rayburn are visiting. I am uncertain what prompted the need, but Gene was instructing us in basic Serbo-Croatian during dinner last night when he was interrupted in that language by the only other patrons in the restaurant—Americans who had come because they found a matchbook cover advertising the place in a Chicago bar. Will their friends believe they really met an American television celebrity in a remote Irish village and conversed in the Slavic tongue? We didn't mention that Fred Astaire is expected next week, or if they continue a bit further towards Killarney, there is the possibility of encountering Maureen O'Hara at the supermarket.

Sometime during his stay with Adele at Lismore, Fred will come down to visit us. Fred is curious to see our place and we're eager to have him. I doubt he believes we're as rustic as we've said.

~ ~ ~

He believes now. When Dellie's driver, Con Willoughby, maneuvered the big wide car around the lowest part of the boreen by the jetty this afternoon, there was a rough high tide and water and spray splashed against the tires.

Fred thinks that anyone who drives a road so precariously near the sea is insane. Though he understands why we love it here, he feels we are ill-met for the lifestyle, that Beverly Hills and London are hardly prep-centers for handling hoe and hammer. We haven't mentioned the well yet. Thank God it stayed wet while he was here.

Although Adele's Mercedes stood in front of the house, we were able to smuggle F. A. down with no leak to the newspaper people, or even the villagers. The locals are too considerate and probably too disinterested to bother us, but we did have one brief

Ireland, 1975. With Ava, Tyler, and Fred.

turn when, as we walked the lane, we were approached by a fellow heavy with photographic equipment. Ava, Ty, and I encircled Fred, who looked as baffled by the sudden formation as did the German sightseer on his way to photograph the old tower. Obviously not recognizing F. A., he must have thought we were performing a quaint Irish ritual. Fred didn't comment beyond an elegantly arched eyebrow.

~ ~ ~

Last night when we found Violet down, we somehow knew this time the old girl wasn't just resting. Coaxing her to her feet by the accustomed grasp of forelock, at the same time lifting with my other arm under her chest, I realized how very frail she had become, and we slowly managed her back to her stable in the lower pasture while Ava attempted to locate the vet. Not an easy matter as he isn't local. He couldn't get here before this morning when, although listless, Violet seemed much improved. Certainly stronger. No less determined, she had refused shelter in the stable all night—at least she was outside whenever I got up to check. But the air was warm.

As he attended her often before, the vet knew it was too chancy to swing his van around the narrow twist of road closest to the water, so I led our little mare down to the main road where he waited to meet us. Rather, she led me. Feeling the halter again apparently stirred adrenaline. She came close to frisking, tugging a bit, nibbling clover along the way; but once there, after she had been examined and he let us listen to her barely discernible heartbeat, we realized her energy was gone and because he felt positive she would soon be in pain, we all decided that the years were enough.

Fred (holding Phyllis-Doris) and Ava at Clonlea, 1975.

Children passing with an assortment of pets asked if we were taking her into the village for the animal show. Today, of all days. And Violet must have thought so, too. As if eager to be away to the heat of competition, she trotted up the ramp into the van without hesitation. Quick, painless, thank God—silent, the hypodermic injection was administered almost immediately.

Violet was gone before we were a few steps home, but her presence shall be felt at Clonlea for a very long time.

~ ~ ~

In order to combat overgrowth of grass and weeds and so their emptiness won't remind us of Violet, we've asked Timmy if he would mind keeping a few cows in our meadows. Cementing our offer forever and to our delight, we learned that in Irish the name, "Clonlea" means "meadow of the calves." Happily Tim installed three calves last week. Happily. Perhaps not wisely.

Ava dubbed them "Rachel, Wanda, and Darleen," feeds them our spinach and is, I feel, becoming overly fond despite admonitions they shall evolve into lurching cows, not lap dogs. Neither she nor Darleen believe it.

Stunted little Rachel won't ever produce much milk, which guarantees a trek to vealtown before long, and Wanda, dim as Phyllis-Doris, sort of ambles with the crowd. I must admit Darleen's affection is endearing. One can't resist scratching those fuzzy ears upon request, but they won't always be such little fuzzy ears, her nudging will cease to amuse once it bruises, and I don't think she should be encouraged. Nor should the wind be encouraged to howl.

~ ~ ~

Among the three or four little markets scattered throughout the village, only one acts as a newsagent, the first place Dick De Neut headed when we stopped to lay in foodstuffs on our way home from collecting him at Cork airport.

After we mentioned that we rarely listen to the radio, have not yet felt the need of television, subscribe to neither magazines nor daily papers and still find the days whipping by, Dick bought all the newspapers in sight.

By the time we reached our turning, fog and the start of night obliterated our location so completely De Neut expressed fears we were entering Brigadoon and refused to accept the piercing clarity of the following morning or that the ocean had been there right along.

The day of incomparable light closed with a ruby, cloud-spotted sunset so vibrant that Dick, who owns the Globe Photo Agency, galloped out to photograph it, stopping only to thank a startled Kitty O'Regan for the beautiful evening. Kitty told Ava she met our visitor and he thanked her for the *sunset*?

Having spent fifty-odd years under these skies, Mrs. O'Regan could not be expected to comprehend Dick's fervor, which is not to imply that the Irish are unaware of the beauty of their land. They are. Very much so. They just don't understand why people are surprised.

~ ~ ~

Dick's moment of truth arrived the evening before he was meant to return to London, when he sighed that he wished he hadn't arranged theater tickets before he came to visit us. Ava changed his flight to a later date before asking exactly how important the plays were to him, then phoned mutual friend Shirley Nightingale in London to advise her of a couple of theater dates on her social calendar, and Dick De Neut didn't sigh any more.

~ ~ ~

Take Notice
Visitors pay at farmhouse
Admission 15p – 10p
CAUTION
anybody that don't go by this keep out

Because I was reversing from the cliffs where—without warning—the road skidded to a halt, I hadn't seen the sign, but Dick and Ava scrambled out of the car before we reached a safe parking level.

Ubiquitous stone fences created their usual patchwork around a small cottage on the hill. Nothing more. Yet, here was this warning posted above a stile in the wall next to the crazy, dangerous road. Having no notion where we were, but intending to "go by this" with our forty-five pence up front, we climbed the stile to find out.

The young farmer is a fool. With eyes light green as the sea, jet black hair, and muscles proportionally giving lie to the wasp waist to which he was stripped, the man could make his fortune simply by posing in his doorway.

I handed over our collective change as my wife rifled her bag for something more befitting a god. I led her away lest she forget our intended adventure and wished to linger, but I need not have held so firmly. The young stud don't go by unnecessary chit-chat either. Promising we would find "it" there, sweeping northerly with one hand and pocketing his cash with the other, he loped across the field.

At an altitude so high gulls circled below us, secreted far from the farmhouse, we discovered the real Twilight Zone. In a marshland plateau bordered on two sides by the Atlantic, a lake reflects the remains of a Norman dwelling—three towers decaying on its banks. Trapped, inverted on the blue surface for centuries, the towers seemed to be survivors from an even older but ageless mythical time. Light, sound and time were slightly out of sync, and conversation would have been an intrusion.

I wondered if we could find our way back to the road.

"Easy," Ava brightened. "We turned left at the black cow."

Dick flew home, leaving the newspapers he purchased on his first day in Ireland unopened.

He urged us to come away with him—before it's too late.

Ava and Darleen at Clonlea, 1975.

PHOTO: DICK DE NEUT

My painting of Kevin and Tyler in the upper field at Clonlea.

Chapter Two

Kevin and Tyler

With Kevin (left) and Tyler in California, 1963.

PHOTO: JAY THOMPSON

Kevin and I retain a strong emotional and mental link, an ESP that cost me my night's sleep. Still unable to settle after breakfast, I declined an excursion with Ava and Ty because, as I told them, I know Kevin is either in trouble or in Ireland.

Born two days before Halloween, the Scorpio son is the

complex one, the one of keen, ready wit housing an often sorrowful spirit I've struggled to reach from the beginning. There is something special about him.

Displaying astuteness beyond his years when he was a little guy concerned about our friend's sister who seemed to never quite belong anywhere, Kevin, one night at a party, stunned us all by asking, "Daddy, why is the lady on the edge of the crowd?" School is out. Now Kevin stands on an edge himself. The real world waits on the other side and I don't have an answer to assure him any more now than I did then.

Maybe this summer's experience will have paved his path a little. I've a feeling we'll soon be enlightened: Kevin isn't very far away. Anticipating my boy's homecoming on this lovely soundless morning, introspection produces a rather bittersweet memory of a portrait I did when he was barely three years old. Sold at a lean time, how I wish I'd kept the painting which, of course, eventually should have gone to Kevin. Though long since out of touch with the purchaser, things have a way of righting themselves and I hold the thought that one day I can buy it back.

I've forgotten when he acquired the silly thing, but Kevin was devoted, then, to a Shriner-type red fez which during waking hours never left his little head, and I painted him wearing the hat and gripping the other indispensable—his security blanket, a particularly weathered diaper he used solely to rub just below the tip of his nose.

We couldn't know it at the time, but the portrait summed up his paradoxical character: shying from attention; crying for it. During the costume party years of the sixties when too many Beverly Hills fathers dressed like Art Deco movie-palace ushers, Kevin's class picture showed him to be the only eleven-year-old togged in Nehru jacket and love beads, yet uncertainty held him back from trying out for the school theatrics that so attracted his more conservative kid brother.

Always enterprising, he canvased the neighborhood for odd jobs and for a while operated a thriving backyard bazaar, selling his own artistically tie-dyed projects. Ava whipped up a caftan for herself from one distinctive blue and white sheet, engendering praise from a noted designer, but when she told Kevin that the compliment was most assuredly due to his talents, and not her abilities as a seamstress, he still needed convincing. Even as a toddler, despite encouragement, if Kevin couldn't master something on the first attempt, he often refused to do it at all, and although I never demanded top grades, asked only that he try his best, I felt he thought his best not good enough and wouldn't make the effort for fear of failure.

Perhaps it's because my work appeared to be so easy and enjoyable. How can you really convey the contrary? Quietly watching me paint, one day Kev asked how I knew where to make a line to get a certain effect and seemed disinterested at the explanation, but years later I learned how much he actually absorbed when I overheard him discussing it with Tyler and saying that he thought art must be very difficult.

With Kevin (top) and Tyler in Ireland, 1980.

PHOTO: BOB WILLOUGHBY

During his first year at the American School of London, we realized that my stubbornly resistant, easily led son had selected as friends loutish kids who we feared might involve him with drugs, and thereafter, except for weekends, Kevin continued his studies away from home under the auspices of two no-nonsense Scots women who ran a boarding school in Suffolk far from the madding lure of some of London's more questionable charms.

Trying harder, apparently popular, Kevin continued to be enigmatic. One of his teachers, the dorm master, and hardly more than a kid himself, told us they regarded Kevin as one of the school's brightest; a leader who spoke with intelligence and knowledge as long as it was casual conversation. In a classroom situation he seemed to retreat behind some private door. But he did make the student council. And he graduated. And I wept.

Although Ava's tears were a certainty, I didn't count on them from myself. That with the fullness of time we had got through it after all; that Kevin was about to be his own man and a good one; the relief of seeing him finish school—could only bring smiles, I thought. Who would have foreseen glorious weather and an outdoor ceremony with roosters crowing during the valedictory? I forgot my heart always leaps to my throat with the opening bars of "Pomp and Circumstance." I didn't expect my little boy to be at once so tall in cap and gown, so poised or as beaming or as full of grace as he came around the old manor house with fifteen other shining young people to take his place on the front lawn.

Nor did I expect him to have a great gash on the left side of his nose and a black eye. It seems he stepped in front of a tennis racket undergoing a last-minute workout before being packed away. Fortunately, photographs were taken previously; they invited me to design his school's yearbook cover and I expect a picture inside of my son's battered face might have tainted the honor somewhat. His bruises were barely visible when he set off for Istanbul, invited to the wedding of his roommate's sister. At seventeen we felt he deserved this excursion. Soon enough he must face the stark streets of Grownup City.

In hope that knowledge gained might offset, a little, the unalterable fact he will never attend university, we always encouraged and arranged as much travel experience for Kevin as possible—in the main, school-organized and overseen tours. But once he worked on a Majorcan pig farm and—being Kevin—soon afterward found his way to a nudist beach somewhere near Barcelona, and he spent the following New Year's Eve in The Hague, a guest of the family whose daughter he helped out that summer. We thought it best not to press for further information regarding his swimming arrangements or a clearer definition of "helping out."

Pleading that he didn't want to be stuck with a bunch of nerds, at first Kevin declined our offer to send him on a European tour sponsored by his old school. "Chances are you'll know some of the kids already," I cosseted. "Chances are I can't stand them," he countered. But when we learned most were girls on summer vacation from the States, he decided it would be an invaluable experience, thanked us for providing such an opportunity to stretch his wings, and couldn't wait to hit the Continent.

I rather soft-pedaled paternal hope he wouldn't abuse the privilege; suggesting it truly could be educational beyond his inference, I made only one strong request: in Florence, he should see David. Kevin had the grace not to ask, David who?

As it turned out, I needn't have concerned myself. After that vacation, for a while anyway, the boy seemed another person. When he came home, Ava and I stared in such disbelief he asked what was wrong. We stared because everything was so right. He was physically different. Glowing.

In observing the behavior of his companions, Kevin did a little self-assessment, and with permission from his supervisor, left the kids to waste time in cafés while he went sightseeing with some young Scandinavians from one of the campsites. Because his new friends wanted to, he visited museums, landmarks, and spoke of the beauty of Venice and the Alps with more enthusiasm than we'd seen before. And he treasures a tooth removed from the skull of a two-thousand-year-old centurion encountered in the catacombs. That alone was staggering, and probably illegal, since he became confused in the catacombs and came out behind a blocked-off section he'd seen earlier. He wasn't alone but there were just two Norwegian lads for company besides the late centurions, and most of Kevin's life has been plagued with fears of one kind or another, especially the supernatural.

All his problems weren't resolved; a few new ones flicker now and again, but Kevin developed courage instead of bravado and a certain physical ease; the old fidgets and tensions—not quite ceased altogether—lessened to such a degree that about a week after his brother returned that year, Tyler approached me confidentially and whispered, "Is Kevin fixed now?"

I think so. I can't say about "now," but after my son's summer of Turkish Delight, I'm anxious to find out.

All day I waited for the bloody phone to ring, climbing the walls until Ava and Ty returned so I could go for a walk knowing someone was there to answer the call when it came. They were home at five, Tyler went fishing, and I hadn't reached the main road before Ava pulled up behind me on her way into the village to collect Kevin. He had been in town all afternoon, hesitant to telephone because he arrived broke and in the company of a German lad, to whom he promised food and lodging without first ascertaining whether it would be all right with us.

True to custom, Kevin spent every cent except the exact fare for the boat trip from England to Cork. He didn't consider the possibility of tariff increases since last he checked the rates. A fiver short, in despair he accepted a young man's offer of a loan, which, typically, he topped with an invitation to stop with the family who would, incidentally, repay the cash. Having not been to Ireland before, Kev knew little about our accommodation or if we had guests already, so a stay in the village gathering courage to explain his magnanimous gesture seemed sensible. He must have felt my vibrations, too.

I took the car on to collect our wandering boy (boys) to show Kevin I had won the battle of the right-sided steering wheel, while his mother returned home wondering how she could conjure a festive welcoming feast from a diminished larder.

His brother provided: In seven minutes Tyler landed as many mackerel. Fortunately, Kevin's benefactor has visited this country often enough to be familiar with roads best favored for hitchhiking. Their journey down from Cork city was relatively swift and without incident.

The firstborn returns rich in experience if poor in pocket, with tales of outrageous, I suspect impromptu, visa fees at every communist border the train to Turkey passed over. After questioning a twenty dollar tab for a cheese sandwich at one such crossing, he was instructed to pay up or be left in Bulgaria. Graciously, they accepted his traveler's cheque, which Kevin says was fortunately for the exact amount. At his age, I had only once crossed a borderline: California into Oregon to visit my sister and even then, Mom warned me about falling in with the wrong sort. Bulgaria indeed!

Perhaps a warning re the "wrong sort" would not have gone amiss. Returning home at a late hour following the Istanbul wedding reception, Kevin tells us, he hailed a cruising taxi and thought the fee unusually reasonable when the driver said it would be six before he got in. When K. learned "six" was English for "sex" with a Turkish inflection, he got out. I told Kevin that, though in no way wishing to beleaguer his worldliness, I'd never confuse sex with a cab ride. Ignoring me, he pressed on, recounting another evening when, as he was about to accept an invitation of accommodation and food from a group of Turkish youths, he realized their campfire conversation concerning blushing lips and azure eyes alluded to him. Swiftly he set up tent near a Dutch couple and their pretty daughters.

His bus ride across Turkey holding two small girls on his lap to save being trampled by gyrating gypsies remains my personal favorite. He was the sole occupant when he boarded, but the first stop brought an entire tribe, complete with livestock, offspring, and housekeeping essentials. Overcrowding only spurred the passengers into singing and dancing in the aisles, and Kevin enjoyed his experience no end, even though many drunks were sick in their tambourines and the little girls swiped his cigarettes.

~ ~ ~

Early in our married life, we took a house mainly because it featured a light, airy room off the attic with a sun porch and separate bathroom. The perfect studio. This was to be its sole purpose. "Although he now works at home," Ava told the children, "your father's studio is as other men's business offices. We, none of us, shall enter uninvited, unannounced, or unnecessarily." A week later I came in from preparing canvases on my porch to find Marni Nittler and Molly Farrell occupying the comfortable chair and couch so thoughtfully provided for respite from the easel. While the ladies praised Richard's sweet workroom, Ava uncertainly carried up Bloody Marys. Omitting reference to invasion of my "office," I inquired about a drink for myself, and though Ava dutifully descended to make one, it was returned by Tyler and Mats, his new classmate from Sweden, while Ava whipped up hors d'oeuvres. Mats and Ty made Cokes for themselves, barely pausing to invite whoever was ringing the doorbell up to Dad's party in the attic. As it was Ted Nittler coming to fetch his wife, my wife called down that he should mix himself a drink on his way upstairs. Only with the arrival of Ted, my business partner, did I mention the sanctity of my working quarters. "I guess I forgot," Ava ventured.

Today, I've been trying my hand at writing and selected the guest room—warm, seldom-used, and with a door which firmly shuts—as my workplace. That closed door calls upon this bunch as magnets to the pole. Granted—they open it with consideration about every quarter hour—but this is followed by staring or throat noises until permission to speak is given and then the old man's voice attracts remaining household members, their friends and just now, the cats who fought around my feet.

I guess they forget.

~ ~ ~

Tyler has always danced to a piper few can hear; therefore I am blessed that under our roof lives someone else to sort out his oracles. Ava immediately understood when Ty addressed "Here, doggie," to his passport case; that was his way of making sure he had it (he would never leave an animal behind).

The day he inquired if his mother thought fur remained on mummified cats, I saw her eyes flicker in serious consideration before I fled. She didn't dispute his theory that caterpillars fall into your popcorn when you sit under laburnum trees, and to her regret, the lady ignored my warning not to investigate when the cheer "Come on, Moose," sounded from his bedroom in London.

My portrait of Tyler.

I remember still the furrowed brow and tight little smile when she returned. Tyler, it seems, sat on the floor behind his rubber menagerie lined up in varying positions on what she took to be a racetrack. The armadillo leading, Ty rooted for the underdog—in this case, the under-moose. Since they couldn't move without his help, Ava asked how he knew who was winning. Tyler said it was easy—he kept score on a chart.

Both boys like

traveling and have enjoyed quite a bit of it, but it never runs entirely smoothly for the second born. Even though we were in possession of his ticket to Stockholm that first summer, at the eleventh hour we learned Tyler hadn't been booked on the flight and the frantic tap dance to right matters I do not wish to recall. For the encore the following year, his arrival date was mismarked by the ticket agent and at destination it was required that Ty be met by an English-speaking adult. We called on his friend Mats' Aunt Laila whom none of us had ever met. That was another tap dance. Tyler wasn't at all concerned. At that age, I hadn't even been on a self-service elevator alone.

I've saved his communications from those two summers.

Dear Dad and Ava,

I am having a great time here in Sweden. I need 5 more pounds. Mats can come to England. I will be at this address for 8 days, then you can't write to me at all on this island.

P.S. Sorry for the mess/keep the stamp.

We weren't surprised by the absence of a signature but the address was written upside down, nearly obliterated by the postmark—and more than half of the eight days had already elapsed. He probably felt posting the card was not of immediate urgency. I kept the stamp and sent the money.

Somehow most of his school friends were Scandinavian—not a prevalent percentage in Beverly Hills—but we decided to discontinue the combination of Tyler and Sweden when he wrote that Mats overheard a telephone conversation between his grandparents and he thought Tyler was to be sent home.

Laila was seldom in long enough to receive phone calls, so I wrote asking her to please find out what the hell was going on and had another try at communicating with Tyler myself. I wrote a pleading letter with small hope he would show it to Mats to translate for his grandmother. I enclosed also a questionnaire for Tyler. A please-check-square-and-return-card-to-sender idea:

- ❐ I can stay here until mid-August
- ❐ I cannot stay here until mid-August
- ❐ I have shown my airplane ticket to English-speaking people in charge
- ❐ They understand I am booked on to Germany and NOT back to London
- ❐ They realize my parents will be in Ireland at that time
- ❐ They know my grandparents will meet me after the 2nd week in August in Frankfurt but will NOT be in town before then.
- ❐ I will return this paper and try to get word to my parents immediately !

Dear Dad and Ava,

I'm in a heck of a mess now. Yesterday Mats told me he wasn't sure if he had to be back in America until the 11th of September, so now he's got to write his mother.

You see he has to stay until I mean if school doesn't start in America until the 11th, then his father will probably want him to stay on because his father is paying half the ticket. If that happens, he can't come. In your letter I didn't find anything saying I could come home but Laila says you did write that. I would like to come home around the 1st of August because I've run out of money, or at least I don't have any to spare. I don't want you to send any more. I've had too much already. Another thing is that Mats is working and I would come help him to work in August but I can't spare the money. You see, I bought a card in July that lasted all month but it will expire soon. It got me free on the busses and tubes. I don't have enough money to get another one and I don't want to stay home for 13 days.

Love, Tyler

Answering her phone at last, Laila quickly sorted things out and assured us Tyler could work with Mats at something, not fully explained, dealing with hamsters. We sent transportation fees plus extra for his weeks under the overprotective wing of his own Grossmama. Before he returned once more to "this island," Ty wrote, promising to board the correct Lufthansa plane at the proper time. But we never learned what happened to that questionnaire.

"Oh-for-pitysake-not-atall-gwan-witye," Kitty O'Regan, the fastest tongue in the west, said after she'd thanked us for the use of our pasture land and I replied that we couldn't even live here if it weren't for their assistance and advice.

We've come to understand most of what the O'Regans tell us—at least the words—but I believed I would never get the hang of Kitty's rapid-fire delivery. West Cork country dialect can be difficult for even the Cork City born, and though Kitty's version whirls past my untrained ears, I'm actually beginning to get most of it now. Herself is a wonderful woman. For the sake of clarity we have to use the local vernacular in many cases, but I've always disliked the patronizing foreigner who adopts terminology for the sake of cute. I regarded "Herself" as too Barry Fitzgerald altogether so I startled myself by referring to Kitty that way in the village one day when I ran into Tim and wanted to ask about her. I felt that "your wife" was impersonal and "the missus" would've made me giggle. "Mrs. O'Regan" seemed awfully formal and I thought that since I hadn't really got to know Kitty yet, calling her by her first name might be too forward. "Herself" covered it all, and Tim didn't look at me oddly. Trust the Irish to come up with the perfect pronoun for just such an instance.

Kitty and I are great friends now. We chatter as we wrestle over the cows' water bucket when I try to carry it to the upper field for her, and I no longer dodge when she releases a barrage of dialogue in my direction. Kitty is world-class mother hen. She frets and worries, clucks orders, comforts, and gathers her brood of six under more than ample wings, and they all attend her bidding, unequivocally. Timmy, too, I wager. Kitty, per custom, demurs to her husband on the surface but I'm pretty sure that Tim is her seventh chick.

He told us that they were children together, married right out of school, and that Kitty is still his best friend. That honorable sentiment, much in vogue these days, and one which I share with my own wife, I imagine is rarely verbalized in this still simple community of tough old chauvinistic farmers. The fact that Timmy would speak of such things to me indicates the degree of his feelings for Kitty O'Regan, a lady of spirit as generous as her proportions. And I am touched.

The combination of Kitty's dark-rimmed almond-shaped eyes and Tim's craggy crooked features produced half a dozen handsome kids: Marie, Billy, Catherine, Anne, Nora, and Donal—in that order, and considering the attitudes of our times, these shyly polite yet bright and friendly, hardworking children might have stepped out of the last century. Donal, the youngest and smallest O'Regan, amuses us the most because we know that when we hear Kitty calling him we'll usually find Donal hunkered down out of her sight behind one of the grass-covered stone walls in view of our upstairs window.

We know Nora best. One evening shortly after we moved here, and filled with the poetry of it all, I was totally undone to hear a child's voice drifting down the hill in song. And there she was, little Nora O'Regan, singing the cows home for milking, a mite following the herd, not even as big as the calves. I wouldn't buy a scene like that in a Disney movie. Nora is seven years old, and likes hanging out with Ava, helping and laughing at the funny way we talk. "I can DO it," she always says when Ava tries to teach her something new or how to use kitchen tools she has never seen before. It's become a family catchphrase, only we suspect that we really can't do all the things that Nora does.

Timmy drives only a tractor, so if something is needed that

May doesn't carry in her shop, one of his kids has to trudge the five miles to the village to get it. Like Mary who has a farm on the hill north of us, and Mary Monica who lives about a mile further on, May is a cousin. They are all O'Regans and all named Mary, hence the need to differentiate, and since there are no identifying signs, the only way you'd know that May O'Regan ran a shop is to be born here or—as we did—notice the bread delivery man bringing her supplies one day when we were going into town to get a loaf for ourselves.

Connie O'Mahoney ties up at the dock near Clonlea after fishing all day.

Dick De Neut wrote that when mutual friends in Beverly Hills ask him how we spend our days, he always tells them that Ava drives five miles to purchase groceries and five miles home, and then if she is lucky she will have forgotten something so she can go back again. Not so. But if she sees one of the O'Regan clan starting down the lane in that direction, Ava will often drive over to encounter the child, and on the pretext of going to the village, she'll offer a lift if the errand is beyond May's shop. This is the lady who doesn't like children?

Down the boreen about a two minute stroll from our gate, the bay forms into a crescent-shaped inlet and plays around rocky shoals and a small cement jetty where occasionally other boats tie up, but usually Connie O'Mahoney's outboard motorboat has it all to itself. Almost everyone addresses him by both names because, in Irish pronunciation, Mahoney's surname rhymes with his nickname and they're fun to say together. Not unexpectedly, Irish family names are quite regional; O'Mahoneys can be found all over Cork, and this particular branch of the clan are the O'Regan's cousins and immediate neighbors. Connie is about seventeen, freckled, angular, with a mass of tousled fiery hair, and waiting with the O'Regan kids on the jetty for Connie to return with his evening catch is our favorite way to close the day. As he stands up in the boat to toss us his mooring line, that head of massive curls ablaze in the sunset is something to behold.

Rarely is Tim without a cap, so *his* fringed bald pate wasn't reflecting in the twilight this evening when I joined him and Nora who were gathering periwinkles amidst rocks in the low tide. Or "wrinkles," as Mr. O'Regan dubs the tiny, pointed snail-shaped molluscs. I wonder what they do with them? We've learned that most of the locals don't eat the seafood living practically in their front yards. Tim suggested that we might harvest the little spiral shells, ourselves, to enhance the garden. It seems that old car tires dipped in cement and encrusted with wrinkle shells make lovely enclosures for bedded flowers and, along those lines, Tim offered to trim one of our wild fuchsia bushes into the shape of an armchair.

"Lads we were when my brothers and I helped the father build this." Tim said, pointing to the jetty. "A fierce task it was. All brought in by beast and trap." And then realizing the lack of drama in the tale he launched into an account of when he was a bit older lad and worked for a Simon Legree type who made the men remove stones from a ring fort despite their fearful protests. "Weren't we all at Death's Door with the sickness soon after and didn't the landlord himself pass through it?" That finished, Tim segued into another story regarding the remains of the old manor house up on the hill behind us. Tim didn't exactly say it was haunted (because someone lives there now) but hadn't he and others discovered a skeleton "hidden in a high room" when they were employed to tear down the portion of the grand house that the pirate had fired upon from his ship in the estuary? I don't wish to paint him a quaint character, but who needs radio or television when there is Mr. O'Regan?

~ ~ ~

"How do you two get me into these things?," Tyler asked on a black side road sometime after midnight.

"Shut up, kid, and lift," his father explained.

We managed to upright the car from the ditch and set it on four wheels again, and I drove it home for the owner who doesn't know how to drive. I couldn't answer Ty's question because I don't know how we get ourselves mixed up in those things: all we did was accept an invitation to dinner at a restaurant in the village.

Relative newcomers here themselves, Keith and Helen Wiggins, who lease the restaurant and run the pub as well, gave a small dinner party and invited the local doctor and his wife, the police sergeant and his wife and—I suppose because we've become regular customers—me and my wife.

We met Dave, the top cop, when we first arrived here and registered with him as foreigners must. Sergeant Dave was on duty and couldn't attend the dinner but his wife, Ann, a first generation Irish American returned to her roots, made a welcoming if rather quiet presence, as did Liz, the Mrs. Doctor. Until now, good health precluded our meeting her husband, Larry, a stocky man in his thirties with a ruddy coloring due, I expect, to his passion for shark fishing, though, with a practice including the population of two whole villages and their outskirts—and with his making house calls, I don't know where the man finds time. The doc's blue eyes indicate a deep compassion beneath twinkling devilment, and I'm sure that no two people have ever received the same explanation as to why he is missing a couple of important fingers from his inoculation hand, but, personally, I like the story that a conger eel got them. We've not heard that the accident in any way interferes with his performance; he jabs as painlessly as the best of them.

When she returned from driving the temporary barman home after mandatory pub closing time of eleven, Mrs. Wiggins downed a neat gin without a word to any of us and she let another half hour slide before announcing that she left the car just outside the village. Seems the young man licked her neck when she drove up the dark lane and Helen turned into a ditch. Being Irish, the lady takes things pretty much in stride, but her blustering Brit husband bellowed, "Woman, WHAT have you done to MY automobile?" just as Tyler arrived to see if we were ready to go home. We were ready to go home, all right, but Larry insisted that the men should attend to the Wiggins' car first, and it was only when we were blindly heaving to, the thought occurred that the only man who could give us medical aid should the car roll over on us was the doctor straining beside me. Fortunately there was too little light for me to see my son's face when we learned that, for all his ranting at poor little "inferior female" Helen, our host had never learned to drive.

As the long, hot summer eases into fall without any sign of rain, water becomes a premium, to be dispersed sparingly only for necessities. Ava has been conserving religiously, but I realize she rates a clean scalp high on the list of priorities. In spite of that, I was not prepared to find her with head immersed in the calves' water trough, an ancient washtub positioned under an ingenious piping system Tim rigged to catch water seeping down from a hidden spring on his land which never goes dry. The water is icy cold and the tub is surrounded by manure, so to complete her costume of terry-cloth robe hitched up around her waist, Ava wore Wellington boots. I trust I was the only observer.

We've been told there is an old law here that one can be

taken away for twenty-eight days of mental observation if three people attest that the person is behaving peculiarly. I accuse her of behaving peculiarly. Ava defends her actions. This is not peculiar, she insists—after all, she rinses her head from a separate pitcher so the calves needn't drink soapy water.

Chapter Three

Dorian Gray et al

Rooting in the richest soil, or harvesting the dill,
Or setting out the kitchen herbs on every bloody sill,
Ava takes to farming
With vengeance . . . most alarming
Dealing death to every slug and fly that dares against her will.

Without Tim's help we should have nothing in the new garden at all. But for a pampered movie brat, Ava grows a mean courgette (zucchini) plus a variety of other vegetables our neighbors view with suspicion. Like most of the farmers around here, Tim regards vegetables other than onions, cabbages, turnips and, of course, potatoes as unnecessary if not actually unnatural. They hold with the odd carrot and pea. But our varieties of lettuces, including the staunch California iceberg, radishes, broccoli, miniature tomatoes, spinach, and squash are looked upon with suspicion and Tim simply does not discuss the artichokes. He is a free spirit, eager to investigate, and though Timmy clearly feels we are beyond our element, he never makes us feel foolish or hesitates to answer our countless queries. Tim prepared a much larger gardening area for us and fenced it off by a beautiful dry stone wall. Secretly, I think, he welcomes the adventure and is as eager to see the results of our foreign planting as are we.

~ ~ ~

"Aren't they lovely flowers?" says Mr. O'Regan, acknowledging the artichokes going to seed in a purple explosion. Thistlebrush crowns erupt on the prickly vegetables in profusion although we've eaten as many as we could manage. I haven't the guts to admit we actually consume the formidable flower, but one day I'll tell Tim to ask Herself how the feat is accomplished.

In the garden among the leeks.

On this side of the Atlantic, many vegetables are known by names different from those we were used to in the States, and earlier on, confusion reigned every time Ava went to the shops (although that is not to be blamed solely on vernacular). Closest by comparison to iceberg lettuce is the firm, British Webb's Wonder, while romaine lettuce becomes cos; and batavia, escarole (or is escarole, batavia?). Beets are beetroot and rutabagas are, of all things, swedes. Contrarily, pronouncing filet steak as "fill-it," the Irish and the English know eggplant by the lovelier French name, aubergine, and Chinese snow peas as mange-tout with equal logic.

Endive is chicory. Chicory is endive.

Few are known or used in our village, where corn is an all-inclusive title applied to wheat, barley and other grains.

Personally, I favor the raising of flowers, which Ava reminds are aesthetically rewarding but hardly filling. I thought flowers would be calming. Never do I wish to feel the rage which darkens my wife's beautiful brow when she catches the white cabbage butterfly eyeing her kale.

~ ~ ~

"What time is it, love?"

"Soon."

It's already too late. I should have heeded Dick De Neut.

~ ~ ~

Life grows increasingly bizarre. Glancing away from the easel this afternoon, I saw Dorian Gray alight from a van by our garden wall. When one is a portrait painter by profession, an unexpected visit from Dorian Gray in the wilds of Ireland shakes reason nearly beyond the pale. It was an eerie moment before the young haughty face of the portrait dissolved and I saw Hurd Hatfield in the flesh. HURD HATFIELD was walking to my door! Where did he come from? How did he find us? And why? We are hardly drop-in-able; ours is not an easy place to locate even with directions and we had not known Mr. Hatfield before today.

He didn't arrive by happenstance. Nor alone. With him were a young black American woman and a beefy German fisherman whom Hurd befriended after they recognized him at Cork airport on his way down here, and—with the reasoning that since we didn't know him, it didn't matter if we didn't know them either—he invited the couple along for the ride. Ava gave them lunch.

The other fellow, it seems, is a comedic performer in Germany—which doesn't explain why he fishes for a living in Ireland, and the girl had little to say except something about the best place to get eggplant seedlings, which triggered enthusiastic response from Ava.

Why any of them were at the airport was not clear, but after a little delving, we learned there was nothing unusual about Hurd's surprise appearance: he lives near Lismore, and now that we have a house of our own in Ireland, Adele is compelled to send any and all new acquaintance to call on us, and then, accusing us of being madly social, wonders—if this is our attitude—why did we move to such an isolated spot?

Following the thread of Hurd's conversation demanded concentrated effort. He tends to veer. We think he is a touch eccentric—in his case somewhat justifiable. Since, to most thinking, his portrayal remains the definitive Dorian Gray, he has been labeled with that image all these years, and he said people don't realize how much he achieved after that.

I expect we shall see more of him.

Hurd Hatfield?

Earlier this week, Ava received a phone call from someone imitating Boris Karloff, who pleaded that she officiate at the opening of the village festival and offer a short discourse on the Brotherhood of Man. "Come on," Ava giggled when the message was repeated after I incredulously handed her the telephone, "Who IS this?" A woman's voice verified that Ava had been speaking to the vicar, who was calling with a legitimate request.

She had to accept or face a promised pummeling from mate and child. Empty threats. Ava is consumed with curiosity dwarfing ours.

The festivities were meant to be held outdoors where stalls, games, donkey rides and the like were set up on the vicarage grounds, a beautiful spot surrounded by lush foliage overlooking the harbor. But as we arrived, so did the rain.

Outside, the building seems handsome, imposing. Inside, it made Miss Havisham's rooms look like Julia Child's kitchen. Later we were told that no one, save the vicar, had walked these halls for years, but we had come to that conclusion ourselves the moment we crossed the threshold. Devoid of other trappings, the vestibule boasts a lone, full-length mirror with its once-fine glass shared and tentatively restrained by a worm-ridden rococo frame enshrouded by cobwebs. Returning an incomplete image where one's lower extremities fragment into stalagmites, the looking glass did not reflect the hoped-for spirit of merrymaking.

Men reassembling stalls had the best of it, as horrified women groped their way through the cobweb fog in order to prepare tea—whipping their brooms and dust cloths with a great frenzy. I shall not forget their faces as they herded the three of us into a side room, presumably out of harm's way.

Nor am I likely to forget the gallimaufric room: furniture upon furniture. Victorian memorabilia. Stuffed dead things. Books stacked floor to ceiling. And a couple of bent biscuit tins, held together by a headset and earphones, resting on the floor beneath an exposed wire fairly screaming for attention. But the vicar arrived before we could examine that more closely.

Sounding less like Karloff in person, the vicar speaks with his palms flat together, fingers steepled as in prayer. Slightly built, though certainly fit, without warning he tossed Tyler a book so heavy it caused him to sit down abruptly from the sheer weight, and the good man appeared to be serious when he suggested Ty busy himself with it. Once dust shifted, the title became legible. Providing you read Latin, Greek, and Hebrew.

With grace, our host proffered sherry. With alacrity, we accepted.

Sensing curiosity (for want of a more apt word) the pastor proceeded to explain why his quarters were in such disarray. DISARRAY?!!

Until her untimely demise twelve years before, he went on, his mother housekept the vicarage for him, and upon her passing over, he vowed to alter nothing except for three reasons: if he married, if the Church wished to refurbish, and—most important—he expected The Savior to return at any time, in which case mother would rise and put things in order to suit herself.

As he spoke, Ava nervously fingered the edge of the sherry glass, while Tyler and I grinned at her and each other behind the vicar's back. We stopped grinning when the color drained from Ava's face and, following her disbelieving eyes, we saw a raven's head edging around the softly opening door.

Small girls ought not to be allowed to play with the stuffed birds when there is work to be done. Deciding our services were invaluable elsewhere, Ty and I, carrying a chair apiece, went out to help the men. As we left, I noticed Ava steepling her hands.

Shortly afterwards, she stood in front of the lethal mirror in the hall where, forgetting man's brotherhood, briefly, prettily, thanking the people for honoring her and welcoming us to the community, she declared the festivities officially begun. And with one quick round of the stalls, where Ava fell upon an archaic meat grinder which she purchased with great delight, we bought some onions and a cabbage and went home in the rain.

With rucksack tethered to his T-shirt sporting a Guinness Stout label on the front, Kevin trudges towards Tralee, where the annual celebrations are just beginning. After his summer adventures, home seems over-quiet and he feels he should see more of the country before leaving Ireland. I think he hopes to pick a petal from the Rose of Tralee competition.

We encourage his hiking because he won't be able to do so much longer, but I have suggested he shed that hump from his back fairly soon. He is beginning to resemble Quasimodo.

Though he missed his mother's performance at the vicarage and the manifestation of Hurd Hatfield, Kevin returned over the weekend in time to meet the Bavarian baroness who rapped our window as we were sitting down to Sunday morning waffles. She didn't announce that she was a baroness; we learned that later. She said to call her "Rudy."

Much of the year, Rudy, jolly as she is fat (very), lives in

Bavaria with her daughters and her husband, Lulu. Swear to God. But she prefers Ireland where she can pamper her passion for the care and breeding of donkeys. A joy she likes to share. Precisely the reason she came to us. And because Dellie suggested it. Not that they know each other, but they do have mutual friends, which is sufficient cause for my aunt-in-law.

Rudy offered the loan of a set of her little beasts until we acquired another horse (we're not) because Adele, uninformed about the calves, among other things, believed we were pining at the loss of Violet. To Dellie's thinking, with Christmas not that far away and all, donkeys in the stable would be so fitting.

Acting swiftly, before Ava could digest the idea, offering waffles, declining donkeys, I accepted an invitation for us to visit Rudy's prize stock at her house (she lives about thirty miles from here) and turned the floor over to Kevin and Tyler who bombarded her with questions regarding Bavaria.

Strangely, some of our friends, who thought we were misguided in taking the children to live away from America, now write their doubts about sending Kevin back to his mother country. People tend to forget the age at which most were fending for themselves and, as I pointed out, in just two months Kevin will be allowed to vote. He hasn't the grades to match his intelligence so Kevin can't attend university, and without special skills and a work permit, he isn't legally employable in Ireland or on the Continent because he is a U.S. citizen. Of course Kevin knows that we will fund his food and lodging until he finds work and gets his own place. Initially, he will stay with John and Rayme Rust, to whom we are all devoted. That makes the wrenching away a little easier for Kevin and me, too, and even though there may be those who dispute it, I believe if my boy can cross Turkey with a band of gypsies, he can cope with California.

Kevin left cheerfully but I had seen that expression in those blue eyes before when a little boy used to climb into my bed after awakening from a scary dream. He is frightened and I think he feels somewhat abandoned since Tyler gets to stay in Europe. Now we prepare for Tyler's departure and a special time in my life draws to conclusion. I realized that it must be an even more special time for the boys when Tyler preferred to stay home when we took Kevin to the airport. Ty wanted a private goodbye because it is possible the brothers won't see each other for a couple of years and by then they could be very different people. The loss of their mother when they were so young strengthened the bond between the three of us, and though we are even closer now, I couldn't share the same feelings they must have had at parting.

Chalet Gloria. Tyler heard about the Austrian school from one of his London classmates who had gone there, and begged to try it; freeing us to more easily address the challenge of bog hopping, and though Albert Finney accused us of sending our kid to a brothel; given the school's delicious title, I personally admire Tyler's selection. A Gloria figured in my boyhood education, too.

A couple of years ago in London Ava asked me to meet her for tea at the Ritz Hotel, and when she joined me in the tearoom, she was carrying a garland of onions purchased, she said, from a street peddler on a bicycle. Now, contrary to most people, I associate "Puttin' on the Ritz" with onions rather than Fred Astaire, and it comes to mind while I watch his daughter braiding onions on the terrace. Thick string attached to the top half of the Dutch door rapidly vanishes as the onions are entwined one upon the other. How Ava gained the knack, one can only ponder. I could ask, but I have come to learn that my wife's answers are not necessarily applicable to the question. I've got to ask.

She learned it from her papa, a garlic farmer in Provence. I should not have asked.

Already festooned with baskets, the kitchen ceiling has sprouted a hanging garden of garlic and onions. I've warned Ava to control enthusiasm should our yield be more extensive next season. She is in danger of becoming the madwoman of shallots.

~ ~ ~

"I have nothing to read."

"Why don't you read the book I just finished?"

"It isn't right to read a book so soon after you've read it."

"Why not? You read the book I read before the book I just finished. In fact, you insisted I read it the minute you put it down."

"That's different. You had just read another book by the same author. I didn't want you to lose the rhythm. Oh . . . why don't I read the book you just finished?"

Silence.

"I thought you were reading that book Rudy loaned you—the one about the horsy English lesbians, not the mystery Henry sent us from his crime club selection that you just finished."

Silence.

"You don't understand. I can't read about lesbians because I laughed so hard at Betty MacDonald's book and I want to stay light."

"The crime club selection doesn't exactly bring guffaws and they weren't lesbians. I'm sure they were of strong fibre. Held high thoughts. They only lived together for a long time and believed in spirit writing."

"In the book you just finished reading?"

"No, the one about the lesbians. Oh, my God. I'm going out to gather firewood."

"We don't have a fireplace."

"I know."

She is right about the fireplace. It's fake.

Although the electric fire, complete with flame effect, glowed on the hearth when we signed the lease, we assumed the Ellisons preferred it rather than the strain and bother of toting fuel upstairs, and if Nigel-Wynn hadn't got himself stuck on a narrow ledge inside the opening about a foot above the electric grate (not turned on), we might not have realized the whole structure was plywood until we tried to light a fire. Chimney, hearth, everything ersatz, except a beautifully weathered bog log used as the mantelpiece and which we shall reinstall when we convert the fireplace into working order. Not an easy prospect because it means tearing out a substantial portion of the wall and building the chimney from the ground up.

Everyone says John and Diana were adamant about the false fire from the first days of construction, ignoring every warning that this is an area where electricity does not always flow at the flick of a switch. In a country where power often depends upon the strength of gales and/or union bosses, it is advisable to have some alternative at the ready. Better to have a working fireplace and gas cooker for the emergency than to freeze and eat sandwiches when the power is off. Sometimes power is cut simply because linemen are doing casual repairs—which, of course, does not warrant advance warning.

The fact that our power source outlet is placed about four feet from the fireplace I accept as yet another example of the Englishman's apparent need to have as many electrical cords on view as possible. In that respect, a lot of English houses are akin to movie sets where one treads with caution amidst the power cables. Fortunately the climate remains mild and the electric fire is seldom in use. Not only is it an unpleasant skin-drying type of heat, it is out of character with the setting and makes me cross.

Ava would say, "What doesn't?" But she shares my aggravation in this respect and envisions stormy nights ahead when we sit snugly by the embers. Not to mention the smell of burning turf, that heady perfume of the Irish village. Here we are in craggy countryside, alone on the moors except for the calves, the curlews, and the cats, living as close to nature as we're ever likely to, and we're expected to huddle around an electric stove which melts our synthetic slacks and singes the cats' whiskers. What could have possessed the Ellisons? Where better to savor the pleasures of a warming, crackling, open fireplace than in an Irish farmhouse by the ocean—for peat's sake?

~ ~ ~

Ever since she hand-fed peppermints to Rudy's donkeys, Ava has tried to rationalize a need for some of our own. I stand adamant. We will be in California much of the winter which would be neither fair to the O'Regans, who have enough to look after, nor to the donkeys, who require loving attention and work. And Tim can use the grazing land. Consider Darleen, Wanda, and How Now (Rachel has been replaced). And no . . . we cannot keep a pig. For the same reasons.

I know what is on Ava's mind. Partly. Now that fall makes such a dramatic statement, rolling those boreens in a donkey-drawn trap is an inviting premise. So much more color than we had expected in an area bereft of trees. Not the dull brown of spent grass, but purple heather fading into complementary yellows—the gorse, beginning its second blossoming of the year. Green giving way to exceptionally vivid orange as ferns die. And reeds become the richness of cream. By far my favorite season here. We haven't really experienced a full springtime in the country when the wildflowers must be magnificent, but I can't imagine it any more beautiful than it is now.

Mushrooms are everywhere—deep red, pink, cerulean, butter-yellow, skinny mushrooms looking like minute umbrellas folded wet after a shower. Mushrooms with great names. Scarlet Hood, Poison Pie, Fairy Ring, and Stinkhorn. Although we gratefully accept all Timmy or his family bring us, Ava and I are not yet secure enough to reap the rewards of our own fields where the fungi spring in alarming number. Not without knowledgeable assistance. Tim advises not to worry. There are ways to test the mushrooms. Observe the birds and animals. What they eat is safe for people. Except the deadly Death Cap mushroom which doesn't bother rabbits. My aged, darling milk supplier suggests the silver test and I recall Mom used to simmer a spoon along with mushrooms if they were picked wild. The spoon turns black when poison lurks. Coincidentally, Ava came across the selfsame practice in a magazine report dealing with old wives' cures. "The field mushroom," we learn, "induces no reaction whatsoever in a silver spoon. Neither does the poisonous Death Cap." Everybody insists the peeling method is infallible. If you can peel it, you can eat it. Safe. Tested, tried and true. Fatal mushrooms are not in the way of being peelable. Excepting, you understand, the Death Cap.

Since to our eyes, the D.C. remains indistinguishable from the delicious variety at the post office, I shall continue to rely on the kindness of neighbors. Ava, meaning to save money without foregoing the potassium value of the mushrooms, selected some of the white pulp and, comparing it to a sketch on the cover of her cookbook, offered it to me with lettuce and cheese.

"Won't kill you just to try it," she urged.

Tyler is home for the Christmas holidays.

Allowed the option, Father would continue filling the bentwood rocking chair by the window; mulling nature's complexities; drawing upon his briar pipe—a gift from his children of a distant, frosty Christmas. But Mother and son warn of atrophy if bodily movement isn't accelerated, smoking causes hyperventilation, and besides, it's a beautiful day. That I hike with them is presented as a moral obligation. I promise to rock faster if they leave me alone.

They don't.

Ava and Tyler are of frightening similarity in thought, deed and speech. Father is somewhat odd-man-out. If I do a little detective work, attended with hard concentration, conversation with either of them on a one-to-one basis, though tricky, is possible. With the two of them at large together, it is not.

So often have I felt like a foreigner searching his language guide manual in the hope of finding a translation that, deep down, he knows does not exist, I have adapted one of my own father's ploys as a safeguard for sanity. When Dad sought peace and quiet, he simply switched off his hearing aid device. Click—and the world was mute.

Although not yet perfected, I have developed a mental hearing-aid—a trigger in the brain that switches to other channels of thought at the first inkling of a sentence which seems to veer from the path of reason. Often I'm not quick enough. But with the practice I've been getting in the three weeks Tyler has been on school holiday, I'll soon have it honed to an art.

"Tyler, did you realize that the Greater Butter Wort is carnivorous?"

"NO!"

"Fancy not knowing that!"

Click

"What?"

"I didn't say anything."

"I didn't think you had."

Click.

"You think that diamond ring is something? My roommate's mother has two ski suits."

Click

"What do you suppose the fleshy part of the bottom of your foot at the base of the toes is called?"

"Cecil."

Click

Click! Cecil?

Some things the mind will not shut out.

Soon after we met him, Hurd insisted that we stop off for tea on our way back from visiting Dellie and he specified the appropriate hour of four in the afternoon. We pulled up his long driveway on the dot. Talk about typecasting: a rookery of tall trees edged on one side of a brooding Georgian manor house in desperate want of attention, which, judging from the large amount of cement-mixing sand next to the steps, would soon be forthcoming.

Stern and dark except for a singular lighted window on the ground floor, there was not an element of tea time cheer in the air, and the longer our knocking and ringing the archaic doorbell went unanswered, the more uncomfortable we became with the surroundings. An operatic aria sounded from a record player somewhere, and when we finally peeked through the lighted window, we found rather an inviting scene: a lady's handbag rested on a sofa, and what appeared to be a very fine, old china tea service sat on a small table in front of it. A fire crackled from an equally impressive fireplace but the portrait above the mantelpiece in this perfect setting for Dorian Gray was that of a lovely woman we supposed to be Mrs. Hatfield—Hurd's mother. That was all we could see and all we did see because nobody ever came to the front door.

We knew we had the right day and time, tea things certainly suggested expected guests, but after forty-five minutes of ringing, calling out and beating on every door panel we could find around the house, mindful of a three-hour drive still ahead of us, we gave up. And because we had nothing with which to leave a note, Ava used a stick to write a message in the sandpile. Late that night Hurd rang—he'd seen our car turning out the gate when he came to check for any sign of us, discovered the note right away, and he thought Ava was very clever to leave the stick standing upright in the sand to draw his attention. He didn't seem to think that such a communication was unusual, but then neither did the person who wrote it. Of course he knew the doorbell didn't work, Hurd explained, and somewhat accusingly added that he couldn't understand why he hadn't heard us rapping from the smoke room at the back of the house where he and a friend were searching through some old clippings.

I believe now we've seen those clippings ourselves. Worried that he might be all alone and piqued by the idea of sharing our first Irish Christmas in this country with the personification of Irish, Oscar Wilde's Dorian Gray, we invited H. H. down for the holiday—scheduling him to arrive the night before in time for dinner. A storm raged Christmas Eve. We weren't overly concerned when he didn't show for the meal; we assumed that because of weather his phone was knocked out and he couldn't ring to tell us he'd decided to wait until the next day, but just as we prepared to turn in, Hurd Hatfield opened the front door. Wind and rain were so savage that this time it was we who didn't hear the pounding on the door or the approach of his rickety van.

Hurd was quite oblivious to our startled reactions and tucked into the warmed-over supper Ava quickly provided while, braving the elements, Tyler and I carried in enough luggage for a fortnight and a box of photographs, clippings, and theatrical notices not especially relating only to him. Hurd hasn't an actor's ego as we know it. Hurd hasn't anything as we know it. Who but Hurd Hatfield would come for dinner in an Irish country cottage during a Force-9 gale at midnight on Christmas Eve, dressed in Austrian-style evening clothes of loden green?

Madame Gloria was all understanding when we rang to advise her that Tyler will be tardy for class. Never did I think I'd be sending a note to his teacher by international telephone, but I couldn't very well write: "Please excuse my son for being late to school. Our alarm clock failed to alert us in time for his flight to Zurich so he went to Mr. Hatfield's party instead."

And this time we were allowed inside the house.

Hurd painted the stone walls of what he calls the smoke room with a type of thick, chalky white paint I've only seen in this part of the world, but it doesn't really alter the spooky atmosphere much. Even though we understand that the big iron hooks randomly studded throughout the ceiling were originally intended for hanging meats to smoke, the presence of an immense museum-quality tapestry covering a large portion of one wall encourages imagery of a darker, Gothic nature.

"Hurd, you can't just leave it like that," Ava cried, nearly falling over the bottom of the tapestry which lay on the floor, still partially rolled up like a scroll. "Think of the damp. Or MICE."

"I know. You're right, of course. It is much too long for the wall but I practically live in this room and I couldn't bear not to hang it. What can I do . . . do you think I should have a dog?

Maybe I should have a dog . . ." Hurd's voice drifted as his train of thought jumped the rails, and though he probably would have taken no notice, I pretended interest in another part of the room, and in my pocket notebook tried to capture a conversation that I knew would be pretty much one-sided. Ava has met her match in H. H.

Standing her ground, Ava cautiously ventured in a small voice: "Do you mean . . . for the mice?"

"Wha-at?" He drifted back. "Oh, you mean cats. I'm fond of cats but perhaps it should be a large dog; I couldn't bear living with someone else all the time; this is family furniture, you see." Sighing at the very thought, his dramatic eyes indicated the room's furnishing, of which, considering that this is his favorite place, there isn't a lot. A Welsh dresser encloses one corner, and by the large fireplace a worn and faded blue Queen Anne chair waits in hope of reupholstering. A few smaller chairs and a nice little bench are scattered over a beat-up and walked-thin Oriental carpet which probably is quite valuable. I think they're supposed to look like that, but where Dorian Gray lives, nothing should age at all.

"There was a house I liked near Santa Barbara once," Hurd continued. "I begged Mr. Mayer to let me drop out of sight after Dorian. People were so odd about that movie, I thought I should leave Hollywood and do a picture in the same mood maybe once a year . . . you know . . . to keep the mystique, but L. B. made me stick to the contract. My agent is annoyed with me now because I keep turning down work at my age, but I have to work again. I have to fix this house and if I had a dog I couldn't go away. I don't know why everyone only remembers THAT movie when I've done so many others. Did you see *Dragon Seed*? No, you were too young."

Not daring to glance at me, her eyes crinkling for control, Ava smiled and shook her head in the negative.

"Perfectly dreadful. AWFUL." Hurd wafted in memory. "We were all supposed to be Chinese. Turhan Bey—A TURK, played MY brother who was married to Kate. That voice. CHINESE?" Braying with laughter and excusing himself to see to his house guests,

H. H. glided down the narrow hallway, his voice trailing in a hilarious bulls-eye impression of Katherine Hepburn's character saying: "I shall not wee-ean my child on Jap-an-ese bull-lets."

Michelina and George Stacpoole, Hurd's houseguests down from Limerick, were already doing most of the menial preparations when we arrived early as promised, and a thought glimmered in my mind that Hurd might be playing a version of The Emperor's New Clothes, testing to see how long he can get away with abject helplessness before we all wise up. But he truly seemed aghast when Ava warned him that a litre of red and one of white is not enough wine to gladden a gathering of forty invited friends. Ambiance claimed his complete focus; and to that effect, he set about arranging more candles around the drawing room than are offered in a house of worship, and pleaded that we search for additional ones when George and I decided to hit the village and organize a realistic supply of booze.

Michelina nicked her finger while slicing the smoked salmon, and since nothing could sway Hurd from instructing Ava in the stretching of wide ribbons across a long, battered pine table destined to hold the food other guests were bringing, she had to search out a Band-Aid for herself. The salmon, I imagine, was a Stacpoole donation, and we popped for extra wine. George and I ignored the request for candles.

As H. H. put the taper to his devotional lights displayed on tables, high shelves and the mantelpiece against dark green walls of the room we had seen that day we peeked through the window, I studied the face of my host reflected in the candle glow. Flickering flames accentuated sculptured brows arching above a slightly aquiline nose. Chiseled bones caught the light, elongating the face and deepening the cheeks in shadow, and a dark widow's peak capped a satanic yet not cruel mask; the lighting is reminiscent of the old black and white films. And totally fitting. His sensual eyelids withstand the natural pull of gravity, and though by no means a young man, Hurd's features remain relatively strong and firm. I must paint that face. Dorian the elder. I wonder if it would bother him?

The most beguiling aspect of his eccentricity is Hurd's ambiguity, the perpetual bewilderment with life in the everyday world. He keeps fit and trim. He is still a handsome man maintaining a patrician elegance and demeanor of the educated and wellborn. When forced to confine word flow to the conversational mainstream, he can be an articulate, knowledgeable and amusing raconteur, but that also requires guidance on the part of the listeners. We are pleased with recent acclaim of his one-man interpretations of Whistler and Edgar Allan Poe, but are astonished that he carried it alone on stage for an entire performance when ordinarily he can't complete a few sentences without veering in all directions.

There is no doubt that—once in harness—Hurd is an accomplished and talented pro but, not long ago, when invited to perform his E. A. Poe in Maryland on the author's birthday, unsure of just when that was and at a loss about how to gain the information, Hurd let the date pass without pursuing the offer. Ava and I find him nutty in the extreme, thoroughly delightful, and altogether suited for his adopted country.

Not pressed into service like the rest of us, Hurd decreed that Tyler was free to roam, and I suggested that if he poked around the many rooms of the three or four floors, perhaps he would encounter a derelict painting, moldering beneath a shroud in a forgotten corner of one of them. Ty took the first three steps of the winding staircase with a mighty bound, but he returned not quite so smug and clearly shaken. In one of the dim rooms, he had come upon an Irish piper standing in silent observation by the window.

Tyler didn't spoil the surprise Hurd had planned to greet his old friend and ours, Angela Lansbury, but that was only because Ty was afraid to ask about the piper, in case Hurd didn't know what he was talking about.

As she arrived, the first agonies of the bagpipe soared and the piper continued heralding her appearance until Angie whispered through her teeth to us, "How do you make him STOP?" The rest of the guests were pretty much the usual mixed

Hurd Hatfield and the Irish piper.

bag of the region: horse breeders, farmers, a German industrialist with his very Aryan son who actually clicked his heels to punctuate each sentence. And lots of gentlewomen bearing casseroles. At once girlish and motherly—they obviously vie for the privilege of providing the care and looking after that H. H. is so willing to accept. And why not?

We suggest that if Hurd intends entertaining often, a light in the loo might be considered before the Chinese raw silk wallpaper for the master bedroom, which, in any case, won't stay up until the walls receive damp-course treatment. And no matter how enchantingly stars twinkle through on good nights, as they did at his party, the openings in the roof afford easy entry to birds, bats, sleet and God-knows-what-else at other times. We personally might cherish the Persian carpet undulating in the hall as draughts from floor spaces give it life, but the child-size hole in the kitchen floor is not to be dismissed beneath a throw rug. People could sue.

Tyler insisted that the bagpiper we all saw isn't the same bagpiper that he saw. Perhaps. Now WE are afraid to ask Hurd about another piper in case he doesn't know what we're talking about.

This time making the Cork–London–Zurich connection with minutes to spare, Tyler returned to Chalet Gloria and we begin to pack up the house for winter. Chilling winds finally arrive but we are in no hurry to leave. The mild warmth of a California January holds little allure, and if we want to see film stars we can always visit Angela. More to the point: through the smoggy skies of Beverly Hills, one seldom catches sight of the real stars, but a step outside on these cold Irish nights and you can almost hear them. We love the dramatic savagery of the Irish winter terrain, but it can be hard and bleak: darkness falls early, and until we install proper central heating it becomes an endurance test. More than anything else, though, Kevin and Fred are in California and F. A. is always so happy to have his little girl home for long visits. We're still not eager to go, but it is important that we do.

Chapter Four

The Movie Stars

It seems we are attending the Cannes Film Festival next week.

No one asked if we wanted to. Fred and MGM assume that after a month on the farm, we would welcome the diversion. Fred assumes; the studio only included us in the package as added inducement. Fred hates this sort of thing, but with Ava along for companionship and consolation and me to run interference, they hoped F. A. would agree to the publicity tour for *That's Entertainment, Part II*. Gene Kelly will be along with some other veterans of the halcyon days. Fred and Gene co-host and introduce the various segments of the film which, like its predecessor, is a compilation of Metro's film clips, and because this is the year of the American Bicentennial, the picture was selected to open the festival. Sure, we're glad to go. Who wouldn't leap at the chance of a free trip to the Riviera? Tim will look after the garden for the week, which at this early stage doesn't require much attention. But we just got back home. Really, we like it here. And the cats will not be pleased to have us leave home again so soon.

Fred Astaire and Gene Kelly in Cannes, 1976, on the publicity tour for That's Entertainment, Part II.

~ ~ ~

I can't help speculating about what foolishness lies ahead. Certainly this premiere won't be as dramatic an evening as was the opening of *That's Entertainment* in Beverly Hills two years ago. That night easily a thousand fans lined Wilshire Boulevard to watch the stars arrive, while in another part of town, five hundred policemen pumped tear gas and bullets into the house where the Patricia Hearst kidnapers were barricaded. We watched the devastation on television with Adele and Fred, waiting for the studio limousine to drive us off to Hollywood's grandest night. After the film, as we walked the red-carpeted paths from the theater across Beverly Drive, up the street and across Wilshire into the hotel for the party, even F. A. was stunned. Fred said he's not seen its equal in all his years in the business. Dellie added a few comments of her own—griping her disapproval of such goings-on from the moment she set foot in the car. Adele commanded my promise to keep close because she is frightened in a crowd, she said.

It was all I could do to hold sight of her, much less act as a bodyguard. Dellie is somewhat of an enigma because she never made a film and is seldom in the public eye, yet she was the most sought after celebrity there. Finally Fred had to yell at her to stop signing autographs because she was holding up the parade. Not your ordinary signatures either—Dellie added extra flourishes. Sketches of swans, daisies and the like. The crowd loved her and she loved the crowd.

The 1974 film itself, a series of clips from MGM musicals made during Hollywood's happiest decade, set the emotional tone of the party. Fifty Metro stars appeared in a formal line-up on the stage to commemorate the studio's fiftieth anniversary. All they had expected to do was pose for one memorable photograph, but with Sammy Davis as master of ceremonies goading them on, the evening grew into a series of impromptu entertainments. As a tribute to Garland, Gene Kelly did the last song he sang to her at Metro. The room, taut with emotion, was hardly ready for the act which followed. Without warning, Fred was suddenly on his feet and up on the stage with demands his sister join him. For an almost unbearably excited audience, he, Ginger, Gene, and Adele

Fred, Ava, and Gene Kelly, Cannes, 1976.

did a change-partners routine. Jack Haley, who produced the film as well as the entire premiere spectacle, had just whispered that I should assure Fred he was not expected to perform, in spite of Donald O'Connor's inebriated pleas to do so, and as I passed the information on to Ava, her father stood up. Fred realized he had no choice but, being the pro he is, hates performing without preparation.

I was seated between my wife and Liza Minnelli. When Gene sang his love song to Judy, Liza burst into tears, Ava grabbed for her hand, and the two ladies remained clutching at each other across me; Ava continued crying as her aunt and father appeared on the stage—performing together again after thirty-four years, and when Liza closed the show with her own tribute to Judy—her mother's "You Made Me Love You"—the entire audience choked up.

For a while we had erased twenty years and the old town was very special once more. As Sammy said, "All we can do is remember this night. It can never happen again."

On the way home, we learned that all the SLA members (Patty Hearst was not among them) who were under siege had been shot or died when the house burned. A sobering and saddening note—that those past few hours had been such high-pitched excitement on both ends of the scale.

Fred insisted that we come in after the limousine dropped us at his house. He opened champagne at three o'clock in the morning! I wonder what lies ahead in Cannes. We'll find out soon enough. We're going over a day early so Ava and I can have some time alone and we want to be there for him at the airport when F. A. arrives.

Two days ago I was sidestepping manure in a vain effort to chase Mary Monica's wandering cattle back to their own road, and now my wife pleads for a definite decision: should she make us cocktails from the full bar provided in the room, or would I rather have the Dom Perignon the management just delivered?

I choose the champagne and wonder. What exquisite deed could I have done to arrive at middle age in this splendid fashion? A lovely, unique woman who, to my everlasting confoundment, truly seems to dote on me. Sons who openly offer their love and respect. A cat who sometimes considers me his equal. What sufferings could I have endured in other lives to earn such compensation? I touch wood.

I, we, are given so much. So many extras, it's difficult to keep the right perspective. I hope the coming years dealing with the sea and soil will prove somewhat of a balance. Whatever. We are grateful. Enough—where *has* that woman got to with the champagne? Ava, I imagine, is roaming the room, rubbing against things in that catlike way she has when abundantly happy. As opposed to bumping into them at ordinary times. Ava is seldom less than happy. But there are degrees.

For me, returning to France is something of an event. Under the auspices of the United States Navy, I chanced to be in Cannes for my twenty-first birthday and haven't been back since. Then, still recovering from the war, it hadn't regained its former glamorous image, but the Riviera is more prosperous and glitzy now. Time has cost it some beauty and perhaps a certain innocence as well. The years have done much the same to me, now that I think on it.

~ ~ ~

Cary Grant and Sherry Lansing at breakfast in Cannes, during the publicity tour.

Breakfasting with Cary Grant above the blue Mediterranean was an okay beginning to the day, but I wasn't keen on how this one was ending. Had Ava and I really spent the last half hour trying to convince Johnny Weissmuller that the barman wanted to close up, and the carpet in the lounge of the magnificent Hotel du Cap D'Antibes, was not the right place to demonstrate the Australian crawl to Donald O'Connor, who is too jet-lagged to care?

Did we really hear Johnny ask, “Howz the water, Mac?” as the king of Sweden emerged from the hotel pool? The O’Connors were nowhere to be seen but Mr. Weissmuller was in fine fettle in spite of his late night carrying on. He may be older and softer nowadays but he isn’t any quieter. We’ve been subjected to the famous jungle yell about every quarter hour through the morning, and just as it seemed his voice was failing, some fool gave Tarzan a throat lozenge.

On the tour, in addition to Kelly, Astaire, O’Connor, and Weissmuller, are Cyd Charisse, Leslie Caron, Marge Champion, all still looking sensational, and a sadly overweight Kathryn Grayson. And, of course, Cary Grant. Gene is a surprise. A Francophile, fluently at ease with the language and custom, he further confused his image by confiding he had first studied to be a lawyer. Kelly likes to say that next to Astaire, he feels like the milkman on a night out.

I knew there was something not quite right about that magnificent suite. We suspected it was a bribe. Suspicion confirmed. Publicity felt the trip will be easier for F. A. if we continue the tour. Two more days in France, two in London and however many we wish to stay in California. None. But Fred was counting on it. Had been all along. The itinerary didn’t allow us to return to Ireland for additional wardrobe, which is just as well. I would rather advise Tim of the change in plans by post than have to look him in the eye. How can he take us and the vegetable garden seriously?

Although we’ve attended many Hollywood premieres and the Oscar presentations often, neither of us was prepared for the Cannes equivalent, a somehow more ominous occurrence. The press, all in evening dress, cameras masking faces, shouted in so many languages when Fred and Gene followed us that it was more akin to climbing the Tower of Babel than the stairway up into the Festival building.

After the screening, Cary joined our group for a secret

getaway maneuvered from an off-stage door and since the two of us, as passengers, had to be backstage while the stars were presented, we didn't see the end of the film. Not to worry. We'll catch it twice more within a few days; in London and—Good Lord—Los Angeles! Though reporters and some fans discovered the plan, the driver managed to move out into the night before they blocked departure completely, and as we raced across the French Riviera with those three famous men chatting quietly in the dark behind me, I marveled once again over the odd chain of events leading me to this position from such a different one years ago when I took all sorts of jobs earning money just to spend a few hours with their images.

To finish me completely, at dinner I sat across from the English actress Charlotte Rampling; looking away from those marvelous cobra eyes only when the sound of someone humming in my ear caused me to turn and collide with the celebrated cleft of Mr. Grant's chin. Up to that point, I had fantasized the gorgeous lady's smile was in appreciation of the savoir faire with which I'd lighted her cigarette, but her amusement clearly was directed at Cary, crouched and leering at her over my shoulder like Harpo Marx.

Who can compete with Cary Grant?

I like Cary despite his incredible good looks but have always found him to be a somewhat more understated personality than one would expect. His general behavior now, however, is in keeping with his screen image. His actions this evening reminded me of another time, at a dinner party when Adele and I were sitting with him and Adele was tucking into his soup.

"Dellie," I hissed, "that's Cary's soup!"

"So it is," she hissed back, and goosed him as he sat down. The familiar Grant reactions and timing were perfect then, too.

Our lunch at L'Oasis was sensational. Though Ava couldn't concoct an omelet during our dating days, her achievement in the kitchen has been honorable beyond measure since. But she will be hard pressed to equal anything we had at L'Oasis. Cary arrived at the table a bit late due to an earlier involvement with his shoes when he accidentally stepped backwards into the fishpond, trying to avoid the crush of bodies circulating outside before dinner.

Although Ava elected to join me in the garden outside our room, I've sent her to bed with a good book after she said that she loved listening to the frogs and I noticed an abrupt pause in the conversation from the French couple in the adjacent garden. "And the crickets, too!" I quickly agreed in a voice guaranteed to carry across the hedges separating our quarters.

Now safely alone with notebook and Scotch *avec* soda, I enjoy the frogs and the French while trying to bring credence to thoughts that the kid who swept sidewalks to make a dime for the movies a thousand years ago and I are one, the same. Surely he never existed. I'm the guy seen with Miss Cyd Charisse, movie star, bumping across cobblestones in the oversized gray Cadillac this afternoon. I'm certain to sleep undisturbed tonight—no dreams can equal the absurdity of present reality. I'll be happy to see West Cork again.

But this is fun.

We got lost on our way to visit the David Nivens and stopped at a filling station for direction. Upon seeing F. A., the proprietor and all his family came out to the car to set us on the proper course with such nudging, Gallic glee, and obvious love for Fred that I thought what a remarkably effective ambassador-at-large he could be. No pun intended; Astaire truly is America's best foot.

The French do not take lightly this business of body-frisking before one is allowed into the passenger areas. Some of our group considered leaving and coming through again and I believe it was Kelly who informed the airport guard that if he got any more thorough, he'd have to marry him.

With Fred and the David Nivens in the south of France, 1976.

I followed Johnny Weissmuller through the queue for carry-on luggage inspection and could have belted the young examiner who opened his suitcase and passed over the autographed Tarzan photograph lying on top of his clothes without a hint of recognition. He wasn't even curious. Many of the airport officials seem to be young kids who wouldn't know him, of course, but watching Johnny close his suitcase, wistfully aware the photo he intended as a gift had passed unwanted, was almost unbearable. I remembered the times I had imitated him—played at being Tarzan—and at that moment I would have given anything if just once more, big, loud, flabby, simple John Weissmuller could play at being Tarzan, too.

During the flight to London, at my request, John gave me one of his biographical resumes and, stupidly, I didn't think to ask for one of his pictures as well. I don't need a reminder that there is only one real Tarzan but it would have been nice to have his autograph.

At Claridge's we've been given quarters adjoining Fred's, and the rooms are so vast they seem to go on forever. We're not knocking it, but it's foolish of the studio to provide two of everything when Fred is really happiest with a small twin-bed room and bath when he travels. He doesn't like rattling around in too much space and prefers neatly arranging his clothes on one of the beds rather than hanging them out of sight. MGM could hardly know that, though, and he wants us to have a private sitting room so he can visit. Visit us he does, too. Even when we're both sacked out with cold towels over our eyes as he found us this afternoon when he wandered through in his yellow terry-cloth robe and said, "I can't sleep, so neither can you." Not deterred that we could barely acknowledge his presence, he pulled a chair next to the bed, ate a banana, and chattered amiably for about twenty minutes.

How does he keep the pace? We haven't undergone the rounds of appearances, photo sessions, and interviews the actors have—and we're bushed. Not Father-in-law. The oldest member of this safari keeps us all hopping and he had his seventy-eighth birthday at the beginning of the tour.

Tonight the picture premieres in London, the obligatory party follows, and tomorrow we'll be once again airborne. Seeing London friends again is a bonus, especially since we can be so grand on someone else's tab. Distributing largess, we hosted two luncheon parties in this room-service heaven and gave away as much booze and fruit as our friends could conceal in the overlarge handbags Ava advised them to bring. I wondered if Fred noticed that, except for the bananas he has suddenly become addicted to, his basket of fruit and a couple of bottles have vanished? Naturally when the accountants settle up, he will be blamed. But who cares? The studio will certainly never bring the matter to him and Fred has given them their money's worth.

As he often does when we're together in a public place, the very shy F. A. asked me to accompany him across the crowded room to speak to his English record producers at the party last night. When he stood up to go, his dinner partner, Shirley MacLaine, pouted, "Damn—I thought you were asking me to dance." He knew she was kidding but he stewed about it even so, and when we returned, he did ask her. Fred loathes social dancing for two reasons: he knows he will be the center of attention, and unless his partner is another professional dancer he isn't very good at it. But Shirley is a pro. I noticed she quickly kicked off her shoes so she wouldn't be too tall for him.

~ ~ ~

Sitting with Gene across the aisle from us on the way to Los Angeles, Fred finally relaxes—five Bloody Marys' worth. His relief is obvious and since they'd been talking steadily, neither Fred nor Gene seemed aware that the flight attendant has been keeping their glasses full. But we kept count. F. A., not a heavy drinker normally, got up to use the men's room and couldn't find the door. Entering the galley archway on the portside next to me, he bypassed the lavatory and lurched out the starboard arch to confront his greatly amused daughter. "Lurched" is not the word. Astaire never lurches. But we have seen him steadier on his feet. Reminds me of one of those German weather predictor things where a little carved figure pops out one side for good days and the other side for bad. This is a good day for F. A.

~ ~ ~

Kevin's girlfriend is a *Playboy* centerfold. Or she will be come December.

I've warned Kev that he can expect to see less of the lady as the world sees more, but he doesn't seem bothered by the prospect and wants to invite her to the Hollywood premiere with the family. Fred agreed at once but Dellie demanded to know if Kevin is "going to marry the bitch," along with a few other unrelated comments Ava told her she couldn't use over the telephone when we rang her in Arizona to find out what flight she would be on. She forgets Kevin is only nineteen. Sometimes he does, too. His girlfriend, he tells us, is twenty-two.

She works as a waitress where Kevin cooks (at one of those quiche and improbable salad places currently mushrooming in southern California) but won't be a waitress for very long. They had a great time at the screening because, apart from the fun of everyone arriving in vintage cars provided by the studio, Kevin and Karen had the added kick of seeing the reactions of some of their friends from work who were moonlighting as waiters for the party after the film. The kids, of course, were sitting at the family table with us, Fred Jr. and his wife, Carol, their son Freddy, and F. A. and Adele. Kevin, wisely, seldom mentions the Astaire connection, so none of their friends knew they would be there with the stars. His phone was ringing when we dropped them off at Kevin's apartment (which he won't let me see although I promised not to tell him to pick up his clothes), which I bet is just the beginning of the flack he is in for, especially at work tomorrow.

Dellie behaved herself and was nice to Karen when she realized how terrified the girl was, having only recently arrived in California from the Bronx. Adele doesn't mind at all about the nude posing, but she did wish Karen would cut her hair. She is very brunette, very exotic, and Fred now views Kevin with an entirely different outlook. We're not surprised, though. One of his girlfriends from Beverly Hills High was centerfold material and he was barely fourteen then.

Well, it's finished. As much as we enjoyed being with Kevin and Fred, life in the film colony has lost its appeal and now seems as unreal to us as it must to those who have never been a part of it. We're eager to get back to the quiet and the green and our own simple brand of nonsense. Until then, we can call friends and maybe pick up some of the hard-to-get things we didn't have room to take back to Ireland last time; we can enjoy the sunshine and try not to think about our vegetable garden and before we know it, we'll be on our way home.

Off season we can drive to the village six days of the week without passing another vehicle, but the seventh day brings out every mode of transportation, often entire families clinging to a tractor on their way to Mass. We return to this peace and simplicity after the carnival of Beverly Hills, and overreact by retreating even further into solitude. "Loathe though I am to say it," Ava says it, "we are in danger of stagnating in a pool of contentment," (Good Lord!), and indicating by inflection the "we" is second person singular, having nothing to do with herself, she is away to hire a television set. She could be right. I am the one who digs in more, weaving my cocoon against these dyspeptic times.

We only have one television channel. Very sensible. And hours of transmitting are few. Amen. But we still are required to buy a TV license even though programs are commercial. I suppose it really couldn't operate without extra tariff here because of the small population, and some areas do have access to other stations including the British ones.

Though most commercials are classy productions, naturally many are geared towards the rural viewer. Some of those advertisements are on stationary illustrated cards, described by off-camera readers; this can be intriguing if the reader has somehow acquired copy which doesn't match the picture on the screen. It's pretty disconcerting if you're seeing pictures of medications for fluke and suck lice and other livestock infirmities while hearing about a sale on lacy lingerie. And we did feel the price of the license absolutely justified during recent televised rowing competitions when, in the last heat, the sports commentator screamed that Ireland was ahead . . . coming in with their cox in the prone position. He changed it to coxswains, but too late. And though crime is never laughable, we find a lovely innocence in a police report that deems airworthy the theft of six hams and a box containing two hundred Romanian postcards.

Irish television can also be innovative, equaling the world's best. It's that kind of country.

Invisible behind the garden wall where she has gone to set celery, Ava calls me to fetch Tyler so they can plant the American flag. I fetch and follow our son to his mother's side where they begin work with little dispatch and less coherence, tracing a rectangular area in back of the house, sprinkling seeds from several packets and referring often to a printed diagram which seems to have arrived by post with the seeds.

I note in silence. This being the bicentennial year, one learns we are expressing zeal with a botanical version of Old Glory. Flowers of appropriate hues strategically placed will burst forth around Independence Day.

I returned to the house. One doesn't wish to dampen patriotic ardor by mentioning the weeds and Irish slugs which will probably chomp the flag before it furls.

Tyler is home for summer holidays, and for all we see of him, he might still be in Austria. He works part-time at a bar and grill in the village, and since Kevin left him his tent, he usually stays in after work camping in a field near the harbor. Not only does Tyler know more local folk than we do now, he knows what they drink. Tonight, he told us, he plans to attend the church dance beginning at midnight, and yesterday when we rang the pub we couldn't reach him because he had gone to a town meeting at the parish hall during his break time. The boy doesn't do anything by halves. But I don't think he is quite so keen on bunking in the great outdoors since an inquisitive Hereford slit his canvas with her horn while he was sleeping, and now he doesn't object to the five-mile bike trek home as much as he thought. He is also bright enough not to suggest I collect him those nights after work unless, of course, we happened to be in the pub as we were at closing time last night, and I've a hunch Tyler won't encourage that very often.

Three large beer barrel tops embedded into the wall behind the bar where Ty presided add to the timeworn country color of O'Keeffe's public house. The dimly lighted room with leaded panel windows looking out on a courtyard enclosed by similar buildings, age-settled off-kilter, and higgledy-piggledy wooden chairs and tables around a turf-burning open fireplace combine into a cozy ambiance where people come for gossip and games as much as they do—as Kitty puts it—"for the drink taking."

After dinner at the restaurant next door, we dropped in with visiting American friends, to offer the bartender a lift home and, waiting for him to finish, indulged in the bar's version of a game of darts where points are scored by tossing wooden rings onto numbered pegs attached to a board on the wall.

"Up yours" growled my friendly opponent when I caught a big numbered peg, and without thinking, Ava, who'd scored even higher, chirped "No, Jack—you mean 'up mine.'" Realizing what she'd said, Ava retired to stand with her face in the dark corner of the room. The two fishermen at the bar spewed Guinness across the counter and Ty, who'd been drying glasses, draped the dishtowel over his head.

~ ~ ~

Declaring that she met a bean, joy in Ava's eyes provokes mixed emotion: pleasure in her pleasure: concern that hours gardening in company of Mr. O'Regan further shift the sands of our verbal comprehension.

"I know YOU can do it—but can a person?" Tyler asked his mother during one of those conversations I try to avoid hearing. The question lingers, God save us—sometimes almost makes sense. Many persons of Ava's background could NOT do it.

Fred once told me that shortly after seeing *My Fair Lady* on their first trip to Lismore, he thought he could correct his daughter's inability to sing in key because he knew she wasn't tone deaf, and for her lessons he selected "Wouldn't It Be Loverly" from the show. F. A. would sing a phrase, Ava the next one. He repeated the notes as they should be but she continued to slide under, above and around them until the end of their visit when the notion was shelved, mutually and for always. Perhaps she didn't learn to sing in an Irish castle, but my fair lady has been in tune with the earth from the moment she stepped into the tiny garden behind our Irish farmhouse.

Though I tend to joke about being out of place amidst wealth and fame, and I truly don't forget meager beginnings—neither do I feel at all parvenu. I've enjoyed enough success and public attention of my own to question our sanity when we first considered this two-hundred-year-old stone cottage. How, I thought, can I judge?

In this country I've always lived in a castle! Yet Ava's positive, immediate assimilation into the extreme opposite from which she was born and bred remains, for me, a puzzlement.

What prepared her? To be sure, she fed us well before, but I don't understand when or from where came this knowledge of the vegetable patch; this creature of real culinary talent who, like Venus emerging from the shell, has apparently arrived fully informed in the blossoming of her first artichoke. Along with Fred's gentleness and Dellie's sparkle, Ava inherited their fashion flair, but her own special Astaire style is produced in her garden and at her table. I foolishly remarked that when Ava prepares fish, it has a flavor wonderfully unique. She allowed it has something to do with dirt under her fingernails.

I asked my wife, in all seriousness, how she learned these things of which she previously showed small interest. In all seriousness, she says she honestly doesn't know and brushes it aside as former existence or genetic memory.

Unlike her peers, I suppose Ava's upbringing was atypical of movie stars' children, indulged, of course, but with restrictions more common of British or East Coast social attitudes. Never exploited or hindered in seeking individuality, she continues doted upon by a much-loved parent and feels in no way reactionary against her childhood, but deep down, there must always have been yearnings foreign to Beverly Hills. A favorite memory of hers features a square balcony used for drying clothes outside the cook's quarters where, as a teenager, she spent many hours alone, sitting in the moonlight.

Weighing grave problems amidst the broccoli, Ava and grizzled Tim O'Regan rest orientally on their haunches, oblivious to the soft rain on this very Irish morning. I watch them and try to equate this woman who hangs curds on the kitchen sill in a mesh bag to turn to soft cheese with a little California girl who once kept her Cinderella and Prince Charming dolls' wardrobes in a blue trunk in a special playroom that was built just for her.

Chapter Five

Aunt Dellie and Lismore Castle

Adele Astaire quit showbiz cold turkey at age thirty and married Lord Charles Cavendish, the second son of the Duke of Devonshire. She came to Ireland as the chatelaine of Lismore Castle in County Waterford, which changed her not a whit.

Lismore Castle.

Then, as now, whatever pops into her head rolls off her tongue in a single movement. Unlike her brother, Adele picked up the theater's more pungent vernacular during their years on the boards and employs it generously. She is the only woman I know who can verbally paralyze a longshoreman without shedding an ounce of dignity. Moreover the inherent Astaire warmth makes it impossible for either Fred or Adele to be truly offensive—God knows, Dellie tries. She is also extremely kind but I never voice that within her hearing. She doesn't know we know.

Had she not lost her children—a girl and twin boys shortly after birth—or remarried many years after Cavendish died, Lismore Castle would have remained her home, but under the circumstances, it reverted to the Devonshires who allow her there so long as she pays rent. Dellie installed bathrooms, modernized the kitchen, and largely furnished main rooms. She employed staff, paid exorbitant rent for the summer months, and the Duke still demanded—gratis—the use of her Volkswagen the six winter weeks he spends fishing in Ireland.

I would love to know, too, the real story of Ava's grandmother. Fred and Dellie can only recall their trouping days through the eyes of the children they were, but what must it have been like for a beautiful, prim woman coping with stagehands, producers, agents, as well as the social attitude of the times? Originally a schoolteacher of stringent moral and religious views, Ann Astaire found no valid reason to change her outlook through the years and remained a beauty until her death at age ninety-six.

We'd love to know the story but we never shall. Adele, in passing, mentioned Shaw had been a beau of her mother's. I have often attempted taking notes, but Dellie's constant self-interruptions with irrelevant tirades make it almost impossible. Ava suggested that if her aunt ever writes her autobiography, she should entitle it *Do You Know What Else I Hate?* Instead of "Good morning," it's her usual breakfast table greeting and one we often hear before seeing her because Dellie's voice always precedes her entrance to a room.

Both Adele and F. A. have long been established in the

Fred's sister, Adele, and their mother, Ann, in the 1960s.

world's Best Dressed Hall of Fame, but Dellie told me that her mother saw over her choice of clothing until she was thirty years old and married. Ann Astaire, as the Irish say, must've been some kind of picnic. Though she still seemed to think of her famous kids as children when they were elderly people themselves, their mother effectively took away Fred and Dellie's childhood when she put them on the stage when they were five and seven years old. The original iron butterfly, Ava's Grannie was still gorgeous when I first met her in her late eighties and she was so annoyed that she'd broken her arm when she fell off a ladder, because she practiced Christian Science and F. A. made her have it treated by a doctor. This woman of patrician elegance who beat the vaudeville trail for her talented offspring was the schoolteacher wife of an Austrian brewer in Nebraska, and it was she who shortened the family name from Austerlitz to Astaire; but other than the story that once when they were on the road there was no food for dinner except a boiled egg which Ann cut in half for her children, I've never been able to pry any of the other colorful incidents out of Fred and Adele that must have been rampant in those days. Mrs. Austerlitz may have been misguided in putting her babies in showbiz, but if she hadn't it would've been the world's loss. They both loved her to the point of adulation, and I'll never forget the day they received the news of their mother's death while Fred was visiting at Lismore. That evening as we were going in to dinner, the septuagenarian Dellie took her brother's arm.

"Oh, Fred," she said softly, "We're orphans."

Dellie was the official Lady Charles, but in the years that Ann lived at Lismore with them she assumed a lot of the care for Lord Charles Cavendish during his illness and I imagine ran things everywhere else pretty much as she wanted to. Dellie certainly would have bowed to her mother's authority in that respect even if she had spent the balance of her life trying to dupe her in one way or another. I can almost see Ava's grandmother, pale and erect, descending those wide stairs, stopping to rub some lavender between her fingers from the antique Chinese bowl of the dried flowers that still sits where it has for years, on an inlaid mahogany table at the second landing. The lady of Lismore Castle that I know, however, all but slides down the banisters.

The loss of her infant children affected Dellie so severely that for years she couldn't bear having small children around her, but when her longtime secretary-companion, a young woman from Lismore village, came with her to the States and married and settled permanently in Arizona, she brought her baby girl along while she continued looking after Dellie. Ava didn't share my astonishment when we first saw the child contentedly crawling around Dellie's feet. "Patricia is no fool," she said "Why do you think she named the baby Adele?"

The doctors couldn't determine why Adele's children died. She was in good health, carried full term, and delivered them with no apparent defects. But Dellie had survived a severe accident when a speedboat exploded as her companion pulled it into dock, and even though she came through it with only the loss of much of her hair, she told me that she'd always thought the explosion actually had damaged her internally and affected her babies. Dellie didn't miss a show. She wore a wig until her hair grew back, and the redness of her scorched face was taken care of by makeup and the footlights. Back then, Dellie allowed that she had to go on, otherwise her brother would've been out of a job. She is an Astaire. They're like that. They care and they inspire loyalty; both Adele and F. A. have had the same people working for them for years.

They weren't married at the time of the boat accident, but I think Adele probably already knew Charlie Cavendish. F. A. and she were much favored by the British royals who I guess were more regular theater-goers than they are now and their attendance didn't create so much hoopla. Fred reminisces less than Dellie, but one night when the four of us were dining out in Beverly Hills, something took them back to the London days and they were laughing about the three men "cutting up" in their dressing room as they tried to get ready to go out with them after the show. We enjoyed the story but hadn't realized who they were giggling about, until it sank in that the "Cut -Ups" were the three princes, two of whom became kings of England. Ava and I begged for more, and surprisingly it was her dad who recounted another story that Ava had never heard either. I think that the Princess Royal F. A. referred to was the King's sister, and she was either reclusive or incapacitated in some way because she asked the Prince of Wales if he could persuade his American friends to perform for her parts of the show that would involve only the two of them. As F. A. said, though, when you're guests in a country, a command performance doesn't require much persuasion, and he and Adele consequently found themselves in a large ballroom, singing and dancing before an audience of one who sat in a little straight-back chair directly in front of them without a hint of reaction until they finished their act, when she rose, thanked them and regally left the room. Dellie said they screamed with laughter as soon as they were alone, and later the Prince of Wales relayed the message that the Princess Royal had enjoyed their performance immensely.

The first time I met him, Dellie's second husband, Kingman Douglass, was in the last year of his life. He was stout, halting in speech and infirm, but he still traveled from New York each year so his wife could spend the summer months in her castle. It was there we met, on my first trip to Ireland, and it was also the last time I saw him. I had met Dellie, once, before Ava and I even thought of getting back together when Ava brought her aunt into my gallery to show her my portrait of her friend, Barbara Stanwyck, in work, and that was my sole introduction before we became in-laws and I turned up at her moat. Despite Dellie's dinner conversation, I worried lest I do or say an "un-castle-y" thing and embarrass my bride of only three months.

After dinner the ladies played a game of Scrabble, leaving Dellie's husband and me to chat. Suddenly Kingman struggled from his chair, opened a door next to his wife and niece, and upon a balcony terrace peed into the night. Neither the bride nor her aunt reacted in the slightest. I no longer find such action unusual; I'm comfortable with the knowledge that outside of every drawing-room door in the great houses of Ireland and Britain there is usually an ornate urn containing a withered plant and I've been known to hasten the demise of one or two shrubs of the manor myself.

"Wake up, you old poop," Dellie would say, punching his shoulder if he nodded in his chair, or, because he was accident prone all his life, "What a Klunk!," and in a classic case of pot-calling-kettle, Ava affectionately tagged him, "Uncle Klunky," a name he carried to his grave. Of course Adele had a string of more colorful endearments as well, but she adored Kingman and her constant needling kept his spirit flashing. One could see it, too: the twitch of a grin when chic, still trim little Dellie, while she perched on it anyway, called him a beached whale because she could no longer sit on his lap. She openly berated his before-lunch brandy every day, but King was fully aware that she arranged for Con Willoughby to drive him down to the pub for a change of pace instead of drinking it at home. Con, a tall, thin as a whip, quiet and kind man, runs his own petrol station and car repair business near the castle, but because he had known and adored Dellie since she first came to Lismore when he was a little boy, he chauffeurs when she needs him, collects her guests from the airport, and houses her beautiful old Mercedes when she isn't in Ireland.

Kingman had to sleep on the ground floor, and though she seemed to allow him little peace during his waking hours, Dellie came down from her room three floors above several times during the night to make sure he was resting comfortably and to check, as she said, if he was still breathing. The castle reverted to the Devonshires once Charles Cavendish's widow remarried. Adele wanted them to just live together, but Kingman insisted on making an honest woman of her. And though she kept her widow's pension, it cost her Lismore Castle in her own right.

Of course, in the final scheme of things, it was for the best. Kingman provided handsomely for Dellie. She will be comfortable for the rest of her life but there will come the time when she won't want to cope with running the castle even for a few months; just traveling to and from Ireland will become an arduous business. Even now Dellie speaks of spending more time with Fred. For such diverse personalities, they are the closest brother and sister I've ever known, and though Dellie is almost two years older, F. A. still calls her his little sister, and now that she is alone he is very protective. He is also wise enough to know that they should keep separate residences and not return to being Fred and Adele Astaire again. Dellie's carefree attitude used to drive him wild, especially when she would arrive at the eleventh hour while he paced the stage fretting that something had happened to her. One night, in frustration, Fred slapped her when she breezed into the theater just before curtain, and because she knew he felt terrible about it, Dellie demanded that he pay her twenty-five bucks before she would go on.

Dellie does have her castle, even its ghost: she once saw a gray lady disappear into the wall on the second landing at Lismore. I'm too much a Celt to completely dismiss such talk; given its centuries and dungeons and wayward monks, there should be a few spooks still floating about Lismore. One evening when everyone else had retired, I had a silly shivery journey up to my bedroom on the third floor. Despite the heavy, somewhat threadbare draperies that befitted the castle image and hid the light switches, the stairways were nicely illuminated. But there was a separate switch for each landing and once there I couldn't find the switch to turn the ones below off again. Cowardice, therefore, decreed a climb to the first landing to turn on the lights then back down to the library to turn off the lamps. The library in the dark seemed a hell of a lot further from the stairs than it did with the lights on. Speed took care of that, but by the time I'd run up one landing, tangled myself in the draperies to locate and turn on the light switch, then ran down to turn off the lights and then ran up two flights to light the next dark landing, then down again to turn off the others, and up again, I was scared, exhausted, and furious with myself for sitting up so late writing letters while the others went to bed and left me all alone in the dark.

After breakfast the following morning I settled with Kingman in the library to enjoy the fire and the newspapers and brought up the subject of the castle's ghosts. "Oh," Kingman began when I laughed about my uneasiness with going upstairs in the dark. His mind was quick and facile but he suffered difficulty in speaking, often with exceptionally long gaps of silence between sentences and even some words. "Did you see . . ." "Oh, God," I thought, "did I see WHAT?" . . . "Mont—,"Ava joined us as her uncle completed the word, "—gomery?" She was malicious enough to observe a shiver before she explained that Montgomery is the gardener who comes in to freshen the house flowers after everyone has gone to bed and who would've had a death on his conscience if I'd run into him on my crazed dash through the library after turning out the lights.

Dellie invited Betty White and Allen Ludden over for their first trip to Ireland, and after spending a few days playing castle together, we'd take them on a tour of the country from there. The Luddens are our closest friends, but ever since Adele and F. A. met them at our house in Beverly Hills, Dellie regards the Luddens as her personal invention and has been dying for them to come to Ireland for a visit. So have we. They've not been under one roof with Dellie for more than an evening before though; I wonder if the hundred rooms at Lismore will be enough space?

After our first tea at Lismore with the Luddens and the lady of the house, Allen and I moved the cocktail hour ahead. All the woman do needlework during tea. A charming scene were it not for the turn of conversation. Betty is closet-evil, dimpling the sort of rotten things Adele belts out, and my wife is given to unseemly guffaws to show her appreciation. Needlepointing or not, they are women to be dealt with. The men are in need of gin. Not tea.

~ ~ ~

Dellie, Ava, and Betty White doing needlepoint at Lismore Castle.

At Lismore, if one removes any clothing that might be wanted again the same day, it must be stashed out of sight. Otherwise hands unseen whisk it away and the article will be gone until the following morning when it reappears washed, pressed, or uniquely folded in an obscure drawer. When we arrive, Con Willoughby always refuses to let me help him unload our luggage, bags which will not be seen again until our day of departure.

This is the pattern: We arrive near tea time. Adele greets us at the door with a kiss and rude comment. After mundane exchanges, we go up to assigned rooms where gear has been unpacked and put away. Some time is then devoted to finding just where our possessions have been distributed, because Dellie's housekeeper's ideas about the order of things change from year to year. Mostly, routine is unaltered. I pack pajamas I never wear, Ava brings a frilly nightgown instead of her favored tatty flannel. These garments will be waiting in artistically draped variations for us at bedtime. In different bedrooms!

Although Dellie assumes we sleep together, the never-observed, ever-observing upstairs maid allots me my own bedroom and huge bathroom some distance down the hall from Ava; she almost always has the same quarters, but if we happen to be the only guests I can never be certain in exactly which room my clothes will turn up. It is assured, however, that Ava and I will be on the same floor. That must be a rule of the game.

Breakfast is at nine each morning. We are knocked up (a phrase to which I've had no little trouble adjusting) thirty minutes earlier on the dot. I've often wondered how the invisible knocker-upper reacts to my gravely "thank you" sounding from Ava's boudoir, and since I'm usually awake before the call, the urge to surprise our grim rapper is nearly beyond control. How I long to suddenly yank open the door and reveal myself right there in my wife's bedroom. Without those pajamas.

A warm bath is drawn before breakfast, whether you want it or not, and sometimes one will be waiting after tea. I don't understand how they know we are coming up or when. But they do. The bath water is never cold. Logs appear on the fire, flowers bloom fresh in vases, and should an unwashable jacket or such be put down just long enough for one to use the facilities, it is properly hung away when one returns. It may not be Big Brother, but someone is watching. Maybe Dellie is a witch.

Allen and Betty were given the room with twin brass beds where JFK once slept, but I warned him not to entertain any lewd notions about sharing the bedroom with his wife. He didn't believe me although I was willing to bet him his gear would be in the adjoining room by the next day. I was right. But they left his toilet articles in Betty's bathroom. That isn't fair. I know the rules.

Although we laugh a lot, the beauty and peace of Lismore does command the respect of silence often. A casual glance from any of the castle windows is still breathcatching. I watch the fishermen spreading their nets out to dry by the Blackwater River's banks and wonder how many times can there be in a man's life when he is able to sit by a warm fire in an eleventh-century castle with just the music of Debussy and burning logs breaking the silence?

Except for the sound of rooks returning to the turrets and the slow scraping of a vine across the window by my writing desk, Lismore enjoys the crepuscular hours quietly. Of course people must be stirring all over the place. Somewhere in these antiquated halls Dellie—for one, I'm sure—exercises her customary evening's rage against the birds: Aunty doesn't regard the rooks' churlish complaints with my amusement but at Lismore Castle I'm always in a benevolent mood.

With the frightened expectancy of kids, we wander through the disused section of the castle; poking into places where Raleigh delved. Since Lismore was once a monastery, a legend lingers that

With Ava at Lismore Castle in the 1970s.

monks walk beneath the arch of yew trees in the lower garden every morning at two, and brave little Ava, when she was thirteen or so, visited the grove at the appointed hour; waited all alone for the apparitions to show up. Crazy little Ava.

Tonight we will tread the yew walk at dark! In the Irish summer that won't be until nearly midnight but we expect to be protected by martinis at tea and wine at dinner. For a kid who grew up in his grandma's cabins, about the size of the castle's bathrooms, Lismore is sometimes unreal.

Betty sang "There's a Kind of Walk Yew Walk that Makes You Happy" until Allen vanished. The only Phi Beta Kappa among us got cute, hid deep in the grove thinking to take us unaware. He might have succeeded, too, if he had been wearing other than white sneakers. I crept up to the tree next to him and, as he was about to do his banshee bit for the very edgy ladies, I tapped the back of his neck. There came the cry of the banshee all right.

That's this evening's fun and games for the silver-haired set. It's a nightcap, giggle, and bed. Dellie decided that if the present duke is cheap enough to make her pay rent on what once was her home (they don't rent the castle out, it's not as if the very rich Devonshires were loosing other tenants during her stay) he can do without her automobile, and she gave the station wagon to us outright. We are driving it off to Galway right after breakfast tomorrow—rather, today!

Following a well-behaved span of driving through the downpour, Betty softly hummed "Look to the Rainbow" and Allen whistled accompaniment just as quietly. A nice sound, terribly moving somehow, and Ava's face streamed with tears before I remembered the song is from her father's film. We are having an adventure in a country we love with people we love, and everyone knows our time spent together from now on will be limited. There is a sweet melancholy.

An absolute topper as we neared Galway: the rain simply blew away and left a double rainbow. A nice welcome for us—especially me, since Ava and I came to Galway on my first trip to this country as part of our extended honeymoon and we're staying in the same inn, actually in our same room we had then. The Luddens are just next door, and since it is so spectacularly placed just above the sea, we're going to take them around the grounds before dinner which unfortunately with these long summer days will be too early for Betty to see the sun go down on Galway Bay as, she said, she has always longed to do.

~ ~ ~

After dinner we were drawn by sounds of laughter and applause into the inn's lounge which doubles as the local pub. Against the far wall sat a dozen men with pudding-bowl haircuts and ramrod backs. Singing a capella at the head of the table were two women and, next to them, another fellow with his back to the room. The "sing-song," as they call it, is a common enough occurrence in Irish pubs, but the spontaneity with which everyone participated, and the beautiful voices of this group in particular, charmed us.

The room fell quiet at one point, a very old man began to sing "Come Back, Paddy Reilly." Such a scene in a movie would send me straight for an insulin shot, but last night the lot of us could've joined "Paddy." The fellow facing away from us, with perfect pitch, saved some of the shakier solos by assisting in impeccable harmony and, displaying an impressive repertoire, they gave us everything from American folk music to Irish rock. Betty White Ludden said that was "Blarney." Betty White Ludden should be put to sleep.

The one person in the pub who preferred talking to singing was a funny little guy called Billy. Although the rest of his group never stirred from their place against the back wall, Billy was all over the room, eventually slid over to our table. Literally. Billy's bottom seemed never to leave the benches that lined all the walls; he edged his way. One minute we saw him with his gang, next minute he was chatting to Betty. Billy asked us all to sing. Ava and I declined. I sing constantly, but within the bosom of my family. Ava faints if she sings. We told Billy Betty would sing. Betty assured us she would not. Billy insisted, his point being that his lady friend in the group had ten kids and if she could still sing, so could Betty.

We agreed and pushed Betty off the bench. She sat on the table, suddenly became Maureen O'Hara. Betty would certainly never have volunteered and swore us to secrecy. But what performer could truly resist such an invitation? Not with that setting and audience. Especially since nobody knew the Luddens are professionals and the locals were including us in their festivities from pure goodwill.

Sitting on a table in a pub in Ireland, Mrs. Ludden sang. The room went absolutely wild and refused to let her off with only one song. They shouted requests and whistled and stomped until she did an encore, this time with Allen. Ava wept, of course.

Ignoring the landlord's harried pleas, no one left at closing hour; instead, brimming with camaraderie and—by then—Irish whiskey, we all formed a circle for a rousing, if somewhat uncertain, chorus of "Side by Side." The men who started it turned out to be some dockers on holiday in Galway. Not locals, they had stumbled upon our place while out driving. One hopes St. Christopher or Somebody up there watched them safely home because nobody in that pub could be trusted behind a wheel last night. Especially Billy.

The dockers have invited us down to their hotel for a "bit of a do" again this evening but we're not going. Any endeavor to repeat the experience would be unwise. Both Ava and Allen sleep while I've been noting Betty's attempts to use a small boat as a stepping stone across the marsh. Our picnic spot is unbelievable. Foals, lambs, a pig, and donkeys amble along the road. Even a family of swans floats on the water. We've lunched in the shelter of white rock on moss, so vivid one doubts its authenticity; truly emerald-like; shades of green interplaying as in facets of cut stone. My God! It's the Fourth of July and I am sitting here listening to the silence—in Ireland.

Betty maneuvered the boat again and joined me on the rocks where we spoke in whispers until Allen awoke, refreshed and determined to buy land THERE—at that very moment. I allowed to help him play his silly game and we climbed over stone fences up to the only house within miles where the old man sitting in the doorway responded to Ludden's enthusiasm with "Get out!" These are land-proud people. There was to be no talk of estate sales in Gaelic or otherwise. I chortled all the way back over the stone fences. They don't take so readily to strangers on their property as they do in their pubs, it would seem.

"Go see what that sonofabitch is up to," Dellie waved us off after breakfast last week. Excepting F. A. and her close friend, Sybil Harrington, Adele sets a standard of four successive days as a long enough visit. Everyone accepts this and we'd planned to tour with the Luddens regardless, but I guess she felt need of a reason for the mandatory departure and asked—no, demanded—we check out a hotel newly opened in Kerry by an Irish Yank she had never met, therefore doesn't trust.

Now that we've a place in Ireland, too, Dellie has it made. After four days, she sends her guests to us on the pretext they should see more of the country and we are family after all. Her guests are forced to leave the comfort of Lismore Castle for a simple cottage, but it really is only for a bit. Everyone is invited back again a few days later.

Upon our return today—though genuinely pleased to see us—Dellie seemed peevish we'd gone away at all, and finally at dinner the truth came out: she knows only four days' worth of menus. If they've been away a while, people won't realize she has begun all over again. In our case, it didn't matter. We are family

With Aunt Dellie, Allen Ludden, Betty White, and Ava, Ireland, 1975.

and we should have "realized that—insisted on staying." God, she is like her niece.

Delia—a local woman who cooks only during the few months Adele is in residence—is accomplished, willing and, I expect, eager to vary dishes since she and Ava exchange recipes almost every visit, but Dellie tries to spare herself and Delia the bother of altering a system that works so smoothly as it is.

We told Allen how the Irish always greet you whether they know you or not, so of course Ludden gave a big hello to the next Irish person he encountered and was met with frosty silence. It happened in the village again today. I'm not overly gregarious, yet I've had people walking ahead of me actually turn around to say good morning. Allen is so willing, so open, the Irish probably don't trust him. Since Betty and Ava receive greetings as well, we've suggested Allen should seek out Mrs. Cooney—still at her post on the bridge, still smoking her pipe. Clothed in black, the crone's crone as it were, Mrs. Cooney may not have the powers accredited her but few pass her without crossing their fingers. Even Dellie, who should know better.

Betty and I decided to explore and discovered possibly the

oldest section of Lismore Castle. Not my favorite part. We peeked into a dungeon or something dark and bottomless where stairs broke off midway into the depths, where red eyes were peering back. Betty asked if I could see anything; I replied we should get the hell out of there and we went to look at our mirror. Our mirror is a huge piece of really fine glass fitted into an intricately carved frame which stands unused in a room behind the chapel. The glass reflects an eerie twilight due, I suppose, to the darkness of the room and the angle at which it's propped, and Betty and I have toyed with supernatural story ideas since we found the mirror. Maybe we should leave well enough alone.

Adele's oldest local friend, Clodagh Anson, joined us for dinner; always a special occasion because the elderly Miss Anson is unintentionally the funniest woman we've ever known. And next to her, my second favorite Lismore character is the jolly fellow who lodges in her shrubbery. Last year her Italian sister-in-law was strolling the grounds when the herbaceous boarder invited the lady into his bushes and, in attempting to calm her, Clodagh explained that he is only the village sex fiend and it's getting late in the year. It seems when temperatures drop, he propositions any age or gender, consequently insuring a warm jail stay during the off season. I asked Clodagh if he'd been around lately. She said she saw him eyeing her rhododendrons just the other day.

After dinner Adele reminisced a bit about her life and we kept her at it until very late. She doesn't dwell on the past, but with four people begging for more, she talked on until past midnight. What a chronicle she could write!

Although her list was edited or added to almost on a daily basis, if Dellie really didn't like someone, she used to write the person's name on a slip of paper and wear it upside down in her shoe. She gave up the practice when a disfavored suddenly dropped dead and she feared it was her fault, but Dellie doesn't stay chastened for long. It seems that, after retiring last night, she read somewhere that an undetectable and surefire method of doing a body in is to shave your leg hairs, grind them finely and stash them in the victim's porridge, and variations on the theme made up most of Dellie's breakfast chatter. "Chops up your guts like ground glass. I have the very someone in mind, too" was the villainous note on which we concluded our morning repast, and I asked if I might have a peek at her bedside reading material.

Though none of us practices organized religion on a regular basis, I accompanied Allen to Mass and Ava went to the Church of Ireland with her aunt who, she said, complained that it was "colder than a witch's tit" in there, and, showing her disapproval of the reformed version of the service, recited the old litany in a raised voice. Betty remained at the castle with her needlework and failed so miserably in her attempt to knit a shamrock from some green wool she purchased yesterday in Lismore village, Dellie commented that it looked like a "willie warmer." Translating, I advised Betty to replace "willie" with the diminutive of my name, and—church or not—conversation didn't improve with Sunday luncheon.

Fred and Adele's schoolteacher mother could provide them little more than basic education while they were children touring in vaudeville, and to this day, F. A. shows hardly any interest in reading for pleasure. Conversely, Dellie, of the more extrovert personality, is somewhat of a bookworm.

I suppose that after she married into the British aristocracy and felt a need to keep apace with her genteely schooled in-laws, and because she finally had the time, Adele studied the classics.

"I'm mad about Jane Austen, of course," Dellie addressed no one in particular at lunch, as she slid slightly under the table, her foot searching for the floor bell to alert the kitchen that we had finished the soup. Finding it, she turned to Betty, "But I've always preferred Emily to Charlotte Brontë, don't you know this fucking bell doesn't work!" Unwisely continuing the tone, I announced that my new favorite bit of graffiti, recently discovered on a wall of the men's room at Cork airport, proclaimed that "cunnilingus is not an Irish airline" and then was forced to explain it. Without understanding the word's meaning, Dellie didn't get the comparison to Aer Lingus and required an explanation at once.

Treading delicately, receiving no assistance but rapt concentration from my rotten wife and best friends, I said that it was an oral alternative men sometimes offer during the love act. THAT Adele understood. Happily supplying the gutter version herself, she demanded to know the clinical term applied to males in a reverse situation. Declaring, in her new knowledge, that she'd like to have a couple of dogs with those names and, substituting "cunnilingus" in place of the song's title, Ava's frail old auntie sang us out of the dining room to the tune of "Fascination."

Those times when I've found her alone, quietly doing needlepoint in the window seat and appearing even smaller beneath the high arched window, with the Blackwater River and her beloved family of swans in the distance behind her, Dellie still seems to twinkle. Thinking I was first down, I was surprised to see her already in the library, sitting with eyes closed, lost in the strains of *Daphnis and Chloë*. Sensing a presence, she looked up, smiled and raised her hands in conducting a few bars. "This is so beautiful," my diminutive and cultured hostess exclaimed. "Doesn't it just make you want to diddle yourself?" For all the service that she must have been accustomed to in the days when Lismore was staffed to the rafters and, as Adele said, there were seldom less than a dozen guests at any given time, she never gives the impression that she takes anything as her natural right. Since I've often heard her larking with the girls in the pantry, I'm not surprised that they nearly chuckle, "Yes, Madame," if she makes a request at table.

Adele installed several extra bathrooms after she came to live at Lismore Castle; the tubs are wide, long enough for a tall man to stretch out comfortably but, since there are no showers, and hot and cold water run from separate taps, it isn't easy to wash your hair. Ava came up with a handy solution when she discovered an old-fashioned glass container in one of the unused bedrooms. Unswayed by the fact that its shape and the nightstand cabinet next to the bed where she found it indicate it must've been a urinal of sorts, Ava had it boiled, and used it to hold clean water for rinsing suds from her hair. I had no quarrel with that until the day, at the end of their visit, when we were leaving to drop the Luddens at the airport on our own way home and the sweet little maid came running out to the car at the last minute. "Oh Mrs. McKenzie." Handing the urinal bottle to Ava, the girl paused to catch her breath. "Your husband forgot this."

Overlooking a stunning panorama, the tall, pointed arched windows line one side of Lismore Castle's dining room which—all things being relative, I suppose—is a less sumptuous feeding place than might be expected under the circumstances but, given the marble fireplace, the displayed collection of Belleek china, the Van Eyck portrait above a carved sideboard, and the crystal chandelier lighting a long polished table also wide enough to comfortably seat two at each end the room doesn't exactly qualify as cozy either.

Adele often has some of the local impoverished gentility in for lunch or dinner, and with most of the Anglo-Irish of that ilk—especially the men—being pompously tedious, she usually does this while we are in residence so she can foist them off on family. Of course, there are the exceptions, Clodagh Anson, and the writer Molly Keane, who do bring a sense of giddy glee to this setting. We're eager to be around when they're invited to lunch. It stays light late enough and Miss Anson lives close enough to manage her way home after dinner without being too much of a menace to the outside world, but it's a wiser proposition if they both just come for lunch during daylight's prime strength. It isn't that the ladies drink. I think it has something to do with being on castle ground when they're behind the wheel. At their departure after lunch today, the two old girls charged out the narrow gate of the courtyard almost simultaneously, waving goodbye and gaily dislodging chunks of wall and bouncing off each other's fenders as if they were armored and mounted for the joust. Wonderful Molly, with her stiletto observations, wit as rich and black as Turkish coffee, was a successful novelist/playwright under the nom de plume M. J. Farrell when she met Adele in the thirties, but she hasn't published anything in years. Following a rare quiet moment at the lunch table, Dellie, ignoring the fact we were eating, asked if Mollie had the real story behind the brains they discovered spattered on Lady So and So's kitchen ceiling. For a woman as soft of heart as she is, Dellie paints some hairy imagery. This conversation didn't fit my fantasies when I imagined myself engaged in witty repartee over luncheon at a vast estate during a weekend in the country. I could hardly cope with it happening for real in a castle where I was a member of the family.

Not waiting for a reply, Dellie suddenly demanded that she write again, and when Molly hinted that there is indeed a new novel in the offing, Adele suggested the people around Lismore were fair game for subject matter.

"You know, those old biddies who are always sticking knitting needles in their canaries' eyes?"

Sometimes those of the Anglo-Irish who've sat at Dellie's table would repay her generosity by a little drinks-before-lunch party which is exactly as it sounds: drinks, usually sherry, and nuts or crisps but never the meal—praise be. After our most recent experience I quake at the very thought. Actually we don't hold much empathy for this sad, pretentious little set of gentility in reduced circumstance, desperately still clinging to a lifestyle that perhaps was not as grand as remembered. I don't think they're very nice people now and suspect that they never were.

Knowing that we were coming up and could lend moral support, Dellie accepted a drinks-before-dinner invitation on our behalf. Other than the fact our hostess was new to us and (unlike similar functions in these parts) she had laid on hors d'oeuvres, all was pretty much status quo: the same old faded faces simpering above outdated frumpy outfits. Little groups, usually divided by gender, arranged themselves throughout the shabby drawing room of a dilapidated Georgian house; a scene Ava and I've seen far too often in this part of Ireland.

Manically animated, our hostess affected an accent impossibly exaggerated. Her jaws parted so widely over each syllable that my eyes were fixed on them to the point of rudeness: I was sure she would spring a hinge. Later Dellie would mimic the woman with deadly accuracy to the delight of the teenage girls serving our dinner, but we tried to turn Dellie towards other topics; as it was, we were hard pressed to erase the creature's monologue from our own thoughts. Lady Felicity's attitude was all the more odious, I felt, because she is somewhat younger than her local counterparts. Sensing fresh blood when we arrived, she pounced.

"Yew will simply nevah guess my secret ingredient which makes these cheesey thingies SO special," she gushed, offering an albino bit of glop on a toasted round, which, too late, we learned to be banana mashed together with Gorgonzola cheese. "As it's yew," our hostess whispered, oblivious to the venom in Ava's plea that we not be kept in suspense one minute longer, "The SEEcret—SHRIEK—is cayenne PEPPAH!" The antidote is another secret. "I barely got back in time to see to the ordoov-rah." We were taken into her confidence once more. "There was I, consulting the muse in my atelier, you know." Mini Muse sprang to mind but I nodded and smiled. "Atelier, Lady Felicity?" "Quite, Deah. One dabbles." I bet one does. "There was I daubing away when the gardener's boy fell into the cess pit. He would push his barrow over the planks covering it, wouldn't he just? One answered his cries at once, of course, but what was one to DO . . . lend him a hand? I mean, Deahs—SHRIEK—it was even in the wretched thing's NOS-trils! Well at lahst one found the gardener and told him to fetch a ladder for his STEW-pid son. I mean, it very nearly RUINED my entarh afternoon—SHRIEK—Relly too tiresome of the boy, yew understand?"

We understood that she wouldn't soil her hands to help a lad who had fallen up to his neck in human waste, and I wouldn't have tried another one of her damned hors d'oeuvres even if we hadn't seen her rearranging them after her slobbering old basset hound licked them askew on the plate. We couldn't get out of there fast enough.

~ ~ ~

On our drive back home yesterday, Ava told an Adele story I'd not heard before: when Ava was seventeen and by then familiar with most of Lismore, she thought to adventure with a hike after tea but explored further than intended before realizing the time and that she still must bathe and change before dinner.

Knowing of a door in the wall facing the river, she cut down from the farmland and returned to the castle from that side—not an easy shortcut, she discovered, involving mud and brambles, costing about an hour and a half. Neither did she know the door was kept bolted, without a summoning bell, and that unless someone happened to be within the immediate vicinity inside, shouting and pounding only accomplished bloody knuckles. Deciding against forfeiting another couple of hours by retracing the long walk around to the front gate, Ava lugged and piled stones to climb up (the senses reel) and finally scaled the wet, mossy wall just as everyone was going in to dine.

Encountering her niece in the hallway—dirty, scraped, and tangled and forcing back tears, Adele's only comment was: "You're awfully late, you know."

~ ~ ~

Years ago, Dellie gifted Ava with a wonderful Victorian toy: a realistic-looking tiger made of papier-mâché which stands on a wooden base set on wheels. Real bone fangs show when the hinged jaw opens and shuts as the animal is pulled along and, for such a delicate piece, it is in such good condition I doubt that any child ever played with it. Rather than chance it in the van with the rest of our belongings, we hand carried the toy when we moved and the little paper beast usually resides in majestic display in our living room. This morning during a fit of dusting, my lady tripped over a sunbeam on the carpet, reached out for nearest support and thereby, alas, hanged the tail. Staving Ava's impending tears, I immediately set to work with paste and paper toweling to repair the damage. God rewards the samaritan. The telephone rang while, holding the appendage in place, I waited for adhesiveness to bind and, because of Adele and my wife, I was presented with the rarest of opportunities.

"Can you get the phone, please, Darling?" . . . "I've got a tiger by the tail!"

Chapter Six

The Short and Happy Life of Nigel-Wynn

"Tyler . . . I need you!"

Ava's plea reverberated through the house, sending me straight outside where I remained in the car with the windows rolled up until the all clear was sounded.

We are in the season of the mouse.

Spring until around mid-October sees the cottage free of rodents, as they still find enough warmth and food in the fields for which they are named; but following first frost, I insisted my family conduct daily mouse patrol before I wander with any degree of confidence about my home. I do this without shame. It is especially ridiculous when one lives in the country but no amount of derision, getting hold of one's self, or knowledge of how stupid this fear is, has overcome my revulsion of these pretty little creatures for over half a century.

So long as I am absolutely certain they are unable to go for my throat, I can observe mice briefly and at a distance (the boys even had a couple of pet mice caged in their room when they were little; that is, when they learned to make their own beds) but rats cause my fingers to go numb at the very thought of them.

We left poison at all probable places of entry, but not long ago one cheeky field mouse marched through the front doorway where Ava, myself, Tyler, the plumber, the electrician, and our boyish architect were gathered, and I didn't feel quite so foolish quaking behind the door when all the guys backed off, leaving my wife to remove the squirming intruder by his tail. She allows the use of poison but Ava won't kill the animals personally or trap them, preferring instead to catch them by the tail. No mean talent that. She carries them out of doors where they do not wish to be (and most likely beat her back inside).

Employed to ward away these horrors, our cats confused their duties: "You are here to protect me," I admonished Nigel-Wynn. "I require no visual proof of your skills and you are to abandon this practice of stacking incomplete rats in the tack room straightaway."

Tyler insisted that cats don't eat shrews because they taste bitter (I didn't ask how he knew) and he might be right; Phyllis-Doris deposited her shrews on the front doorstep for me to stumble over, but they're tiny and not as scary as the mice.

Not gale, nor sleet, nor dark of night would deter the meter reader from his appointed rounds unless, of course, he chanced upon members of the O'Regan family, in which case he asked them to ask us to read our electricity meter ourselves and drop him a line with the details when we were of a mind to. For the last reading, though, he came out in person, arriving after ten p.m. amidst black and raging skies, shouting above the wind as he knocked, "I'm not a burglar in the dark." In this respect, he isn't unique. The electrician has been known to call with several teenage apprentices well past dinner time; the contractor appeared mostly before breakfast; our architect discussed blueprints between goal points during Sunday night's repeat of the big game on television; and the plumber preferred to consider our pipes following Mass on Sunday morning. I have often discarded jeans for the flowing ease of a caftan robe when, suddenly, one of their respective vehicles eases around the bend towards our house, and I've learned to change from Arab to patched-elbow tweeds in a twinkling.

Ava had cajoled for years that caftans were masculine, even biblical, before I accepted them for the comfortable garments they are. But no matter what she says, I am not about to let an Irishman catch me wearing a dress. After Tim moved the calves down to the lower field last week, I decided we were enough out of sight for me to fill their water tub without changing from my caftan so I pulled on some wellies, drew the water and was pouring it into the cows' tub when we heard the O'Regan children approaching. Kitty sent Nora and Donal down to water the stock and they had cut across the back field for quicker access. Fortunately my wife was laughing too hard to find the camera when I tossed the half-full bucket into the air, picked up my skirts, and ran for cover as quickly as the wobbly boots would allow. It would have been worse to let an Irish CHILD find me in a dress.

Ava had blind faith in all things Irish since she was simple-minded enough to marry one in the first place, but certainly, I should have questioned an Irish builder's word. I should have remembered that though my dad could achieve wonders with a trowel and plumb line, twelve years wasted before he and my oldest brother, a building contractor, finally completed the one-day job of installing the archway between our kitchen and dining room that they had promised my mother throughout my adolescence.

When we elected to extend the cottage to include a working-studio-cum-escape-hatch for me, everyone warned against it, to forget having anything built in this country unless we wished to join the like-minded society burgeoning at the madhouse; and genetic surging should have alerted me, but ignoring all, we stepped stage center of a black comedy and called in a contractor.

"Have my men out of here under two months," jollied our friendly builder as we settled the deal over a hefty swig of Jameson's.

Bejaysus, he is a man of his word. Six weeks after groundbreaking, there wasn't a workman in sight.

I believe they will return to complete my studio one day, but until they do, we must continue to live with the smell of oil paint in our living room where the study of Kevin and Tyler standing in the upper field is beginning to take shape. My aim is to portray the boys surrounded by wildlife indigenous to this seacoast, a painting that progresses as I observe and learn about the area. It'll play hell with composition, probably, but to

In the living room at Clonlea, at work on a painting of Kevin and Tyler.

PHOTO: DICK DE NEUT

adverse criticism I'll always have an answer: "It isn't finished." Actually the idea was born from parsimony. I found a large expensive linen canvas had been damaged in transit. In order to save the canvas, realizing it could only be for use within the family, I considered reproducing the fencepost standing askew in the upper field just outside the window, its gray, aged grain being beautifully weathered and the knothole a dandy camouflage for my terrible job of patching the rent in the linen.

Ava spoke her doubts regarding the merits of a portrait of a rotting fencepost in our brightly decorated living room, especially since a four-foot-square picture tends to catch the eye. She suggested a few things to go with it. "Why not," she offered, "do the landscape behind the post and paint the boys looking Irish in Aran sweaters and Wellington boots with spring flowers?" I associate muck and mud with Wellington boots, but I like to be agreeable and asked that while I was at it, why didn't I just include all the seabirds as well? I'd like nothing better than rendering little feathers with a Number One brush and magnifying glass. Ignoring sarcasm, giddy with the idea, Ava said I also could put in the bramble bushes growing just below the fence because she intends making jam soon. And rabbits, too, because we almost have to kick them out of the way when we're strolling, and maybe a mouse because they're so dear (ugh) and bugs and butterflies only not the Cabbage White. "What a nice painting," she squealed, slapping her hands together like cymbals in a "that's that" gesture. "Several nice paintings," I pointed out, adding that I had never more than dabbled in landscapes before.

"Richard, put in another magpie at once!" Ava whispered behind me as I was about to dab a purple-blue flash to the tail of a magpie in flight. "One is for Sor-row . . . Two for Joy,"

"What are you on about?"

"Nursery rhyme. YOU know . . . One is for Sor—"

"Cut that out. I haven't the foggiest notion what you're saying. Sounds as if I left out an ingredient for the Blackbird Pie.

WHAT rhyme?"

"Now you're being silly. You can't have four and twenty blackbirds and a magpie pie."

"I think I don't want to have this conversation."

"It's superstition. Very bad luck to see just one magpie. I don't remember the rest of the poem. Did you know the Irish word for superstition is 'pishogue'?"

"Will you and your voodoo get out of here? I have curlews and ravens to consider."

My day was off to such a happy start, too. Two for Joy, huh? Well, there might be room for another magpie; it's a big field. Not only has Ava created compositional problems, from now on, every time I see a magpie I won't rest until I find its goddamned mate.

Will those builders never finish my studio?

Most mornings I have coffee by the sitting room window and watch the curlews make their spindly way through the tall grass. Speckled brown, the size of hens, with their over-long scythe-shaped beaks and knobby knees, they provide comic relief from the vivid little songbirds flocking among the bramble and other wild berries. Often the curlews are joined by oystercatchers. Slightly smaller, these seabirds' similarly shaped bills, like their webbed feet, are bright red while the plumage is black and white. I expect they really do feed on oysters, although they can unearth precious few in our pasture and I recently made the error of telling Ava that the bird book describes the oystercatcher's call as sounding rather like "kleep." "Oh," she asked, all interested, "is that kleep with a C or a K?"

Black and white seems a prevalent combination of so much of the animal life around us, wild and domestic. Nearly all the cattle, the dogs, even the few cats, the ubiquitous members of the crow family, and my favorite, an exquisite little fowl, aptly named wagtail, who looks more a Japanese pen and ink interpretation than a living creature, are mixtures of this color scheme.

Despite their fragile, etched-like quality, the wagtails enjoy our coldest seasons as well as summertime and, along with consuming curiosity, possess a sense of fun. One entire family of these cheeky little birds has recently taken to racing, or rather leading, the car to at least as far as the first turning when any of us drive away from the house. Dipping close to the bonnet, darting just out of sight below the headlamps and back, may be great crack for them but unsettling for the driver, and they remind me of porpoises pulling similar antics at the prow of the ship when we rounded Gibraltar in my navy days, a hundred years ago. They were black and white, too.

Crack. Funny how quickly we slip into native vernacular even though we'll probably never understand their customs. Nor they ours. Actually, "crack," in this instance, loosely translating as "fun and games," is to me harsh sounding, not in keeping with its colloquial meaning, but it's seen often enough to be unconsciously assimilated. I never use it purposely but pub signs everywhere advise food, drink, and crack for the ultimate evening out, and I've heard Ty agree that something was "good crack" in conversation with his friends. Both Kev and Ty have an ear for languages and parrot dialects unconsciously. Once, when I heard two West Cork men talking on our back terrace, I went out to investigate and found Kevin in serious conversation with Timmy O'Regan, and Tyler's ear is such that he has to be reminded not to slip into local dialect when we pick up hitchhikers lest they might feel he is imitating them. He is unaware when it happens.

Thumbing is a main—and often the only—means of transportation in this part of the world, and what a joy to be able to offer someone a ride without fear and to know that our kids can travel on the roads in safety, too. We always say "lift" because offering a "ride" has a sexual connotation in this part of Ireland. Sometimes the thumber doesn't require a lift; it's often no more than a request to take a message into the village or perhaps just to post a letter. On one of his more recent visits Dick De Neut accused me of staging it for his benefit when I was waved down to help with wandering cattle, easing them forward with the car to keep them on the intended path while the herdsman dealt with the more adventuresome. Dick said we were putting him on; the whole place is a Warner Bothers back-lot film set, and he refused to accept that people actually do these things and talk this way. Especially us. We are as comfortable with the Irish terms of bonnet and boot as we were with the American automobile counterparts of hood and trunk, and Ava keeps an extra pair of Wellingtons in the trunk which, in the case of the Volkswagen, happens to be in the front. Dick could only hang his head and somewhat forlornly repeat Ava's request that he please fetch her boots from the bonnet.

~ ~ ~

Returning from a shopping excursion miles away, Ava bemoaned that we couldn't have the paté she intended making because she was unable to locate all the required ingredients save one—pork fat. No brief dissertation this: she babbled as I nodded in sympathy and unpacked the groceries. She finished wailing about the lack of pork fat—"when you've driven miles"—as I came to the final item in the basket which was underneath her cardigan.

"And what is this?" I inquired expectantly as she unwrapped the parcel.

"Pork fat! PORK FAT, Richard?!"

"Don't look at me. I haven't left the house all day." Maybe shamrock pollen is an hallucinogenic.

~ ~ ~

Girlish giggling brought me to the window and the sight of my wife skipping rope with Nora. They were supposed to be weeding the vegetables and Ava should never, ever skip rope.

~ ~ ~

Nigel-Wynn didn't nag outside our bedroom window heralding the beginning of my day, which was serving the cats' breakfast, and although he had been tardy before, depending I guess upon what unfortunate he might have feasted on earlier, he didn't come in for his midday snooze next to the storage heater either. An unalterable routine. Now with twilight darkened by a sudden fierce squall, his continued absence causes anxiety. He loathes storms.

Last week while I lazed in the rocking chair by the window with the sun robbing my head of thought, he climbed onto my lap and—briefly—held me in a gaze of unbridled devotion. A feeling I returned. As far as it could be understood, between us was love of the purest form. Only a moment of a strong electric exchange but something I hadn't believed possible on this level between a man and—of all creatures—a cat.

Because the timbre of her voice indicated how very disturbed Ava really was even though she kept assuring us of his safety, I haven't mentioned it, but as surely as I knew I felt his love that day, I know that I never will again.

The storm raged through the night and part of today. Now Phyllis-Doris was nowhere to be found. Either she went in search of her brother when the weather cleared or else misfortune claimed them both. We've seen no foxes in the immediate area since we've lived here, and the neighboring dogs, who would discourage predators, also lived in harmony with ours and sundry cats; yet the thought that a fox or stray mongrel might have come for our pets is finally given voice. From the beginning, we accepted that country cats could not be housebound despite the hazards of their nocturnal roaming, but all this time and the knowledge they preferred spending most nights on a security blanket in the tack room fostered complacency. We were unprepared. Not that one is ever conditioned for a loss of any sort, but our defenses were totally down.

Just as we took our breakfast coffee outside, Phyllis-Doris labored over the back wall. Alone. Exhausted. Away forty-eight hours, how far could she have traveled to be in such weak condition? Evidently returning just for the food she downed more desperately than usual, the cat started off again and I followed. But we didn't go far. I couldn't get through the gorse-covered places she attempted and she was confused, too unsteady for much effort herself. When her legs finally folded, lucidity fled and I carried her back to the house where, limp as a rag doll and with about as much sense, she slept around the clock.

Phyllis-Doris hasn't sought her brother again; has hardly left the confines of the terrace. But I believe she found him before. Please God, not trapped. Probably the victim of poison some of the farmers set out for vermin. Remaining with him until the end I think, she came back to show us where he was.

Tim told us later that his whole family searched for Nigel-Wynn, too, and with country awareness, had watched the landing places of the carrion birds, something, of course, we wouldn't have thought to do. These country people, as a rule, don't coddle their animals. Pets work for their keep like everyone else, but old Nigel-Wynn, refusing to accept any such folderol, managed the

Nigel-Wynn, who wouldn't take no for an answer when it came to cheese . . .

. . . nor would Phyllis-Doris.

family O'Regan as easily as he did us.

I miss him. Our roughhousing. He liked his tail pulled and being held under his front legs when I swung him as I would a child. We went for walks together and he came when I whistled—a jet blur returning like a shot across the meadows. Embarrassed to call out such a ridiculous name, I always whistled, and although he did react to his name or just my voice, I never understood how he knew the whistle was intended as a similar signal. Or even came from me. He was my good friend, never entering a room without greeting me loudly. For Ava he was different. Entirely chauvinistic, he held her beneath the conversation reserved for males, but allowed, accepted, expected her caresses and, at times of special favor, he would cup her face between both paws to nip her lightly on the chin; something he did to no one else.

Wondering what to do with Phyllis-Doris now that she is alone and also such a reminder of her brother, we've considered trying to find some nice old lady who might take her in for comfort and companionship. Kevin and Tyler both threatened us with bodily damage if we gave her away and we really didn't want to, but she shouldn't be left by herself and the next cat will have to be a working barn cat like the farmers'. No more pets. How could we expect another cat to stay outside if Phyllis-Doris had the run of the house when we were here and access to the tack room when we were not?

~ ~ ~

No question. Phyllis-Doris stays.

Ava went to fetch some garden tools from the barn and found her curled on straw in the corner. A barn cat. We never saw her there before. Any notion of gardening forgotten, Ava streaming tears with the cat clutched to her bosom, ran back to the house. Poor, demented little Phyllis-D., with her rolling eyes, exposed fang, and slobbering appreciation, couldn't be much consolation, but I believe that little black P.-D., so seldom with us in mind, is going to stick around in body for years to come. And in spirit, Nigel-Wynn hasn't left.

~ ~ ~

"Do you think I should see what is on television at six-twenty because next week they're rerunning 'The Conquest of Everest' at that time? Or do you think I should read?"

Fortunately Ava punctuated the sentence with a martini so I merely suggested she busy herself elsewhere and thanked her for the drink. I offered that since our lanes were replete with blackberries she might try making up the few jars of jam just as a filler between books. Ava said that sounded like a very strange sandwich and they were bramble, not blackberry; and she intended to rearrange the linen closet.

What a small seed it takes to produce the flower of discontent. I was so pleasantly absorbed with gulls and surf before. Now I had to know what was on the box at six-twenty.

I could only find television listings for the upcoming week, but it really didn't matter because what was printed is not necessarily what was programmed. This rarely bothered Ava but, my tolerance crumbles when I've planned an evening around a particular showing only to learn that it started twenty minutes earlier than scheduled. To give them fair dues: when the main transmitter in Dublin blew out canceling the country's viewing of the ending of an espionage thriller, the network screened the crucial last few minutes of the film following its newscast the next evening. I suppose it all equals out in the run.

Nigel-Wynn can't be replaced but we found a companion for Phyllis-Doris in a feisty little marmalade-colored tom from the village. Orange or redheads are called ginger-haired here but there is no way we would name an animal Ginger. He comes to us already dubbed George. Simple enough. We can use it and not care if anyone else is within hearing distance.

Phyllis-D. wants no part of him. Keeping mostly in the protective confines of her basket by the hearth, which until George's arrival she wanted no part of either, she rebuffs efforts towards friendliness, but she had better change her tune quickly because she won't have size advantage very long and it appears George doesn't accept that difference even now. At first he retreated, cringing before her snarls, but finding her asleep, he sidled up to the basket, batted her across the head and swaggered away leaving her blinking. We will have him neutered, of course, which will probably make him grow even larger than his stocky frame already indicates, so P.-D. had better exercise diplomacy while ahead of the game. Although he had not ridden in a car before, George settled easily into

My study of Ava holding George, with Phyllis-Doris at her feet.

Ava's arms for the ride home from the pub where he was born, and once here, he walked into the house as if he owned the joint. Arrogant and gregarious, he should pep up Phyllis-Doris' winter no end.

As Ava said, "He is a satisfying cat."

~ ~ ~

Vet's bill for George's recent operation reads:
Mr. McKenzie
Castration
£ 5.00

Chapter Seven

Tall Enough to Hold the Pyramid

We talk to each other a lot, my lady and I, sometimes late into the night, about how we came to be together. Funny about Ava and me. Born and reared polar opposites, we're almost alike in our difference. The flip side of the same record. Basically, we each were influenced by a single parent: her father, my mother. They both came from Nebraska, were middle-aged when we were born, and neither was formally educated beyond grade school.

Before we return to the green fields of our particular Land of Oz, I indulge a time warp. A glance over the shoulder. Ava's, too.

~ ~ ~

I recall so much about my family's lifestyle because in our cramped quarters there was no escaping. We were all very much a physical part of it. No less loved, but by virtue of a different set of customs, Ava often given into the care and training of a governess, the wonderful Zella—Mademoiselle Kohl, who remained her close friend and confidante until she died a few years after our marriage.

Mom would send me to the butcher for a quarter or fifty cent's worth of stew meat—brisket. The Astaire kids had their hamburger meat especially minced in their own separate kitchen.

Ava with her Aunt Dellie (left) and Great-Aunt Maud in California, 1940s.

In my neighborhood, kids spilled into the streets, yelling, laughing—crying, too—with great regularity but, for their own safety, the children of movie stars couldn't enjoy such freedom; usually playing and seeing each other by arrangement when not in school, and though a large family of children lived directly next door to the Astaires, their properties were separated by a wall. Zella liked to recount how the very little Ava used to hear one of the daughters crying all the time—how it distressed her until one day she thought she discovered the cause: "Geraldine," she confided, "just doesn't like the Chaplins."

At sixteen I learned to drive in an Oregon hayfield where I had a summer job. At age ten, Ava drove a tractor at their ranch but trained to drive a car on the back lot of Fox Studios and because she would be away visiting her aunt on her sixteenth birthday, the inspector came up to the Astaire house after hours to test for her driver's license.

I had rabbits, cats, dogs, and once, a pet opossum. Ava had two horses and a pony.

Until I was eleven, I spent birthdays with my grandmother because she thought it was cute that we were born on the same day. Ava remembers circus parties with Liza Minnelli and elephants and disappointment because Hopalong Cassidy failed to show up, as promised, on her birthday. The Astaire cook made serious Austrian concoctions of incredible chocolate cream. Mom baked a coconut cake for Grandma and a chocolate cake for me every birthday. We seldom had cake other times, which probably accounts for my sound teeth because, being a rotten baker, my mother compensated for the lack of symmetry by extra dollops of frosting on her lopsided layers.

My stepgrandfather—the only grandfather I knew—used to hold me on his knee and threatened to burn a hole in my arm with a finger he heated next to the wood stove. Clark Gable dandled Ava on his knee when he visited their ranch on weekends.

Mom dressed my flighty six-foot-two cousin, Ernest, in drag and took him to a barn dance. Ava's family didn't attend barn dances under any circumstances.

I nearly broke my neck searching the Christmas tree for a teddy bear. Ava gave her teddy to a children's hospital and still remembers her despair when she saw him riding away on top of the other toys her mother gathered and knew she couldn't ask for him back because it would seem selfish.

Once a family of summer people who manufactured candy brought down a kid-high barrel of their best-mixed over which we clawed and fought, trying for the caramels. Ava says that's like the barrels of oysters Hermes Pan used to fly in from New Orleans and they all searched for pearls. No it isn't.

Every Sunday, Mom and I joined Grandma to hear "One Man's Family"on the radio. Her grannie listened to "One Man's Family," too, but Ava, the cook and the maid watched Gorgeous

George wrestle on TV in the cook's sitting room.

Mom always diagnosed a case of the "Highflinkykafloris" when I was sick. If Ava wasn't up to snuff, her dad introduced himself as Dr. Crackinbones and took out hammers and saws from his tool box.

I played in the turrets of a fake castle on the beach. Ava slept in the tower of a real castle in Ireland. They both had bats.

~ ~ ~

I guess it couldn't have been what you'd call an unstable childhood, but we sure moved a lot when I was a kid. My roots were hardly damaged at all, though, since we didn't travel the world, or the country, or even much of the town, and I always attended the same schools. We just kept changing houses about the neighborhood. All probably within a radius of some eight blocks or so. I've never quite known why.

Prices must've been pretty much the same everywhere in those times, too, especially in that section of town, and with my mother's almost religious attitude toward the prompt payment of rents and insurance premiums, I know we weren't evicted. Sometimes we stayed at my grandmother's

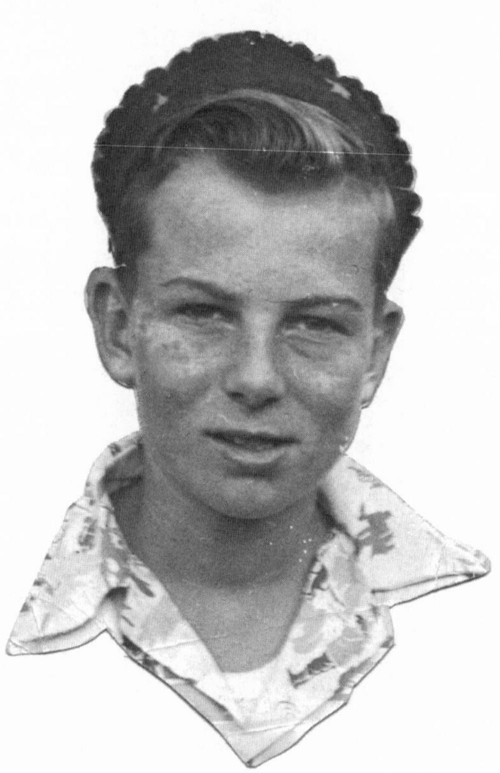

Santa Cruz, California, 1930s.

house or, rather, one of her cabins (Grandma lived within the radius), but those were usually brief stops to give Mom a chance to case the area for fresh prospects. I suppose, in Mom's eyes, the grass constantly looked greener in someone else's yard and if, by chance, that someone rented us his house for any length of time, the grass looked taller, too.

Scrupulously clean about her house and person, my mother was none-the-less haphazard regarding the general order of things. Not so much untidy as disorganized. Still, I suspect we might have cut our grass if we'd ever owned a lawn mower. Although little attention was given to our own weeds, Mom and my father once, in a fit of civic-mindedness, decided to burn the dry grass in a vacant lot next door to us. It wasn't even our property, but they insisted it could be dangerous and they were right. The whole wooden-structured district would've burned down if the fire department hadn't arrived in time. I don't know who called the firemen since I can't remember anyone around there ever having a telephone.

Actually, there weren't all that many lawns either because most of the places were elevated slightly back from the sidewalks with large semi-enclosed front porches and steps filling up the bits of ground not devoted to flowers. The backyards had all the space, which people needed for clotheslines and kid pens, and were where most of the family life centered. Flowers shot up unrestrained everywhere. The little orange California poppies, intermingled with blue and white lupines, enchanted our fields in springtime, and at one section near the trestle bridge, sweetpeas covered the hillsides on either side of the railroad track. Oddly, I have no images of anyone formally controlling them. I suppose they must have done, but no member of my family would dream of interfering with nature's whims, even Grandma, who had lilies and hydrangeas and wild poppies and fuchsias growing in places no one ever saw. And, although you could sure see the roses climbing all over a side of my grandmother's considerable house, you'd never find any in her parlor except the ones my brother's second wife made out of toilet paper dipped in paraffin wax, and some cellophane poinsettias. Like the flowers, we popped up all over, staying a season or two, fading away, only to appear again on the next block.

Since my friends remained the same, all that moving wouldn't have mattered much if Mom's version of Bekins hadn't been my wooden wagon. It wasn't even a big, sturdy conveyance made of substantial metal, it was a little kid's wagon. It was red, though, which is probably all that counts in wagons. And it was, sure as hell, brave. I think my mother just liked it. Because of the unique transportation, moving day was usually in the plural with the packers and shippers being Mom, my sister Charlotte, and myself. We brought out such belongings as Mom thought the wagon could sustain, her ideas varying widely with each trip, stacked them into a pyramid and set off towards the new dwelling. The load was put together like a Chinese puzzle, where all the pieces locked in. At least I believe that was the general idea since nothing was ever tied down with anything so sensible as rope, and it didn't work very well because Charlotte had to keep returning for the things that fell off. Even though it was never any great distance, the journey always took some time, as I was pulling the wagon. And I wasn't very big. Charlotte, who is eleven years my senior, would have pulled, except she and my mother walked on either side to hold the pyramid in place. You needed tall people for that.

We made several trips a day, of course, but even so, it sometimes took us a week to move and we must have amused the neighborhood no end. It was fun, though, keeping us laughing all the time. I loved my silly mother. Many people, at first, thought she was my grandmother because by the time I was born, she was forty and had already seen one brood into adulthood. As she had little formal education, Mom could be of small help with my schooling but she taught me a lesson during those days of "musical houses" that hasn't often failed yet. She taught me to laugh at myself. Laugh at life.

Naturally, we didn't put the stove or refrigerator on the wagon, but the three of us literally moved everything else, because

I guess the males who owned the cars in the family were at work when Mom's nomadic feet itched to get on with it. We only used ice boxes, never actually having a refrigerator except once when one came with a house, and I remember that place more than the others because it was the nicest we ever rented. It had front hedges and a lawn and we lived there quite a while. I made Kool-Aid ice cubes, had my tonsils removed, and won the American Legion award for eighth-grade boys while we lived in that house. And the lawn topped the hedges.

My award decreed I was selected because I was "found to possess, among others, those high qualities of character—honor, courage, scholarship, leadership and service—which are necessary to the preservation and protection of the fundamental institutions of our government and the advancement of society." I memorized it, but nobody else was much impressed.

Although the move to that house was the last one on my wagon, for the first time, I felt embarrassed about it. I had grown stronger, the task became easier until, finally, I was tall enough to hold the pyramid. But I was self-conscious and, despite Mom's philosophy, it wasn't fun anymore.

Zella told me of Moving Day—Astaire style.

They built a house on property adjoining the only family home (aside from their ranch) Ava had known, and when it came time to change residence, not only did they walk a short distance, everything was in place, the staff having shifted a room at a time, putting everything in order immediately.

Ava doesn't recall any of it except that she was upset because she didn't want to move at all.

We never had a real sofa (or chesterfield, as people called them) but somehow we acquired one at the time of our move to the house with the refrigerator. I was too old then to want any part of a kid's little red wagon, but I did want that sofa and its matching chair more than anything in the world. I hauled them on my wagon and I looked everyone straight in the eye. The sofa and chair weren't exactly overstuffed, either, since they were made of knotty pine wood, the sort of pieces usually found in beach motels, and had cushions that were full of holes as well. Two coarse blankets of an Indian motif pattern appeared along with the furniture, and though Mom envisioned them as carpets, I tucked and stuffed them around the cushions and got furious when anyone sat on them. You weren't supposed to sit on them because, in order to pass for real upholstery, the blankets had to be kept as taut as possible. I suppose we got the sofa and chair from someone who wanted to throw them away, but it didn't matter. I loved them.

I do remember starched, dotted swiss curtains with, for several years, blackout curtains behind them gracing our windows in abundance, but we never had rugs or carpets. Only great splashy linoleum which I always enjoyed unrolling at the end of each moving day because it was often new and meant we were settled for a while. Actually, there was a great deal of furniture but, before the sofa, I can't recall anything really comfortable except a rocking chair, and that remains unforgettable because it refused to ride more than a half a block without rocking out of my wagon. Two pieces we never transported were permanent fixtures in Grandma's four-room cabin. One was a brass bed which filled up much of the small living room, and I'm not likely to forget or forgive that bed because I caught my head between the bars at the foot of it Christmas morning when I was attempting to see if there was a teddy bear in the Christmas tree. The bear was there but I nearly had to spend the day in bed anyway.

The other item was really a piece of lawn furniture that my Aunt Irene made in night school and had lots of slats. She called it a love seat, a term justifiable only by the devotion with which it was created. Even though my uncle married three times, I don't think she was ever truly my aunt. Aunt Irene was just his girlfriend of long standing, but she was jolly and I liked her very much. I don't know why she built lawn furniture at night school.

Memory is rather clouded about our living conditions in those days because we kids practically lived on the beach during the summer months and, since the population of our household ebbed like the tides depending upon how many brothers and sisters, if any, were in residence, I can't quite sort it out. Now that I think about it, that probably was the main reason for the shifting around. We needed room for however many were at home at a time, and since Mom wouldn't waste anything, including space, we took smaller quarters as family departed. Only to move again when they returned. And my brothers and sisters, gregarious all, usually returned in tandem. They brought friends, cousins, various spouses and eventually, of course, children. I came to do the same thing in later years but being of a quieter nature I more often tended to observe rather than participate in my family's lifestyle.

We usually stayed in the four-room cabin between houses, but if that was rented to a tourist, Mom and I sometimes lived in Grandma's two-room cabin. I can't imagine what we did with our belongings during those periods, but I suspect much of it was stored in the big house with my grandmother's furniture. Naturally, since the cabins were often rented, Grandma didn't put any good furniture in them—certainly none of her comfortable couches or chairs. Their cut-velvet, rose patterned, rose colored upholstery was slip-covered in chintz for protection, which was unnecessary since no one ever sat on them anyway. Unsullied, they stood in Grandma's parlor awaiting guests. Friends and family were not guests. I suppose it was the same with all the elderly widowed ladies who knew each other so well, it was considered unfriendly to entertain in the formality of the parlor. Or, indeed, to even call at the front door.

Dad was an Irishman who drank and didn't live with us for long stretches at a time. Not that he was off on a bender so much as he was chasing rainbows, or simply working in another town. My own feelings regarding my father ranged the full emotional scale, finally ending in pity; but he was a nice enough old guy and during the very early years I enjoyed the times when he would take care of me alone. I still remember the gray rubber rat he bought for me and the snake he made to go with it by stuffing one of Mom's cotton stockings. The rat was probably for our bulldog but Dad gave it to me and I happily played in the gutter with my snake and my rat for a long time. I loved him then, I guess. He just kept us poor and my mother had to work very hard because of him. They got along fine unless he was sozzled and then she couldn't cope at all; but they managed fifty-four more-or-less happy years, more-or-less together, before Mom died. And her last spoken thought was of his well being. I never wondered where the others went while we lived in the two-room cabin but I do remember Mom and I visited Dad in his tent on the beach during one of those times. He was down there panning for gold.

Grandma owned three cabins, but she only rented two of them because my uncle kept his printing presses in the one closest to her house. He was her favorite son, but none of us liked him very much, and if he had any saving grace, it was because of the women he attracted. Even I wondered how such a pompous, boorish man could appeal to the pretty, warm-hearted ladies who were his wives and girlfriends. But apparently they knew something I didn't. He certainly couldn't have won any prizes for looks or personality and wasn't exactly over-full with the milk of human kindness. Yet I was usually solicitous in his company because he had reams of fresh white paper for printing in his cabin, which was like a chamber of gold to me. Sometimes, when Aunt Irene found me with my nose pressed against the cabin window, she made my uncle give me a bundle of paper, and occasionally the old bastard, after I'd shown enthusiastic interest in the machinations of the printing world, handed me the treasure of his own accord. I disliked him, but I would have forgiven Aunt Irene anything. Except her lawn furniture.

I kept my Fellowship of the London Zoo when we moved to Ireland but the London Zoo doesn't compare to Mr. Walker's zoo that was once just three houses down the block from ours in California.

A leathery little man who preferred animals to people, Johnny Walker fortunately didn't include the neighboring kids as people, and those of us who showed proper respect for his menagerie were allowed visiting privileges at almost any time. Mr. Walker's zoo—not for the public at all—consisted mostly of tropical birds, a monkey who detested anything female, and an anteater that loved having the back of its head scratched.

Because the monkey fell into screaming fits when girls came around, visits to Mr. Walker's backyard dwindled off to a few boys and ultimately to just me. I became a champion head scratcher and the anteater's delight. He'd almost purr when he saw me. I never knew him to have the slightest interest in ants, however, even though I brought him some in a jar from time to time. I'd coax them out near his nose, but he ignored them, nudging my hand like a cat, and the ants would get away.

One of the parrots learned to call my brother Mike's name. Like my wife, my mother invariably remembered one more thing she meant to say to anyone departing the house the minute the door closed, and since Mike was always away at full speed she had to raise her voice in pursuit. The parrot learned to mimic her and Mike was forever running back to see what she wanted. Other than my brother and Mrs. Walker and her daughter, who were understandably not fond of the monkey, no one complained about the animals and Mr. Walker's zoo remained undisturbed until he moved away to larger quarters of his own accord.

To this day I can't see a Johnny Walker whiskey label without thinking of anteaters. I seldom mention that to anyone.

Since our table was always covered with condiment containers awaiting the impending family meals, my favorite drawing place was the middle of the living room floor; a constant source of irritation to all but my mother. Yet Mom was the one I had to be most wary of whenever I acquired a packet of paper because she invariably took it away "to keep it for good" and gave me a penny for butcher paper instead. The butcher's assistant was my brother, Michael. You got a lot of heavy white paper from the butcher's roll for one cent, and though I liked it well enough, it still had to be cut into workable size—always becoming crinkled in the process. In no way could butcher paper compare to the pristine bond, and I always managed to hide some of that before Mom found out. She didn't want the paper for herself, nor could she have understood, really, how I felt about it . . . that I actually had a gut reaction at the sight of the first pencil mark on the virgin surface. (Besides, if I tried any explanation about physical excitement, she would have thought I was talking dirty.) Mom, with her aversion to any sort of waste, simply wanted me to save the special paper for special drawings and/or rainy days.

Though she meant well, my mother never understood that it doesn't work that way. Mom never quite understood me at all but she suspected I had something her other kids didn't have, and she intended to protect it at any cost. If I wanted to draw instead of helping her with work, I could. I could draw and paint late into the night without intervention as long as my school work didn't suffer, and the other work got done eventually.

The street where my grandmother's house was, and where we and Mr. Walker and the man who built the castle lived for a while, was lined with acacia trees. As the blossoms fell, our sidewalks became bright yellow velvet and, firmly believing in the Land of Oz, I often imagined it to be yellow brick on its way to the Emerald City. Yet the most magical moment I'd ever encountered was not in imagination, or books, or movies, but the day I came out of our house and found a fawn-colored greyhound standing motionless on the yellow carpet, wearing a light mantle of acacia. He was glorious. I was very young but I didn't want the illusion shattered, so I went back inside quickly, before he could move, and refused to go out front the rest of the day. Usually I was screeching in the streets with the best of them, but I often found my singular world more rewarding, and on the day of the greyhound, instead of trying to record what I'd seen, I drew my greatest love—a mermaid. Mom was putting up preserves (nearly a constant occupation) when I drew, colored, glued onto cardboard, and cut out my mermaid and showed it to her. She seldom read, having little imagination as I knew it, but something that day kindled a startling inspiration in her and, to my horror, she dipped the mermaid in the hot paraffin used for sealing her jam jars. I couldn't protest because you didn't yell at my mother. She produced the mermaid perhaps not as vividly colored but magically waterproofed and I spent the remainder of the day watching the lady swim with the aid of a long thread, right where she belonged amidst the goldfish in our fishpond.

She had lots of horse sense, my mom, and I miss her to this day.

But she was peculiar.

Although our own tall grass would often be bending in the sea breeze, I was still a champion mower, keeping other people's lawns carpetlike. And I swept miles of sidewalk to earn a dime for the Saturday movie. Mom made me sweep our sidewalk of the moment for nothing, however, unless we were living in one of those places (and there were many in our part of town) which had no side pavement at all. Only a small road ran by Grandma's cabins, but there was a proper, very wide, concrete walkway in front of her house, which my mother designated as family territory, thereby falling under her sweeping jurisdiction. I always resented the chore of Grandma's sidewalk, being only a little thankful at the same time that she favored rock and shell instead of lawn as front yard trimming. Thank God she didn't have a lawn mower either because we would've borrowed it no matter where we lived. We always owned a broom.

Saturday was Flash Gordon Serial Day at the movies, and though I was Flash himself, commander of a driftwood rocketship after the movies, I was a pavement sweep before them. Many Saturday mornings would see me, broom at the ready, knocking at the doors of my regular customers. Mostly I worked for old ladies, but sometimes kids would hang around, talking to me while I swept their walks and collected my fees from their mothers. Their mothers, indulging the kids, were also being charitable to me, I suppose, but it never bothered me because we thought we were putting something over on the grownups, and because I was popular, I knew my friends wouldn't go to the movies without me. The mothers might have thought it pretty strange, but they didn't realize I was their children's captain in outer space.

Mom didn't believe in paying for her kids' services at all, and because of our yo-yoing circumstances, she couldn't give a regular allowance, but she usually came up with a dime when the chips were down. I didn't like to ask her for movie money; not so much because it was a hardship, as it was providing her with a super weapon. If I came to count on something which could be withheld during those times she thought I was wising off, I knew I'd be in real trouble. If I earned my own money, she felt I deserved the movie,

I was always pretty certain of funds for movies and coloring books because one sweet old girl who admired my industry would pay me to sweep her walk five times a day if I so desired. Mow her lawn, too. All a bit of a con, since the pavement which ran up in a path to her porch was so neat the concrete glistened, and her lawn was only a couple of green patches on either side of the path. We liked each other a lot. I liked her because she was a demon with the pinball machine at the drugstore, managing to shift it around without lighting up the tilt sign, and even more so because she constantly encouraged my drawing. I called her "Absolutely," for her favored word which she spoke slowly, putting equal stress on each syllable and assiduously included in every sentence. Sometimes, after making absolutely certain "Absolutely" knew I was there, I'd sweep her walk (using the broom from her tool shed) and sneak away, leaving the broom in an obvious position, naturally, warm in the knowledge of my good deed. We both knew better, but we played the game anyway, and she never mentioned the free sweep. Of course, I didn't call her "Absolutely" to her face because she wouldn't have tolerated it. And Mom would've belted me. She called me "Son" ("Absolutely"—not my mother) and always, following my "good deed," when I could somehow be found sitting in the field in full view of her kitchen window, she would call out, "Son, I'm off to the drugstore and ab-so-lute-ly need company." That meant a free pinball game for me, which I never failed to tilt almost immediately, which was "Ab-so-lute-ly tough luck, Son" and guaranteed a penny for the more lasting candy, jawbreaker.

Besides hauling household goods and the weekly load of food staples from the big market which was not in our neighborhood, my wagon and I were in charge of supplying driftwood and other burnable refuse for our Franklin stove. One house, I remember, had central heating, because I stupidly walked barefoot over the hot grate, which caused my mother to sit up all night applying canned milk poultices to my sole. She used condensed milk for sunburn, too, but I don't think it was very effective in either case. Most times her weird concoctions worked. Nevertheless, we were usually warmed by the stove which had an insatiable appetite during the rainy winter months. January's lusty high tide filled our cove with driftwood, bringing Mom, me and my wagon out the moment it receded. In full battle dress—yellow hooded slicker for me and any number of protective combinations for her—we'd be down on the beach with other locals, picking it clean of any flotsam that could be dried and burned. Mom loved stormy weather and this gleaning time was exciting; in a way, a social outing for her. Because we were pretty sure, but not altogether sure it was okay, Mom and I went after dark one evening to gather shingles from a demolished building. Dad was at home at the time but, as he was somewhat deaf, we found it easier to do most things without him. Especially things outside, where the air swallowed much of the sound he could hear.

Anyway, we came home to find my father, obliviously reading by the stove while a neighbor lady waited in the rocking chair, rocking with uneasy determination. She had dropped in to call on Mom, but couldn't tear herself away when my father told her she might as well wait, since we would be right back. We had only gone out, he declared, to pick up sea gulls for the fire.

I've never ceased wondering how Dad could've actually accepted the fact we were "going after sea gulls" even though that was what it sounded like to his faulty ears. He was sober, too. When he drank, I couldn't abide him, but he did have long dry periods, and if he was home during those times my presence would often incite his paternal feelings. I tried to indulge him, but really hated the moments of father-son togetherness because he was old enough to be my grandfather and couldn't hear very well. My brothers and sisters knew him as a young father, but I had to overcome an age barrier as well as the sound barrier. Usually I didn't mind fishing with him, because I wasn't expected to talk much. But we still shouted at each other all the way home. Dad thought the world was hard of hearing like he was.

On the last of the very few fishing expeditions we shared, he insisted on walking clear out to Black Point Rock instead of using the river or the wharf in town as everyone else did. An especially dumb place to go, in that it was far away and waves crashed against it even in the calmest weather. All kids were forbidden to go there. Of course we did, but only because we were told not to. And none of us would have dreamed of fishing there. Almost immediately upon our arrival a big wave broke over the rock drenching Dad, who lost his fishing rod, and which annoyed him so much he tossed my pole in the ocean after it. We walked the long distance home in stony silence.

I didn't mind. I preferred drop-line fishing off the wharf because there were lots of pelicans around and sea lions in the water, and people sometimes caught octopus, and I used to go there with Jeanine who was French Canadian. She had a shifty little brother and a tiny, excitable mother. Everybody pronounced her name "Zhah-neen" because that's the way it resounded across the neighborhood when Madame summoned. That's how we were all called; our parents simply opened the door and bellowed our names, but Jeanine's mother's voice is the only one which remains in the mind's ear. Ever in a glass-shattering, Gallic dither, her tones reverberated the blocks, and I liked her because she wore wigs. Actually it was just the one wig, chameleonlike by virtue of its many visits to the dye pots, and which she often misplaced. Jeanine's mother, particularly nice to me because she admired artistic ability of any sort and thought I was underprivileged, liked all kids and was forever handing out cookies or pennies. Still, people made fun of her. You couldn't help it, Everybody liked her; we just laughed at her, which wasn't as rotten as it sounds, because her husband and children did, too.

Compared to some of the kids I suppose I could've been considered underprivileged, but I don't believe we were a lot poorer than the rest, certainly my grandmother owned one of the larger properties. The general living standards were scarcely more than lower middle class at best, and though I hadn't many of the things my friends did, I never felt particularly deprived because our homes were really the beach and the streets.

I did envy some of the beautiful big houses on the cliffs, but they belonged to the "summer people" who were of another world, not just folks like us year-rounders. Unlike the others, however, who I doubt ever gave it any thought, I knew I belonged in that world where people owned separate houses for separate times of the year. Now, as I spend seasons in separate countries, I remember my wacky wonderful mother and hope she knows I've learned it is one world after all. Immensely popular, Mom never realized she was regarded so highly, never paid a social call as such, or visited anyone unless they were ill or in need of assistance. Yet our kitchen was rarely devoid of neighbors. All the kids laughed at Jeanine's mother, but I honestly don't think they ever laughed at mine. Lord knows why though. She certainly gave them cause often enough.

Mom's views of child rearing could be considered somewhat perverse in that she would not leave me alone of an evening in spite of the fact our neighborhood was so safe we never locked a door. I can't recall ever using a house key and feel the entire district probably didn't either. At the same time, my mother would allow me to walk on the beach at night or to sit on our cliffs just staring at the ocean until all hours without turning a hair although we were subject to earthquakes and, once, a tidal wave. I doubt the possibilities of my falling down the cliffs or being snatched away by a great wave ever occurred to her since her principals remained whole. She was at home where I needed her—with the lights on.

I was never bothered by the dark if I was outside, and Mom wasn't afraid of it anywhere. But she probably instilled such fears in half the kids on the block. Although empty lots and little fields appeared abundantly along the small streets, most of the houses were clustered close enough together that any crying out would bring immediate assistance, and we felt private but never really alone. Be that as it may, the times are countless when I've seen my mother storm into a neighbor's house to turn the lights on for a child so he needn't enter a darkened room alone. That most parents were usually visiting nearby or just at the movies, expecting to be home before any kid would even consider coming in, made slight difference. Mom considered it gross negligence. I suspect she got away with so much because she cured people with her crazy medicines, dubious though they may have been. She got together some pretty odd concoctions, but nevertheless, if Mrs. McKenzie wrapped bacon about your finger to coax out a deeply embedded sliver, you left it there. Nobody questioned it and your parents didn't make you take it off.

Being a good deal older than my friends' mothers, she had already raised a family, gaining her medical skill from experience, some of it from instinct while, I guess, most of the unorthodox treatments were based on old, long-proven country remedies. Everybody believed in her. I don't know where she got the notion that coal oil mixed with sugar was cough medicine, but I warned all the kids to stay away if they had a cold. I caught bad colds all the time before my tonsils were removed, and I nearly exploded trying not to cough where Mom might hear me. I can understand the need for awakening me in the middle of the night to accompany her if she had to go fetch the doctor for Grandma, who was given to spells of kidney or gall or some kind of stones that only happened at dawn, but I still fail to understand why I had to go along when Mom herself was called out to help an ailing kid through the night. Not only did I lose sleep but, as I usually remained in the same room with Mom and the sicky, I was exposed to all his germs. I guess she reasoned I was safer there than sleeping in my own bed—alone—in the dark.

In later years Mom developed a fear of the cliffs herself, but once I found her sitting in my Tarzan tree, a large oak which grew diagonally out from a foot path above a small canyon near our house. We kids loved to shimmy over its branches until we were extended over the ravine. Mom rarely read or went to the movies and didn't quite understand about the Lord of the Jungle when I showed her the tree where I imitated him, but she didn't lecture me about the dangers of such foolhardy play either. In my wildest dreams I would not have expected to find my mother curled up on a limb of the Tarzan tree and—of all things—reading a book. Happily, I was alone when I did.

Mom's most valued possession was an enormous volume she called the "Doctor Book." Always within easy reach should an emergency arise, the book with its graphically illustrated pages and beautiful color overlays of intestines fascinated me. But there was no sneaking looks without strict supervision, I would not be corrupted by a glimpse of the human body's private parts. Years later, when I was studying anatomy in college, Mom came across one of my books and remarked that she guessed "they were right when they said art was nude." I don't think that is quite what she meant, but I thought it probably prudent not to pursue the matter any further.

A lot of hours are spent by kids waiting for other kids so they can all hang around together, continuing, once they are together, to hang about waiting for something to do. Sometimes such waiting reaps rewards, as it did the day a group of us waited for Jeanine to finish her piano practice and her brother came out to tell us they'd swiped their mother's wig and stashed it in the piano bench. Whenever the poor woman passed the window we, led by her son, succumbed to falling down in hysterics. Not that she looked particularly funny, since her head was protected by a bandanna, a common sight among most housewives. But we knew she hadn't a clue where she left her jet black (at the time) hair. Unlike her unfortunate mother, Jeanine was blessed with luxurious chestnut tresses, which she promised her father she wouldn't cut until her eighteenth birthday but reneged when the hair fell below her waist at fourteen. I was as sorry as her dad when her braids went under the shears, but that was for sentimental reasons. Jeanine was our eternal Dorothy Lamour when winds rose on the beach, and got lashed to the big driftwood stumps a lot. Sometimes she wafted around as a lady vampire when we played Dracula on the castle, so by the time she was fourteen I expect she was tired of having sand in all that mass, and wasn't very keen on suffering rope burns in honor of the Jungle Princess any more. I guess we were all past it then, but I hated seeing her with short hair. It wasn't right somehow, even if Miss Lamour did cut and auction her own locks for the war effort soon afterwards.

You always went "on" the castle, never "to" it, a term that has gone unquestioned for so many decades there seems little reason to challenge it now. I imagine, however, it's because the huge building was erected on a small cliff site above our cove and, often enough, we were on it as opposed to being inside the rooms, which were really shops. Only open during the summer months, the castle was mainly for tourists. Besides a hot dog grill and soda fountain, there were a couple of gift shops, and a drugstore which

The "castle" on the beach (during driftwood harvesting time) in Santa Cruz, where I played as a boy.

dealt chiefly in suntan lotions, dark glasses, arty bathing caps and pith helmets. I wore one of the pith helmets when I played Jungle Jim by myself in the small, untended park just behind the castle, but I can't imagine why the drugstore featured so many. I never ran into another Jungle Jim, although occasionally you'd see a behelmeted stout summer person, who invariably rounded out his baggy trunks ensemble with straw shoes and dark sheer socks with clocks up the side. The lifeguard wore pith helmets, too, but there was only one of him and always towers of helmets at the drugstore.

Running the castle was handled in rather a cavalier fashion altogether, since it was open for just two-and-a-half months, boarding up its windows the day after Labor Day, and there was a banquet room and dance hall on the second level that never opened at all. During the winter, especially those gray stormy days when waves crashed against its outer walls, the big structure looked very much like a real haunted castle, and many a November evening found us scuttling under the archways, frightening ourselves silly. Other times, we climbed into the turrets with Gloria and weren't scared at all.

According to Absolutely, "You and your friends don't live near the ocean, Son, you ab-so-lute-ly live in it." An observation which was practically fact. From the minute school let out for the summer until we were hustled into unbending back-to-school new overalls, we skirmished in the surf. With skins ranging from copper to chocolate, except for white noses caused by liberal smearing of zinc oxide ointment, and withered pink fingers from over-exposure to salt water, we ricocheted the beach, June through August. If we weren't battling waves, we were jumping off smaller cliffs, or rolling down dunes in the sand, which meant diving back in the water to wash it away, starting the whole process all over again. The zinc oxide, ostensibly meant to keep the nose from burning, was really a badge to distinguish us as learned locals, and not dumb summer people who fried themselves in oil. My nose constantly peeled anyway, but the chalky beak remained a must.

Towels were seldom used to dry ourselves because they figured importantly in our activities. A beach towel, knotted around the neck, hanging the long way down the back, became a passable cape, and capes were almost mandatory when you had castle steps to descend. I didn't wear a cape or zinc-oxide on my nose when I was that master of the deep, The Submariner, my favorite comic book character. But I only became him when I played alone. At such times I would swim the distance from our cove, emerge from a shattered wave with steely dignity, and scale cliffs or sneak through caves in pursuit of evil-doers and, indeed, many an evil-doing couple was startled by the hard-eyed Submariner who, without benefit of tide or telephone booth, instantly converted to a rotten kid and ran back to his own beach faster than the speed of light. Such goings-on always topped our day and, afterwards, we boys stayed together to talk dirty. We had to lie on our stomachs then, for reasons the girls understood perfectly well, although they pretended innocence and insisted we go in the water with them. Realizing that the girls knew, and knew that we knew they knew, only prolonged our conditions, until with yelps and sudden leaps we'd dash for the shrinking safety of the cold water.

A substantial river concluded its journey to the ocean through our town, allowing us the somewhat unique choice of swimming in fresh or salt water, and though it wasn't at our local beach, the river was still close walking distance for even the smaller kids. Most of us learned to swim there. It was great. Once you were good enough, you could swim or just be carried down the river to the dangerous junction where the waters met and where you got clobbered by the choppy surf because you never waited until you were good enough. Because a strong undertow pulled beneath the waves at that rough water intersection and could carry you out through the natural rock bridge, we stupid kids were given a dangerous combination we found irresistible. Oddly, no lifeguards were posted at that point. Perhaps the town fathers considered that any of us lost in such a foolhardy place would only be the population's gain.

I learned to swim when I was six years old because I stepped over my head into the riverbed and there was no alternative but to swim out of it. I swam out, straight across to the other side where older kids were diving off the rocks, though that had not been my intention. For the rest of the day I splashed around the rocks, finally returning to the shallow beach side without a qualm. We all learned to swim in much the same manner.

Although Mom loved the dark beach when wind raged and surf pounded, or calmer nights when phosphorous, caught in the moonlight, shimmered across the arched waves, she rarely went during the daytime (excepting the driftwood harvest).

But she did join us one Fourth of July at a big family picnic by the river. By then I had been an accomplished swimmer for several seasons, spending most of my time diving off the rocks between submerged old railroad pilings when not bodysurfing through the highest waves I could find. Leaving my usual spot on the rocks that day, I dove into the river as a couple of cousins canoed by and tagged along, dog-paddling next to their boat, when my mother began shouting for them to save me. Apparently she had suddenly realized I was no longer on the rocks where she'd waved to me earlier. No matter how I got to the rocky side in the first place, she had never actually seen me in the water; therefore, I could not swim. I didn't laugh as I swam to the shore because she was so frightened. But I did wonder why. Each summer day, without fail, Mom had sent me off to the beach with some joke regarding severe punishment were I to come home drowned and miss supper. All the while, it hadn't occurred to her that I actually could swim.

I never told her one of our favorite sports involved jumping into the river off the trestle bridge just before the train got to us.

So much has gone now. Not just the years and Mom and Dad but the durable things, those which one expects to remain beyond memory. No one was hurt, but the caves eventually proved disastrous when the cliffs above them collapsed one winter and sent a great many beautiful old houses (fortunately empty because of the season) crashing onto the beach. God may have been expressing his disapproval of the caves' secrets, but I expect the ocean, after all the years of swirling and lashing, finally penetrated far enough underground to claim the cliffs. And the castle is gone, too. Man-made, it could withstand the elements for just so long, and I didn't grieve as I pointed out the bare rock where it once rose high above the cove to my sons, but I could only stare in stunned silence at the river which seemed dirty (man-made as well) and forbidding; no longer roaring into the sea.

The last house we lived in (which we bought) has been torn down, and Grandma's house and cabins were lost in a fire. I don't miss them—the visual signs that I had passed this way—or the people, really. But I am sorry my wife and children couldn't share a little of what I remember.

Chapter Eight

Little Gloria Galore

Every time I think of Gloria, I remember how Mom wouldn't let me see the Doctor Book.

Gloria and I were generally considered to be the nicest kids in the neighborhood. To all appearances, we were. She had long blonde curls, dimples, and terrific manners, while I, a freckle-nosed towhead, wore a beanie (which later gave way to a black silk mandarin's skull cap with a red topknot) and carried packages for old ladies. We were both excellent students, and I imagine the only reason we weren't loathed by the other kids when their parents pointed us out as virtuous examples is that the other kids knew us better than their folks did. We were all about nine or ten, and though the majority of us played elaborate games inspired mostly by the motion pictures, Gloria remained an earthy sort of person. Never one much for fantasy play, her feet were firmly on the ground. Well, that's not true either—she was not without theatrical flair.

Off-season winter months Gloria lived with her grandmother on our side of town, but during the summer she stayed in a small hotel her mother managed down by the boardwalk. There, she studied acrobatics, and one of the amusement pier performers who lodged at the hotel taught her to do a little routine with a parasol. She proved to be a competent dancer, I guess, because for a couple of seasons thereafter Gloria backbent her way across the

Richard and little Gloria in Santa Cruz.

stage as a warm-up for the real show which was usually something Hawaiian.

The best thing about Gloria's grand-mother's house was a closet between two bedrooms—the kind you could enter from one room and come out into the other. It was marvelous, and when Gloria lived in my area, lots of hours were spent in that closet as we hid amongst the clothes, took a flashlight and went over each other's private parts like mad. We were really rotten. I did my best, but Gloria was rottener, and we spent so much time in the closet, it's a wonder we didn't get hung up on the idea.

Like all seaside resort towns, ours featured a plethora of awful gift shops, one of which was owned by a crippled, grumpy old man. He made and sold terrible abalone shell jewelry on the boardwalk, and most of the local waitresses also had him make up their names in twisted copper wire, which they pinned over the floral handkerchiefs ever-exploding from their uniform's breast pockets. Gloria acquired quite a hoard of abalone and copper before I realized she didn't have any money to buy the junk and tried threatening her into an explanation. But Gloria never really needed to be bullied into anything. All you had to do was ask. I think she was just waiting to see how long it would take me to wise up.

The old guy's name was Mr. Swift which later amused me a lot when I discovered what Mr. Swift had been getting up to. And without even leaving his wheelchair. Little Gloria, who fancied an abalone pin or two, told me how she had dimpled her darling way onto Mr. Swift's lap, and encouraged his craftsman's fingers—a demonstration I was avidly determined to witness, especially since the pinch-mouthed Mrs. Swift was a crony of my grandmother's. I demanded Gloria take me along the next time she needed her name in twisted copper, and I guess she blackmailed him because, after that, Mr. Swift occasionally let me visit his workroom with her—but there was never any demonstration. I believe she was an honest sort but I had to take Gloria's word that she earned her jewelry. We were not yet pubescent. I imagine he knew that I knew because later he always seemed wary whenever I passed his stall on the boardwalk with a hearty "Hi, Mr. Swift," or an even more enthusiastic salutation if Mrs. Swift happened to be with him. He remained mean and grumpy, but he winced every time. We probably had him counting his days.

Gloria's grandmother owned a male collie, a big friendly dog that suffered many a winter's discontent while his mistress's little granddaughter was about. Not that there was any actual culmination, but Gloria used to work him up pretty well with some of her more inventive acrobatic dance numbers, and she knew she could count on my riveted attention on those occasions, too.

Now that I think on it, I suppose we were awfully jaded for our tender years; the more bizarre aspect being we didn't find any of it particularly unique. To smoke, drink beer, or get a C on your report card—those were really bad. But it didn't seem to us that a small girl's sexual cavorting with an elderly paraplegic and a shaggy dog—for the benefit of a small boy—was anything unusual. We had our own version of "show and tell" which was hardly confined to classroom activities since she spotted my first dark pubic hair and I was second only to her mother at viewing her training bra. In fact, the two of us became so close during those formative years that we stopped fooling around with each other and more or less got together just to compare notes. Gloria's, of course, being always the more colorful. But she was a generous girl—good about sharing and giving pointers.

At that age, none of us thought about homosexuality as any more than curious playing around. No one was held to be gay, or queer, and even if the subject had come up, those weren't the terms of the times. Not to our group, anyway. Stanley Davis put his hands inside my pants and then asked me not to tell. He fell out of our fig tree the same day and broke his arm, so I didn't tell. I didn't understand why he wanted to keep it secret, though. It felt nice. But we did have a friend who everyone said was a sissy. Alwyn was a sissy. So what. We rather admired him, at least Gloria and I did. A few parents remarked about his "sneaky" look, and although we knew there was some basis for the allegations, Gloria and I defended him because, mostly, he was just shy. He really was a nice kid when you got to know him, and we remained friends until he died tragically in his early twenties. By then he was a virile pilot in the Army Air Force.

Alwyn's father, a handsome giant of German heritage with, I suspect, balls up to his jutting jaw, was all man. He let everybody know it. And the one thing his only son wanted most in the whole world was a Sonja Henie doll with ice skates. We were sincerely sympathetic when he confided in us because Gloria and I knew his father, and there certainly was no doll in Alwyn's future that we could see. We always maintained that Alwyn was just quiet, not sneaky, until the day he quietly caught his mother kissing the man from the car repair garage and immediately told us. Recognizing the knock of opportunity when she heard it, Gloria sent him straight home to speak to mother of his heart's desire. Although it wasn't Sonja Henie, Alwyn got his doll—and one every Christmas for the next few years. Gloria even gave him some dolls she had no further need for which Alwyn gratefully added to the growing collection that he kept in a suitcase under his bunk bed.

I can't imagine how his mother ever convinced her husband, but Alwyn showed his appreciation by never exhibiting his dolls in public or the living room, where his father immediately constructed an elaborate electric train set which remained on permanent display. Even Gloria and I played trains sometimes if we weren't performing operations on Alwyn's dolls. We were long past playing doctor with each other. Ab-so-lute-ly. Well, Alwyn wasn't. I doubt that he ever did, although he told me that once during a card game behind the couch, Gloria took off her underpants. Naturally, such information sent me flying to her side where I learned there was a bit more to the story. They were playing a game of Go Fish behind the sofa all right, but Alwyn neglected to mention that his parents had company who were sitting on it at the time. Because she knew he couldn't react audibly, Gloria removed her panties and hitched up her dress just to unnerve him. And I'll bet there wasn't the slightest quiver in her sweet voice as she called for the cards. She was really something, that girl.

Shortly before Gloria moved to another town and out of our lives, we decided to set Alwyn on the right track, so to speak. We had both come into puberty, barely, but with great glee, and thought Alwyn must at least have a go at it. I spent as much time with the innocents of our neighborhood as I did with Gloria but, as she shared other confidences in the peppier part of town, she arranged for a girlfriend to seduce him in her grandmother's garage. We had every intention of being around at the awakening but, realizing Alwyn's nature could never cope with our presence, voyeurism was added to our sins as we watched through cracks in a packing box brought in for the occasion. It all turned out a dismal failure, however, proving such an ordeal for poor Alwyn that, later, we two pooled our money and bought him a pair of doll's ice skates. Although our friend was no longer playing with dolls, he was touched that we remembered. We didn't tell him we'd been in the packing crate.

Even though we, in fact, gained the confidence of most of the local kids, Gloria and I never told anything to anybody except each other. I guess the fact that no one actually had anything on us is one of the main reasons we remained high in the esteem of our friends and their parents. To our credit, I think we were also basically understanding, warm hearts, helpful if we could be, and never did any real harm. Unless you count the time Gloria drew a tattoo in Tangee lipstick around Wanda's private parts and left her to clean it off as best she could without getting caught by her sisters. That was probably vicious.

After her grandmother died in the spring of our seventh-grade year, Gloria's mother gave up managing the beach hotel and they moved away permanently. I never saw or heard from Gloria again, so she never knew I received the award for "those high qualities of character—honor, courage, scholarship, leadership and service." But she would have expected no less.

I got through the usual terribly serious, terribly innocent string of high school romances typical of the forties war years, but there was never another Gloria. Actually, I didn't think much about her until one night almost a dozen years later when a shipmate and I were returning from liberty in the Bay of Naples. We were twenty, worldly in our knowledge of women and eager to exchange experiences. Most of the Sixth Fleet frequented a raunchy Neapolitan club aptly named The Red Lantern, and my buddy observed that the Lantern ladies tended to greet me somewhat more warmly than the other sailors. He wondered why, but before I could explain about basic training with Gloria, he launched into the wildest experience he could remember. Seems he had once met a pretty blonde at a school dance in the suburbs of San Francisco and when the dance was over, as any nice girl would, she took him home to meet her mother. After serving cocoa, mother went off to bed and things developed with considerable alacrity. The little blonde took him into a clothes closet where things happened, he said, I wouldn't believe.

I believed him. I damned near cried.

Chapter Nine

The Beverly Hills Kid (Tap Roots)

I am ever amazed how—as it was in my family, too—one child can be so unlike the rest. Other than the fact they prefer quiet places away from the public, for the most part, the Astaire children could have been separate stock.

With interests and backgrounds so acutely diverse, it is understandable that my brothers-in-law and I don't really know each other, but I doubt if they fully perceive their little sister either, that her style is not really jet and fast lane though it sometimes seems so. I could settle easily amidst baronial trappings. Ava could not. My wife is happiest in the kitchen or curled on the window seat of a small and patterned room. Ava, the Astaire of most positive nature, considers her cup half full rather than half empty unless, of course, she carries it in which case it may well runneth over. She may not have inherited her dad's mobile agility but Ava has his grace of spirit; and her honesty, generosity, lack of bigotry, and shy yet effusive quality seem to me a happy blend of her father and Aunt Adele.

Ava and her brother, Fred "Freddie" Astaire Jr.

I didn't know their mother but I expect Ava's brother is not a personality combination of anybody. As often noted by F. A. Sr., "Freddie is one of a kind." Bearing that particular name must have been burdensome to one who prefers flying or ranching to the entertainment world, but the elusive, soft-spoken Fred Astaire Jr. has always been extremely independent and very much his own man.

A dozen years her senior, Ava's half-brother, Peter Potter, long a member of the sheriff's department, retired to raise avocados for a bit and once, in partnership with Fred Jr., purchased a tourist site featuring a moaning cave which ceased to moan almost immediately following the business transaction. Out of the cave business, Pete devotes a lot of time to an island property acquired off the Washington State coast while Freddie—whatever he chooses—will undoubtedly continue to plot the course the way he sees it.

Had he not died still an infant, six years before I came along, my brother Clarke would have been the closest to a sibling rival of any of my brothers and sisters. I've often wondered what impact he might have had on my outlook. Probably not much.

Given that same age variance between Ava and Freddie, with their essentially disparate views on nearly everything, there can be small doubt we all compile individual lists. We are what we are. I like what we are.

~ ~ ~

Rather than hot water bottles which she didn't trust, my grandmother heated sand in a skillet to toast our beds of a blustery winter. Tied up in flour sacks, the sand seemed never to diminish in temperature, and if contacted, scorched your flesh. I hated staying overnight at Grandma's house. The beds were too hot, and since she used the same skillet for frying, Grandma's meals often required extra measure of chivalrous character as well. As regards my grandmother's special roast beef hash, the term, true grit, aptly, doubly applied to the texture of her offering and magnanimosity of the consumer. And to this day, I shun all save body heat to warm my resting place.

Well enough disposed towards hot water bottles, Ava employs them almost immediately following the swallows' departure southward, but in the matter of clothes washing machines, my one and only keeps apace with those other nutty women of my boyhood: Ava, it seems, requires a specific type of appliance the better to spin-dry her lettuce.

Now and again, when quick enough, I bring to her attention our orange plastic lettuce-drier or its wire counterpart, both created for that express purpose; both sitting idle while salad greens, securely wrapped in clean toweling, continue to find their way into the washing machine during its spin cycle. Though, naturally, no actual laundry is in progress at such times, occasionally the towel loosens slightly and I have come to overlook the odd bit of cress consequently discovered lodging in a dress-shirt pocket.

Considering my upbringing, It couldn't be otherwise. We seek our own.

In the second week of our marriage, we were invited for dinner at Chasen's with Barbara Stanwyck, a lady I'd been commissioned to paint a few years earlier, and who had become a friend during the process. After the meal, we continued conversation over a nightcap back at Barbara's place, thrilling my bride so much she forgot her own heritage and swiped a monogrammed book of matches as a souvenir. It was pink, initialed simply B. S. but Ava cherished it.

Painting Barbara Stanwyck's portrait in the early 1970s in Hollywood.

Barbara told me that she, herself a major celebrity at the time, once followed Garbo for a few blocks and at a discreet distance in New York City, but even so, Ava's behavior was hardly that expected from one who as an eight-year-old sometimes took tea at the home of Theda Bara and played with her collection of Kewpie dolls.

Oh, the hair trigger of memory! Sorting through Mom's things after she died, Charlotte and I discovered two pairs of black lace stockings and a loving cup containing six enema syringes and a Kewpie doll. My mother never wore make-up; she didn't know the meaning of the word décolleté and her hosiery, at best, would be considered seriously bland. But perhaps in her heart of hearts,

Mom out-vixened even Miss Bara. I hope so.

The few times during our marriage when Ava had been interviewed regarding life as a movie star's daughter, she asked me to sit in. Knowing no other existence, she isn't objective and can't relate to what writers may consider of public interest. Unlike my mate, who didn't read film magazines although she was often in them, I devoured the nonsense and act as prompter—suggesting it is the names of the game they seek and, along those lines, from time to time, have pressed my own interrogation.

Except for her fondness of old houses, antiques, and old me, Ava is a now sort of person, unconcerned with the past; I can't get her to unload much—certainly haven't managed to convince her to write an equivalent to my recollections for our family memory scrapbook. She truly doesn't recall a lot but over the weeks and some glasses of wine, I've wheedled and coaxed, probed slowly for information. Ava is extremely articulate—at times can't be silenced—and her letters are clever, but other than to her best friend, Molly, she doesn't write the way she talks. Perhaps that is just as well. I see her point.

If Mr. Gable pretended to be the ranch hand and your parents fished for marlin off the Mexican coast with Randolph Scott whom you knew as Uncle Randy; and if Merle Oberon, swathed in green satin, came to your bathroom and embraced you good night while you performed a bodily function, embarrassing you forever or until you grew up and forgave her; and if you and your best friend Cynthia, as school girls, arose at dawn to ride horseback across the desert with Cary Grant; and if Mr. Sinatra placed you next to Elvis at his dinner party and you didn't stumble when you curtsied to the Queen of England at the races; if you remembered Marlon Brando as having a squeaky voice, always addressed Dinah Shore as Mrs. Montgomery and didn't realize that the nice Mrs. Swope you'd known all your life was also Dorothy McGuire you admired in movies—then I suppose it would be difficult sorting out what to tell an interviewer. If that which is everyday normal for one person is thought unobtainable and fascinating by the majority—how can one relate?

Few realize it, but Ava's lineage on her mother's side can be traced back to Robert Livingston, Governor of New York, who also signed the Declaration of Independence. Because of such status, she was invited (and declined) to join the DAR, and although her society debut was listed, accepted—expected—in New York, London, and the International debutantes' ball at Versailles, Ava politely turned them down as well.

She came out in Los Angeles because her father wished it, which also may have been a bit of a statement. In spite of their dads' celebrated positions in the community, Ava and Anthony Quinn's daughter were found acceptable debutantes only because of their mothers' social bona fides. In an area so entwined with the motion picture industry, as recently as the late fifties, film performers and their ilk were frowned upon by old-monied Los Angeles; a weird double standard extending to the school Ava attended from second grade through graduation.

Ava and Fred Astaire with friend, 1952.

Fred was actually called in and advised that something must be done to quell such thinking when his daughter had written a school paper indicating she might want to become an actress. They suggested her governess was probably putting such nonsense in her head and should be removed. Her father knew how invaluable Zella's guidance had been through the years and wanted to remove Ava from their clutches instead, but since she had invested so many years already and there could be ensuing publicity, she elected not to change. Shortly thereafter, Alana Ladd was expelled for taking a small film part during the summer holidays, yet the school's most proudly acclaimed alumna was Shirley Temple.

Had Phyllis Astaire lived to see Ava into young womanhood, I seriously doubt—adorable as I am—that I would have been allowed anywhere near her daughter. Theirs was a world foreign to me where, for the most part, the less privileged were not encouraged to venture, and even though Phyllis died when Ava was barely twelve, the successive years under the watchful eyes of her dad and Zella, and somewhat guided by her mother's aunt and uncle, followed pretty much the pattern established for a proper young lady of the time.

Ava's was an all-girl school of strictly enforced—if sometimes silly—rules; where a dress code was mandatory and why, even now, she feels edgy wearing a certain shade of blue. Dates were chaperoned, organized outings with boys of like-circumstance from all-male schools. No rolling in the sand under the boardwalk for them. Once I mentioned I had a job making sno-cones on the boardwalk when I was a kid, a statement eliciting rare and impromptu reverie from my wife: somewhere around age twelve, the first dance to which she had been asked was scheduled at the end of a day of school fete, known as Harvard Day, and with anticipation, Ava had meticulously prepared her very best outfit.

Early in the afternoon, her escort, who attended the Harvard Military Academy, bought her a grape sno-cone which flipped when she tripped over a step and up-ended smartly on top of her head. Ava cleaned off the melting ice as best she could but she wasn't allowed to leave the grounds, and a very miserable little girl spent the rest of the day and went to her first dance with her hair glued a sticky purple mess.

Some few years later on her first—and only—date with a star, the then teenage heart-throb, Tommy Sands, took her to her first nightclub. As they entered the Copacabana, Ava tripped yet again and bounced down the stairs to land unscathed in a mortified and very young seventeen-year-old heap in full view of jaded old New York. She said Tommy remained cool and concerned—a perfect gentleman, but rather soon thereafter married Nancy Sinatra Jr.

Accordingly, as befits the "Quality," Ava trained for all the divertissements with which she would eventually be expected to while her hours. She was given lessons in riding, golf, swimming and diving, ballet and ballroom dancing. Singing was ruled out but there came a coach for drama and speech. Another for tennis. She studied piano and—of all things—the auto harp; everything, it seems, other than the culinary art in which she excels. She is a strong swimmer and she sits a horse nicely, but the last time she played tennis, Ava came home with an image of the mesh fence which encloses the court imprinted on her upper arm.

Before I knew her, she went out with Churchill's grandson, Winston II, the same year she divided time between several prominent eligibles, including a scion of the Singer sewing machine family—heir to its fortune, and Johnny Payson, nephew of the distinguished John Hay Whitney—Jock, her dad's buddy, then U. S. Ambassador to the Court of Saint James.

Her polish, contacts, and breeding are such to provide Ava a top-rung toehold in the social echelon had she chosen, but the lady is too classy to be class-conscious and early on, seeking other directions, she quietly withdrew from a scene where often these things mattered.

Judging from Hermes Pan and David Niven's raves, and in fairness to a mother-in-law I never knew, Phyllis Astaire was probably less enslaved to social nuance than her mother-in-law.

Fred's mother couldn't have been more gracious to me but always with the hint of the grand dame. Unlike her fragile bones, her will remained unbroken—apparent even in the last years when she once again lived with him and still regarded Fred as "Sonny."

When we married, Ann Astaire—Grannie—confided in me her pleasure that Ava appeared so happy; that she could now be a mother—but she wished her granddaughter hadn't such a thick neck. She was nice, amusing, and though I liked her quite a lot, I doubt that Ava's grandmother gladly suffered the nearness of any other female who might claim her son's affection. It seemed to me she cared for Ava well enough—blood was, after all, blood. But she didn't allow her too close. Grandma—my grandmother—was the same. She liked us; loved in her way, but even when she read me Uncle Wiggly stories or told with dramatic effect about the time a giant snake escaped from a circus and crushed her picket fence, I knew her very being revolved around one son—the arrogant Uncle Frank. Towards the rest of us, her affection was matriarchal and a little constricting.

Both women were deserving, they had to be tough to survive. Ava's grandmother was the world-class champion stage mother, possibly of all time, and my grandmother had been all but sold in marriage to an older man she didn't love because he was a man of property, considered a good catch. He was also a closet artist according to Mom, sneaking at sketching birds because he considered it unmanly. Good Catch ruled with the tyrant's manly hand and I wasn't curious until now how Grandma, with their five kids, finally escaped him and Nebraska. Now, it's too late to ask Mom.

Grannie Astaire presided sweetly but firmly, and when she invited us all to dinner, Ava very cautiously requested we might have roast beef, Kevin's favorite which he seldom got because Ava and I ate mostly chicken or fish. Roast beef was duly granted as a surprise for Kevin, and Kevin eyed the entire evening with trepidation. Instructed to employ top manners if they wanted ever again to sit a bicycle with any comfort, the boys reacted quietly under scrutiny, didn't fidget with their ties, kept jackets on, and accepted Grannie's warm welcome with less quaking than expected from guys who viewed Mr. A.'s mom with equal measures of awe and terror.

Fred and Ann headed the table with Ava and me flanking her grandmother—the boys seated on either side between us and Fred. Kevin, next to Ava, accomplished the soup easily but became so nervous when informed the roast beef was ordered specifically for him, he mis-manipulated his cutlery causing the initial slice to lift off his plate like the Concorde and head on collision course towards Mrs. Astaire. Before he could form a prayer the earth should yawn and swallow him whole, the errant bit of meat landed back whence it came, swiftly as a boomerang. Some of Ava's lessons paid off. Stopping it mid-flight, his mother had returned Kev's serve with the neatest backhand ever to wield a dinner fork while, regally unaware, Grannie continued holding forth—even snickering a tad when, in discussing validity of birth signs, she said Adele wasn't a typically tidy Virgo and Tyler asked if she didn't keep the castle clean. Later, fortunately out of Grannie's hearing, while watching Fred vigorously chalk a pool cue, Tyler also inquired if he had to wash his balls often and we decided to call it an evening.

Needing to get away after his wife died, wanting to get closer to his daughter, Fred took Ava to visit her aunt at Lismore Castle—her first trip without Zella and alone with her dad. The closeness Ava and Fred maintain deepened into a great sense of fun as well as devotion during those crucial years following their mutual loss and they continued to travel together whenever possible. During one school holiday, Ava visited her father in Paris while he made *Funny Face*, and when a quirk of studio management somehow released the film in Japan almost simultaneously with *Silk Stockings*, she accompanied him to the Orient where he had been requested for some double-barreled publicizing of both his movies.

Thinking she should taste the flavor, Fred arranged for Ava to address a theater audience with a newly learned sentence in Japanese, and to fill in some other engagements he felt she could

Ava and Fred traveling, 1950s.

do as well as he. Consequently, Ava, terrified and fifteen, found herself being interviewed on Tokyo radio and an Armed Forces broadcast where, meaning to convey a ladylike image in a preference for dresses rather than trousers in public, she confused her words and announced to the brave defenders of our country that whenever she went out, she never wore any pants.

The first Christmas season I knew Ava, I noticed there were piles of presents on their living room furniture but no Christmas tree. Holidays had become especially difficult for her father, she told me, but this was usual procedure even when her mother was with them. Of course, there was always a tree when she was a little girl but only her presents were beneath it. Freddie's family's gifts grew on one sofa, Pete's on another. This was a different

Ava and Fred Astaire in Carmel, California, during the filming of The Notorious Landlady, early 1960s.

PHOTO: BOB WILLOUGHBY

house however, with only Ava and Fred at home. He never had the spirit again and she didn't try to force it. Guess that is why she goes to such lengths during the holidays now.

Fred was never thrilled by the social life himself, and Ava's interest in his business pleased him. He told me he would like to see her follow in his footsteps. Not exactly footsteps. He felt she could act. But after she had—fully dressed—backed into their swimming pool when the ample lawn was free of other bodies or obstacles, and her skirt fell off when she stood up to leave the table at Chasen's, and during the father-daughter dance at her debut, they—with everyone's attention—waltzed around the room in the opposite direction from the other couples, I believe he correctly reasoned that his mobility and Phyllis' nobility little affected their children. Occasionally upon seeing a peer's performance acclaimed, Ava wonders, what if? But she is quick to concede she neither really wanted it nor was temperamentally suited to perform.

As Ava was always sensitive to his needs, Fred was to hers. She acted production assistant on his specials and he named his record company and television production company for her. She took some extension classes at UCLA but Ava eventually opted for a practical business course instead and her dad didn't press for university. Though so like himself in many ways, Fred realized his bright and gentle little girl was every bit as individual as his son, and if always available for comfort and advice, he didn't attempt to influence.

Ava with her father at the 1975 Oscars, the year he was nominated for Best Supporting Actor for his role in The Towering Inferno.

Ava sought her own roads, but for all their detours and twisty bits, the path she eventually followed led back to the place where she first began the journey with her father—Ireland.

With newborn calf and mother, Fourth of July morning at Clonlea.

Chapter Ten

The Zenith of the Universe (in which Fred makes a picture)

While moving the heifers, Tim mentioned he was confining three of them to the lower field near the house because the smallest one was due for her first delivery and he thought there might be a problem. If there were, he said in passing, he would be obliged if I gave him a shout; a statement to set the urban heart quaking and obviate thoughts of anything else. How could she be pregnant? She was still a baby. What constituted a problem? How should I recognize it and if I did sense difficulty, would there be enough time to get up to Tim's farm? I was certain to make an ass of myself crying calf for all the wrong reasons.

Many nights had gone uninterrupted by sleep and my nerves were filed to the point that I'd not left the poor little beast a moment to consider her cud with any degree of contentment, but the attention paid off and I hope she understands that this nut was only trying to help after all.

Around half-past five in the morning, my brain cleared enough to realize a cow was lowing with some regularity, and trying not to disturb Ava, I groped for my watch to time the calls. I wasn't sure bovine labor pains even occurred that way and, since I'd already proved myself foolish in country matters on too many occasions before, I hadn't asked. As her complaints definitely came at evenly spaced intervals, I stumbled into jeans, boots, a pullover, shook Ava not too gently and ran out to the pasture where the little cow was indeed in trouble.

Resting on crossed hooves, the calf's head protruded to just above the eyes, its tongue out. Exhausted, the mother obviously had given up pushing and I was hesitant to assist by pulling in case I would harm the baby and wouldn't know what to do if I did manage it free. When she attempted lying down, I ran for the O'Regan farm, uphill at a pace courting cardiac arrest and once there, after setting off every alarm dog and rooster in the place, still had trouble raising an O'Regan.

"PROBLEM!" I shrieked when Tim's head finally appeared at an upstairs window, and without stopping to see if he understood or heard through the racket of the livestock, I shot away again. My presence at such an hour was enough explanation, I thought, and I wanted to get back in case I could do anything although I hadn't a clue what. Though it was all downhill I returned at a more sensible pace and was glad I'd conserved my strength; when Tim arrived, the real workout began.

We got the confused animal on her feet but only long enough for Tim to pull away the calf, and from then on all the attention was to the baby. Tim and I manipulated, pumped the legs as a form of artificial respiration while Ava, at Tim's instruction, poured icy water on its face and in its ears for shock value. I thought you always boiled water for births.

When he saw the half-emerged head, Tim knew immediately the cow had been accidentally inseminated from a breed too big for her, but we saved both mother and daughter and, for added fortune, the calf is of more valuable stock than he had bargained for. Valuable or not, preferring to forget the entire matter by way of a nap, the cow ignored her baby completely, and since various O'Regans had arrived by then, they packed it into the back of our station wagon and Ava drove it back to the farm where it will be hand-reared.

Tim insisted that the cow must be brought to her feet and his departing words to me as they all piled into the wagon were, "Just rock her back and forth—firm like. Convince her to get up." Sure. I convinced her she was right all along—the man is balmy. And I convinced myself I am not thirty years younger, that there must be better methods for toning stomach muscles than wrestling cows at dawn.

She convinced me she would stand up when she bloody well wanted to, which was late in the day long after I had given up and crawled back to the comfort of our kitchen, creaking, dirty, beat and—glowing from the most exhilarating Fourth of July in my life, I wondered if we would ever spend this holiday in America again.

It was mutually agreed that Tyler should be nearer home and he has been accepted by a boarding school which is less than an hour away and—praise be—a third of the cost. He is mad about his school uniform, the standard gray trousers, blue blazer affair; a regimentation that Kevin hated so much, he did everything he could to undermine his school's dress code. We know that once it becomes mandatory, this love affair with the school uniform will die quietly and we try not to dissuade Tyler before classes begin, but he displays himself in uniform so often, we're concerned that it might disintegrate before then.

"There is a perfectly good reason our flatware is in that jar in the postbox . . . if you'll just let me explain."

Maybe we should have Tyler tutored at home and I wouldn't feel so terribly alone. No. He would never give up the uniform.

Another cold, dreary morning but it doesn't deter the carpenters as they bash out windows, exchanging the rotting old ones for more resilient teak frames. Winds dance in the living room because panes have yet to be installed. We're promised that all will be completed by quitting time. There aren't many hours left. Do they think I have no memory? If I must throw myself in front of their van I shall make certain the windows are covered with something substantial before they leave, on chance of the odd hurricane whipping in suddenly. Once this crew departs, when they return again is anyone's game.

Think I'll just check with Tyler regarding the projected weather forecast. For reasons kept to himself, Ty is avid about not missing such information on the news programs, and he also comprehends Celsius and centigrade which to me is perverse, like Ava's distaste for chocolate.

When I asked Tyler if he had a current rundown on the weather, he replied that it was four minutes past eleven.

"No, Son, you misunderstood. I asked . . ."

"I know what you asked me . . . but I wanted to tell you the time, Dad."

Perhaps he should have stayed at Chalet Gloria after all.

Decided to wear my hair on the longish side. Not that the hairdresser isn't perfectly capable, but her large dog resting his head on my knees and following her every move with great sad eyes while the baby constructed complex miniature automobiles from Tinker Toys at my feet on her kitchen floor required adjusted thinking. The little boy can identify makes of cars beyond the knowledge of most adults, always remembering what family friends drive; he often knows who pulls into their driveway by the sound of the engine and he is still pre-school age.

If he weren't such a nice kid, he'd be scary. His dad, the

only electrician in the area, sometimes comes home for lunch while his wife is cutting my hair, so I mustn't be too hasty about the long hairstyle. Often the only opportunity to approach the electrician and pin him down to definite dates for lighting up our lives is while I'm getting a hair cut.

~ ~ ~

Fred couldn't keep his promise to attend Adele's seventy-ninth birthday party at Luttrelstown Castle near Dublin because he fell off a skateboard and broke his wrist.

~ ~ ~

For all my boyhood fantasies, and they were considerable, nothing is more unreal than present reality. Although I daydreamed to excess, never did I imagine living in a castle, and in one week I've been a guest at two.

After four days at Lismore, we are spending the weekend at Luttrelstown, a castle more opulent though not as massive as Lismore. It's big enough. My God, we don't even know how many people coming for Dellie's bash are actually staying here since some arrived late last night, and no one can get acquainted at breakfast because we are all required to take that in our rooms.

Without room numbers we didn't know how to describe where we were when we rang for breakfast until the housekeeper, or whoever answered the call, informed Ava, in tones to chill the grapefruit, that Madame was in the Fuchsia Room. Spirits weren't exactly soaring in the kitchen this morning, I'd wager. At Lismore, if more than toast and coffee is desired, we advise them the night before and we always come down to breakfast to save the girls climbing with heavy trays.

Rules are stringent here, one hesitates searching about or examining the fascinating, beautiful objects d'art found everywhere for fear of replacing them wrongly. There is a feeling of calculated effect; that everything is displayed where it is meant to be right to the centimeter, yet, conversely, a foreboding that all is slightly off-kilter permeates the house. More than a foreboding.

The butler told us that our hostess wouldn't be here until the party this evening. She flew to Paris to have her eyebrows dyed.

~ ~ ~

Peering from beneath thick, very orange brows, our hostess had mistaken me for the butler all during lunch, which was certainly okay if a little baffling since we sat side-by-side at table and I doubt she runs her house in quite so democratic a fashion. I served her drinks on request anyway while the real butler winked at me behind her back and took care of the others. Seemed easier that way.

The era is probably best over but for a while last night I decried the passing of such a time of grace. Seeing those elderly ladies with their poise, elegance, and style was rather like watching a tableau, being caught up in a painting by Whistler or Sargent. They overshadowed the many attractive young people in attendance by far.

Dellie seemed to be truly touched by my birthday gift: since they were on the road so much as children and traveled with costumes and props, there was never any extra space for toys, so little Adele Astaire's only playthings were paper dolls. Ava kept her aunt involved elsewhere while I sneaked into her closet at Lismore, sketched some of her outfits and then made a water-colored paper doll likeness of Dellie complete with attachable wardrobe.

A columnist once wrote that time had kissed Adele lightly on both cheeks and never was that more apparent than at the very end of the evening when we found her dancing alone in the corner of the ballroom—an old woman, once a star, dancing wistfully without music while her chiffon scarf floated around her. How very sad that could have been if her movements weren't so exquisite or, when she realized she had an audience, she hadn't mugged, kicked like a chorus girl and collapsed laughing. Or if she hadn't looked so glorious.

~ ~ ~

We bought a little farm in order to experience a lifestyle other than Hollywood offers, so why in the name of God are we touring Ireland with a French-Italian movie company at the start of winter? This is about as far from rationality as I care to wander and already suspect we may have reached the point of no return.

It happened so suddenly: the call from Fred announcing his arrival to commence filming in Dublin, even though his wrist hasn't quite shrunk to normal size yet; that our rooms were waiting at his hotel and, as a condition of his contract, we were expected to be in them.

His contract? We just signed a contract of our own for a new well which they promised to drill any day now. I planned to be here to see if they chose the same spot Tim and I discovered with our water-divining powers. His water-divining powers. I did little more than drop the wish-bone shaped branch when it quivered in my hands and scared me silly. Where in Tim's grasp the stick danced violently, it only shuddered in mine but the shudder continued all the way down my spine. I guess I'm not as divine as Mr. O'Regan, who was only experimenting out of curiosity to see if he had the ability because he knew the well driller brought along his own diviner and, unlike me, Tim is not one to accept such mysteries unquestioned.

"'Tis a mystery, too," as Tim says. Why does wood react for some and not others? There must be validity to the method: well-drilling is an expensive operation but on the diviner's word, our contract guarantees not only freshwater but an estimated amount of gallons per hour. If we don't receive the minimum, we don't pay . . . and not having the gift himself, the big business-man uses a man with a stick. We would love to be home to see if they select the place where the divining rod nearly twisted out of Tim's hands but that is an excitement we must forego, because by the time the well digger gets around to our land, we shall be in the extremes of Connemara or some equally distant, forlorn, and probably freezing countryside. While visiting Fred in the States I read the script and know it calls for a Galway location but such are the ways of filmmakers, they're almost certain to select other areas because

Galway doesn't look enough like Galway.

Usually Fred will have a general idea of scripts when his agent submits them, but he reads only the parts pertaining to his character, and if he finds those appealing, often he'll ask me to read it in entirety and give him a synopsis and (which still knocks me out) an opinion. Ava thinks he believes I'll be more objective than she is. She refuses to acknowledge any suggestions that her Dad rates me of higher intellect, and now that we find ourselves in this position, she may well be right. Suggesting that he accept this part may prove not to be the smartest thing I've ever done.

With the exception of Peter Ustinov whom I am most anxious to meet, the gang is all here and wherever we're going, the call sheet decreed we depart Dublin for the first location bright and early. Well . . . early. The cast isn't large. Mostly just the stars and crew are at the hotel; extras will be recruited along the way and bit players will arrive when needed since actors can come from Dublin on short notice no matter where we might be.

Besides F. A., the players consist of Charlotte Rampling, France's Philippe Noiret, Mr. Ustinov, Italian ingenue Augustina Belli (whom we have also not met because she is currently in hospital with a back problem about which details are few and rumors rife) and the young American actor Edward Albert. Equally eclectic, the crew comes from France, Italy and, of course, Ireland; a technologically creditable mixture, I'm certain, but it appears to us outsiders that we might encounter some major problems of communication as time wears on, not the least being the handsome young director, Yves Boiset. Yves' air of eager bewilderment enhances his charms if not doing a lot towards expressing his wishes, and although he professes fluency in all three languages, it has been suggested, for reasons of clarity, he should stick to French and let the rest of us work it out amongst ourselves. I don't know where he learned Italian (nor apparently do the Italians) but his admission that he acquired English while residing in Japan hardly came as the surprise intended.

Looks like interesting days ahead. I'm glad now we were brought along for the ride, and perhaps if we are very good, we shall be allowed to go home once in a while and savor life down on the farm.

The Renvyle House Hotel, a comfortable old family-oriented place which had few out-of-season guests except the locals who frequented the bar, welcomed us and valiantly accepted our intrusion. Especially the trusting little lady who leased her cottage kitchen and bedroom to be used as a set. She didn't know what such a venture entailed. Not only is her own kitchen off limits for fear she might unwittingly move a prop, she didn't understand why she couldn't speak for long periods of time. Her neighbors didn't hesitate to speak their resentment about the lease money she was paid instead of them, but she had hand-painted the interior walls in multicolored swirls and her cottage had the most flair. She deserved every penny, too; her house will never be the same. If we hadn't actually seen it, Ava and I wouldn't have believed so much equipment and so many bodies could fit into those two small rooms, but they managed to shoot, and even though conditions were difficult, Fred was more relaxed after he worked a day. At least he was warm for a change.

I came up to our room on the first floor next to Fred's to find Charlotte emerging from a room on the other side.

"Didn't realize we are neighbors," I said in some confusion, remembering she told us they were at the back of the building.

"We're not. I can't resist peeking in open rooms," the lady offered without guilt. "But I knock first. Yours would have been the next unless you can lock it. I don't lock mine because the key sticks. Most of the rooms have been unlocked so I expect it's the same all over. Shall I see your place, please?"

"Have I ever denied you anything?" And I invited the beautiful Charlotte Rampling into my bedroom. It is a warm, cozy room and last night Ava and I managed a quiet evening reading in bed even though F. A. insisted he heard his daughter's voice in the hall long past what he considers a respectable hour. His daughter's voice sounded in our doorway as I was about to mention that to Charlotte.

"Someone just told me you were singing in the bar after closing time, Darling. I said it couldn't have been you . . . Hi, Charlotte . . . Daddy accused me of keeping him awake . . . now I'll have to convince him somebody here sounds like both of us . . . Charlotte? . . . I just left Richard in the lobby. How did you get in our room with my husband?" Ava's voice ran down while she caught her first breath since entering, and before she could begin again, a small crowd of Charlotte's household—her secretary from New Zealand, her English nanny, the French nurse for the continuity girl's child, and the Vietnamese friend who reads tarot card for a living—gathered at the open door with such discord of prattle and accents, I begged them come in and made my own exit.

For term holidays Tyler asked to join us on location, knowing full well we couldn't refuse since there was no one at home and none of the other boarders were remaining at school during the break. We cautioned it would involve some intricate maneuvering on his part: "Don't miss the train! There is a connection to be made and the west-bound goes only once per day." Ty offered to thumb to Renvyle but he hadn't realized the distance or that hitching through County Galway at this time of year is positive thinking worthy of Norman Vincent Peal.

Fortunately a schoolmate had come to see Tyler off when he missed the train, else he might never have known to phone his friend's family-owned car dealership or found the foreman restless and itching for a spin west in order to test-drive a new Bentley. Besting us and the railroad system by a good forty-five minutes, Ty continued traveling in style when Fred asked his driver, George Penney, to collect him at the station in his Mercedes.

I think Tyler actually welcomed the thought of returning to school if only to get his blood circulating again. Much of the holiday he spent with Fred on location huddled over a gas lamp in the trailer during lengthy waits between shots, or freezing outside with the crew while his grandfather was filming. We thought Ty would be more adjusted but he griped about the elements as much as F. A. who seldom leaves his house in sunny Beverly Hills without a topcoat.

Ava asked if I thought it was any milder in our part of the country now? We've begun packing up for the next shoot tomorrow which will be close enough for a fairly easy drive home. Hope the next stop will be as much fun as this place has been. I think a lot of the population here will be sorry to see us go though possibly not the village post office staff, who threatened strike if the hotel switchboard didn't curtail a portion of the international phone calls bombarding them at the end of the day's shooting. On the other hand, since more and more locals joined us in the bar each night, I wouldn't be surprised if the post office ladies were included in the group of sturdy girls dancing together this evening. It's good to note there were fewer of the dark glances that came our way at first.

This was an unusual experience for us, but what must it have been like for some of these people who have spent their entire lives without leaving the mountains, and hold Dublin to be the zenith of the universe?

~ ~ ~

We're berthed at Ashford Castle. Thank God it's out of season; this place must draw tourists like flies during the warmer months. The setting is beautiful—amazingly so—but the building, compared to Lismore, is contrived, more suited to Disneyland, which, considering that the lobby will be doubling as a sound stage, is not really inappropriate. As a hotel it's fine, but only a small part of the original castle remains and the rest, though imposing, smacks of papier-mâché. I read that pheasants are provided for those of a shooting notion. Although I've never classified killing as a sport to begin with, this removes even the vestiges of chance and, so far as I'm concerned, is simply slaughter.

Cables, booms, arc lamps rendered the hotel's entry hall useless for traffic but the management still insisted upon jacket and ties for men in the dining room. Normally I don't challenge policy of this kind, but the place is not operating under normal circumstances, and on days action is required outside the crew barely has time to remove weather gear and wash before dinner as it is. The company is bringing in business far beyond the usual winter's expectancy and these people need to relax after a long rigorous day in bitter temperatures. I'm not sure some of the guys even brought neckties. So far we haven't seen young Mr. Albert in anything other than turtleneck sweaters and the jeans and boots his part calls for and a sheepskin coat that looks as if it originally served Air Corps duty in World War One.

Since just after breakfast Ava and I have been making our way across the hotel's sizable lobby while Miss Rampling causes a commotion with the desk clerk. Now, at mid-afternoon break, there is talk of extending the scene and providing us with another day of employment tomorrow. Fred, Philippe, and Edward viewing from beyond the camera range gave us a hand following the first action, perplexing some tourists who watched our moves during the second take to see why the stars applauded the extras.

I hope they never learned the connection. Working as extras eases our guilty twinges that someone else is paying expenses while we're enjoying ourselves so much and have the bonus of being with Fred during the months we're usually separated. Even though we realize that Ava is great comfort and companionship for her dad, therefore of value to the production, it is still good to be doing something more apparently constructive. Especially for me.

Ava on the set of The Purple Taxi, *1976. Fred Astaire starred in the movie, which was filmed mostly in the west of Ireland.*

Other couples pretending to mill about are Major and Mrs. Blackwell of the Crosse & Blackwell food products; Cathy, Charlotte's secretary, and a young man who spends his time in the real world searching the seas for shellfish worthy of Blackwell soups. Securing extras is never a problem. Nearly everyone wants to be in a movie, ourselves notwithstanding, and I think, in that regard, I must have a sharp word with Charlotte later about the way she is hogging our scene.

Fred's worries about his last scene, where he must run into the hotel and up the long staircase in high agitation, turned out to be valid. They couldn't use the shot but not, as he feared, because he was too winded to continue dialogue. In a single take, to a round of applause from the crew, he managed with such ease it looked like a dance number and no matter how convincing an actor he is, that was unmistakably Astaire—not an elderly Irish country doctor—on those stairs. The grace of movement so uniquely his is even more identifiable from the back and Fred has never quite understood that his walk is as recognizable as John Wayne's. I remember once how touched he was in a restaurant when a young boy came to our table and politely asked just to shake his hand and when the kid left, Fred asked quite seriously, "How do you suppose they know an old bird like me?"

Fred during filming of The Purple Taxi *in Ireland.* PHOTO: AVA ASTAIRE McKENZIE

He is as incapable of inelegant motion as his daughter is of falsehood. Not that Ava is without elegance herself or lost on the dance floor, but we don't speak of her everyday mobility. That she has been seen to open a taxi door and knock a passing cyclist into Madrid traffic in a single action hardly merits mentioning. Claudine, the dazzling continuity lady for the film, was so resplendent in a turban at dinner last night, Ava stopped by her table to tell her so, tripped and stuck her finger in the startled girl's eye. Claudine laughed, so I guess it wasn't as painful as it appeared, and for once Ava had the presence not to giggle, her usual reaction when acutely embarrassed.

~ ~ ~

We were browsing the hotel boutique, a cottage situated over a little bridge a short walk from the main building, when the little terrier that lives there began whimpering. Two loud reports rang in succession, the dog cowered close to its mistress . . . then another explosion. "Gun shots!" Fred said hurrying over to the door while I snarled that it was probably some brave man shooting sitting ducks and Ava, not yelping at unexpected noises as she usually does, uneasily insisted that we wait in the shop until we were certain the hunters had gone. Lightening up a bit, she reminded her father that since he often referred to himself as an old bird, we'd better not chance it. Strange how the terrier seemed to anticipate the shots.

We lingered awhile allowing Fred to purchase souvenirs for his housekeeper and secretary in the States before we somewhat cautiously returned across the bridge to the hotel but there was no sign of any hunters. Last night I noticed three sort of surly looking civilians in the dining room who didn't strike me as the type we've had around lately who come to see the funny movie people, and I remarked that maybe they were here for the pheasants. But, I thought the game-run surely couldn't be as near the hotel as those shots sounded.

Fred often refers to me as Richard, the Interrogator, and he demanded I go ferret out information straightaway.

The whole place was buzzing. Indeed the men we saw at dinner were hunters and the obese one was responsible for the gunshots. Only he didn't kill a bird. At close range, he shot a dog the entire unit had befriended . . . a little black and white mutt belonging to one of the waiters. Barely more than a puppy, he spent each day sitting by the entrance until his master came off duty, but he went for walks, played with all of us, and this lout, who supposedly heard that a dog was taking the slain pheasants, saw the trusting little guy waiting at the hotel door, actually called him over and shot him twice in the head. Point blank. A couple of lads, hired to flush the birds attempted to intervene but they were threatened with equal treatment and wisely backed off as he shot the animal once more and threw it in the river. If the monster's friends hadn't checked him and themselves out immediately, we might have had an international crisis when the crew returned from location.

A pall has settled over the company and we can't get out of here soon enough. Ava and I will never return to Ashford Castle again. I was wrong. It isn't like Disneyland at all.

Kenmare, County Kerry, was meant to be a short location shoot before the final wrap in the Dublin studios, but we arrived here so far behind schedule the producer advised us to plan for Christmas in Dublin.

And Charlotte grows larger. Her early stages of pregnancy wouldn't have mattered if there hadn't been so many rewrites and last-minute changes decreed by our endearing but quixotic young director.

Delays allowed full recovery time for Augustina, though, and she was able to join us the last few days at Ashford just when it was feared they would have to scrap her earlier footage and recast the part. She is lovely, very soft spoken for an Italian, and so relieved to be away from the hospital where she couldn't understand a word that she took off skipping across the lawn soon after we checked into the hotel this afternoon. Comprehending only one of the languages immediately screamed at her, she apparently got the message and has been walking rather timidly ever since.

Through most of the story, the girl's character is mute, but as Augustina knows only Italian, comes the time she is meant to regain her voice she'll have to be dubbed in both French and English. Philippe, Charlotte, and Ustinov are at home in either language (Peter Ustinov, in almost any language); Fred and Edward have enough background to lip-sync dialogue shot in French. The double shooting has been our main delay. Ah well. Not to worry; Clonlea isn't too far away. Ava will remain with her dad. I'm going to beat it for home tomorrow where I intend to indulge the cats, squelch the rising damp, and sink into the relative sanity and sanctity within my own walls. Maybe I can develop some of my location sketches into something more profitable before I return on the weekend when tuna sandwiches and a quiet bed will have lessened in appeal.

~ ~ ~

Home! Not quite bliss. The cats haven't ceased wailing since I scrunched Phyllis-Doris against the storm door when the three of us attempted simultaneous entry against a Force-6 westerly. Perhaps they're telling me all that happened during my absence; God knows they're hardly less intelligible than some of the English I've tried to decipher these past weeks.

I'm glad I didn't come home until today because without alerting anyone of his arrival, Mr. Ustinov calmly ranged into the hotel breakfast lounge as we were being served, surprising Fred so much he spilled oatmeal on himself. Compounding her dad's embarrassment, using my shoulder for support, Ava climbed onto a window sill in order to photograph the two stars as they chatted across the otherwise vacant room.

"Mr. Ustinov," she said trying to focus, "you're in the not enough light!"

"And you, my dear," he replied, "have been in Ireland too long."

Considering that he had only half an hour before concluded

a non-stop solo drive from Spain, Ustinov was amazingly amiable. I trust next weekend we shall meet again under less ludicrous circumstances.

Fred and his costar Peter Ustinov in Kenmare, Ireland, during the making of The Purple Taxi.

"I should like the number for O'Brien's Television Rentals shop, please."

"Yes, sir. Which one?"

"O'Brien's Television Rentals."

"There are two O'Brien's Television Rentals. Which one do you want, sir?"

"I don't know. I thought there was just the one, you see."

"Grand . . . I'll ring through."

"O'Brien's Television Rentals? My name is McKenzie. I didn't realize there is more than one of you and my wife isn't here . . . that is—she always deals with you. I hope it's you. Look will you check to see if my name is on your books?"

"What color is your card, Mr. McKenzie?"

"You want to know the color of my CAR?!"

"Your car-dah, Mr. McKenzie."

"Good Lord! I'm not sure we have a card. What color should it be? My wife is away, you see and . . . AHA! Are you the O'Brien who operates your TV repairs service in a different village from where the main shop is located?"

"No, that wouldn't be us."

"Then can you please give me the number of the other O'Brien's so I can tell the operator?"

"Now I couldn't be doing that but you might try the O'Brien's Television Rentals on Bridge Street."

"Great. Thank you very much. Is that B-R-I-D-G-E Street?"

"Yes, sir. But you'd better ask for Nolan's."

~ ~ ~

They probably wouldn't have come to fix the television before I return to Kenmare anyway. Herself can sort things out when she comes home to prepare for Thanksgiving, and I think I'll forget to mention my little exchange with the outside world since for years Ava has been convinced I'm helpless on my own.

~ ~ ~

Perhaps the stay at home should have been longer. I'm not certain the picture presented me as I entered the lobby wasn't too much of a cultural strain when one had been isolated as I had down on the farm. Peripheral vision caught Father-in-law shooting pool with a cigarette-smoking nun while ahead was my wife in a phone booth with Peter Ustinov.

Ava explained she was assisting Mr. Ustinov in obtaining a phone number. His need for aid in that direction I most certainly understand, but I can't comprehend how they were both able to squeeze into the cubicle together. I don't see how the distinguished gentleman could even manage it by himself. The nun with Fred turned out to be a costumed extra from the hospital scene, but I think the next time they play they should close the recreation room door before she lights up a smoke or chalks her pool cue. This hotel is big with tour groups even off-season and enough people back in the States labor under misinformation about Ireland as it is.

~ ~ ~

Thanksgiving Day.

Keeping her promise to give the very homesick young Mr. Albert an American Thanksgiving dinner, Ava prepared the proper meal, but not with the turkey Kitty raised for us as a gift. After it followed her around the O'Regan barnyard looking for a handout, Ava implied that the celebration was canceled due to work schedule changes and we purchased a bird of less personality from a butcher in the next village.

Giving truth to the lie, Edward rang this early afternoon; they were moving to a new location to take advantage of the unexpected bad weather—an upcoming scene requires a storm on the beach. He and the girls couldn't come to us. Ava turned off the oven, joined me and the cats around the real fireplace in the new little library room. We would work Thanksgiving Day in another time. Edward rang. It proved too stormy to shoot the storm, they were coming after all. Only not the expected Amanda and Kathy who speak English. Edward had invited Augustina and Talya who do not.

Ava turned on the oven. Edward rang. They were lost. Ava removed the bird from the oven. She would return it when she thought remaining cooking requirement matched estimated traveling time, provided her directions were heeded. Edward rang from the village. They were drinking in a pub. Though Ava pronounced the turkey now decently mummified, it turned out one of the best ever. I think she said that when Edward and Co. finally arrived, they poked the bird with a fork and poured in honey. Probably there was more to it than that.

Around ten o'clock, as we were finishing the meal and the storm really gained momentum, we heard voices in the wind. The door opened: Yves and the assistant director literally blew in. "Once more from the top," he shouted, before collapsing into French where he and everybody else, including my wife, happily remained while I stacked dishes in the kitchen.

Edward helped Ava tidy the kitchen and had a nightcap while the others raced back through the mountain pass. I mustn't dwell on that. The girls intended to stay over with us, but Yves needed Augustina for an early shoot tomorrow and thought it easier to risk an hour's drive over the ridge in utter darkness and appalling conditions than to telephone. He could be right about the phone, but they were all returning tomorrow and it would only have meant an earlier departure. I think Yves really was more interested in the pumpkin pie.

It's nice writing here by the fire. No Latin commotion. Just the sound of a Force-10 so incensed against the windows. Soothing by comparison.

~ ~ ~

As we returned to the hotel from our walk, we waved up to Fred who stood at his bedroom window sewing; he had tried to shorten a tie by cutting a piece out of the middle and stitching it back together. His daughter and I suggested perhaps now was a good time for him to come home with us, since he isn't needed for a couple of days and we can drive him up to Cork airport for his next scene. F. A. agreed.

Thank God we had the small electric heater acquired in Galway because even the rooms in Renvyle House were too chilly for Fred. The heater seemed useless at first when we found the only power outlet was in the unused room next door, but Ava spliced together flex, making an extension long enough to reach Fred's bedroom, not an easy task given the tiny size of the electrical goods shop where heater and cords were purchased. The proprietor held one end of the flex, Ava took the whole roll out of the shop and up the street until she felt the distance was close to that required. While she chatted with interested passers-by and neighboring business persons, I investigated the windows of shops on another block.

We drove F. A. to Cork airport for the shot; George Penney took him on to Dublin where it was confirmed we would be spending Christmas, while Ava and I returned home to arrange for the cats again and collect our tree ornaments before making the long haul to the opposite end of the country.

Fred didn't mind not being home for the holidays, he just wanted to be warm again. The heater worked fine, but he confessed he used all the comforters and some of his clothes as well. Neither of us felt it was especially cold, but it was damp, of course, and Fred shivered automatically at the thought of being so close to the bay at this time of year. Ava knows now there is no chance of ever luring her dad back here in the wintertime. We, he said, are candidates for the Home for the Bewildered . . .

Yves' request for fifty ships on the runway for today's shoot was met with horror until someone had the sense to realize he wanted a herd of sheep. Fortunately he couldn't get them; this country isn't quite that quaint. Bereft of sheep or ships, the shot went smoothly enough except that Charlotte's scene boarding the plane required rain and the rain had to be manufactured when the promising, gloomy Irish clouds suddenly blew away, leaving everything sunny and dry. Next stop, Dublin.

We were wise to bring the Christmas decorations. The tree in our suite brought cheer to a lot of otherwise unhappy folk who thought they would be home for Christmas.

Fred found a toy English taxi, painted it purple to match the one he drove in the film. He wouldn't tell us how he managed the exact color, but he was obviously very proud of his effort which was a welcome addition to the memorabilia-ornaments we hung on the tree. The original cab was stolen from location in County Kerry, and when the police found it soon afterwards, they were regarded with astonishment when they asked the company for a registration number as proof it was the same taxi. Requesting an ID for a vivid purple, English-type taxi cab found in the Irish back country is so good a story that the police laughed themselves. All the same they requested the producers not release the incident to the press—there are enough Kerryman jokes in Ireland already.

Tyler again joined us during school holidays. Contrary to character, he balked at attending a big function at Luttrelstown Castle, even though I told him I thought he'd want to meet the Guinnesses, considering he had pulled enough of their pints working as a barman. The biggest surprise was his hesitation to wear evening clothes. Fred shared his feelings. They both went under duress, but we learned later, from Ty's dinner partner, as the meal progressed Tyler overcame shyness at being the youngest person there.

Unaware that the grandmotherly Eleanor Lambert often dined with the most celebrated people in the world, he confided that he guessed he didn't mind being charming. Knowing my son, he meant to say he didn't feel so out of place as he thought he would. The evening wore long for Fred though. He hates being charming.

F. A. got out of it somehow, but dinner at Sybil Connolly's last night found me wondering what the hell I could possibly discuss with Alfred Biet when the ladies retired—as I knew these would, leaving the men to port, cigars, and dirty stories, none of which I manage easily, and I am even less at home in the high-powered business world of the likes of Sir Alfred. I could ask about his famous art collection, but I really wanted to hear about the theft of some of the paintings and his kidnapping by the infamous Englishwoman Rose Dugdale and her IRA companions. It had been all over the press and I was dying to hear the story from the horse's mouth, but to ask Alfred outright about the dramatic events seemed of questionable taste.

The ladies fluttered away, he filled the vacated seat next to mine, lit a cigar, stared long. "Tell me," he growled, "do you know Bette Davis?"

~ ~ ~

They wrapped the picture. F. A. returned to Beverly Hills. Warm at last, he was determined to replace weight loss he could ill afford and was taking a Bourbon old-fashioned whenever the mood struck him. Especially on Sunday. Never much of a tippler, Fred liked to unwind with one or two of the cocktails before dinner, a drink for which I shared enthusiasm, he decided, and whenever ordering one for himself, he did the same for me. During our month and a half stopover at Dublin's Royal Hibernian Hotel, this was a manageable request six days of the week, but on the seventh, when the Hotel's Grille Room rested and we were forced to dine in the more opulent main dining room, it became a contest we always lost.

The small bottle of bitters, an important ingredient, was locked up when the Grille closed after dinner Saturday night, not to be seen again until Monday lunchtime. We decided against purchasing a bottle of our own on principle, and as weeks progressed, ours was a challenge of wills. The hotel never gave in and we didn't buy another bottle. On Sundays I was allowed my martini. Fred stood stoic. On our last weekend, Ava remarked that in a way it was understandable, probably there was no call for bitters at the bar other than by us, and two bottles would be considered wretched excess. "No, Madame," a waiter clearing the adjacent table corrected, "the Bishop drinks gin and bitters here all the time."

But never on Sunday.

~ ~ ~

"Oh I wasn't talking to you, just then."

"We might have grown accustomed to lots of company and conversation in several tongues recently, but we are home now, and when we are seated at the breakfast table—just the two of us, away from urbane society and even the cats, I hold that when you speak aloud, it is a valid assumption you are addressing me. You must promise you shall make every effort to speak to yourself when you are by yourself. And only then. There's a love."

Timmy's latest tidbit, that the always-muddy little patch at the corner of his lower field is said to be a holy spring with healing properties especially benefiting eye problems, brought Ava scurrying up the studio stairs, two at a time, but she said my reaction to her information would guarantee my sizzling in hellfire for sure. Why? I agreed that it must be a site for sore eyes.

"George, let go! All right, which one of you caught it?"

I think I'll not go downstairs. Ava is preparing the evening meal; I do not wish to encounter other than that in the kitchen.

With February nearly upon us, we'll soon be in California. The Irish weather has turned bleak and brooding and good painting light is fleeting. More importantly, F. A. has urged us to come almost since the day he got home. A deadline for my exhibition there was set some time ago, and I shall be happy to complete the rest of these bucolic studies of old Erin in that little room off the kitchen in Fred Astaire's house where I needn't worry about what the cats drag in.

Painting is the art form which requires application, more physical than mental, so my concentration wasn't broken when Ava brought me a cup of coffee—already talking (as Dellie does) before she entered my little hideaway next to Fred's housekeeper's quarters behind the kitchen. My concentration was, however, badly shaken. I was sure we left this line of conversation in Ireland where it belongs.

"Richard! I've got a sore throat."

" Not another, darling? You just got over one."

"No, this feels like the kind that goes away before I get it."

"Go upstairs without me, you'll get in trouble," she warned on the flight to Los Angeles. But I went anyway to escape the movie.

He was a large man, beyond portly, the oxygen tank between his knees—mask at the ready, not dimming an attitude of privilege. I sat two seats away in the nearly full lounge, picked up a magazine. Too late. I know better than to make eye contact with strangers, especially when it appears there might be a situation brewing. There is something about me that cries out to the world's crazies; it's caused no end of bother all my life, so Ava wasn't exactly untoward with her admonition. "I wonder if I might ask of you a favor?" he boomed across the woman seated between us, gaining instant attention from the other passengers. The favor being that should he be overcome by a fit of gasping, I was to retrieve an attaché case from below and fetch it to him like a good fellow.

He foresaw no trouble but he had been traveling for forty-eight hours and there still remained traces of respiratory infection picked up in Africa. Should there come an attack and the oxygen proved insufficient, I was to remove from that attaché case medication in the form of suppositories, assist him into the lavatory, and administer same like the fine chap I am. Whimpering something to the effect that I didn't feel qualified to accept such responsibility, after informing the flight attendants I crawled back to the protection of my wife, and when they finally got hold of themselves, the cabin crew advised that I was not allowed to administer aid of this nature, nor were they. Nor would they, if they could. The gentleman, it turned out, had been guzzling champagne by the tumblerful for quite a while.

You were right," I whispered, slipping into my seat next to Ava, but didn't tell her how right until we were disembarking and passed the old boy snoring and wheezing loudly.

Betty Ludden said I should have told him what he could do with his suppositories.

With Ava at Clonlea.

PHOTO: DICK DE NEUT

Chapter Eleven

Que Sera, Sera . . . Begorrah

Either the twenty-ninth or thirtieth of May is the Farrell's wedding anniversary—an event Ava feels significant enough to shatter my reverie, but she can't remember which it is because it is also my sister Charlotte's and Ruta Lee's birthday and the day Paul Hauge joins his father at a reunion of Norwegian-Americans in the Midwest, and what do I plan to do about it?

I suggest we ignore the month of May altogether. We're back at Clonlea. What else can possibly matter?

We found not much changed this trip other than Kevin's girlfriend. This one was thirty-five, separated, and a past runner-up for the Miss Universe crown.

Fred had sent us a photo he took of Kevin in his chef's toque, but we hadn't thought how he happened to have it until Kevin told us. Neither of the boys trade upon their relationship to F. A. and Kevin said he was having his own lunch in the restaurant when a waiter rushed up to the owner and stammered, "Fred Astaire is in the kitchen asking the dishwasher if he can see KEVIN!" Fred loves to putter around the hardware store and always parks in the alley behind it. He knew Kevin worked next door and wanted to take a picture of him in his cook's hat.

F. A. was in great form and my show was more successful than I could have hoped. Animal studies, a relatively adventuresome attempt for me, were especially popular and provided Ava a new outlook. "Paint more sheep!" she kept whispering at the showing, but it was a sell-out of everything and meant I was back in harness again for real.

With Ava and John Travolta, early 1980s.

This to-ing and fro-ing could get pretty schizophrenic. Not many of the L.A. contingent credited that we strolled misty moors in the company of a cross cat and an affectionate cow any more than our Irish neighbors could grasp that we are often in the audience at the Academy Awards ceremony when they see it on television. Everyone knows that Ava is F. A.'s daughter, but around here, the lady in the cabbage patch is the one they relate to.

Although I think the use of weaponry is a contrary hobby

for a messenger of The Lord, we can't, in fairness, fault the vicar's target practice on the rectory grounds. But when we saw him heading towards town wearing what appeared to be a long brown-and-white checked flannel dressing gown topped by a deerstalker hat, and in company with a disheveled Great Pyrenees, we began to worry about the man's marksmanship.

Hurd Hatfield and the reverend fascinate because they legitimately teeter on the edge of an exquisite eccentricity that sometimes I've encountered in my own backyard as well. If one gets down to basics, I suppose the vicar's ecclesiastical garb really isn't that much different from his bathrobe and deerstalker cap. Substitute the robe with the ankle-length black cassock he usually favors and replace the Sherlock Holmes headgear with a peaked affair that resembles a Hershey chocolate kiss; add pointed sideburns bits around the ears and you've got the clerical dress. Unless there is wind whipping his robes against his legs, I'm never convinced that reverend actually progresses under his own steam. He seems to glide down the street and even if he is laden with parcels, in my mind's eye his hands are always steepled in supplication.

~ ~ ~

In the sitting room at Clonlea.

"Inch by Inch. Row by Row. Every Little Seed I Sow."

My wife's singing reaches the open studio window as she crawls about the vegetable garden. Any endeavor to aid the larder must be endorsed but that song has got to go, and though Ava inherited her father's and her aunt's ear for music, hers misses in the translation; she shouldn't sing anyway because she tends to hyperventilate when she tries. We don't want her swooning in the swiss chard and frightening Kevin O'Mahoney. He is out there, too, but as I hear no derisive hoots, I expect she furrows somewhere downwind of Kevin's good ear.

Kevin O would never suppress comment to anyone, employer or not. Though he often tugs at his hair, menially protesting that the gardener can't sit at table with the quality, he is far from being just the gardener: he is the fellow who allows us to live amidst the displays of his genius. I don't use that term lightly. What Mr. O'Mahoney brought forth from this bogland in such an incredibly short time surpasses ordinary gardening. But K. O. is far from ordinary in every way. Kayo: not a bad moniker to distinguish him from our son and all the other Kevins abounding in this country. Cork born and bred, the son of professors, he has no sign of the regional accent unless he puts it on, is knowledgeable in the arts as well as geography, history and, I'm sure, mathematics; though he claims his Greek is rusty, he is fluent in six languages, speaking them all with an acid tongue, but his soul—I swear—is Japanese.

Kevin reclaimed land, uncovered great stones, playing their severity against flowers and plants new to us, especially the many and various poppies. Other stones he brought in and cemented them so subtly into the hillside they seemed to be natural steps and places to rest. The formal bits and herbaceous borders blended naturally with the savagery of wild gorse and meadow grasses and extend beyond two ponds he created; the higher feeding a lower one, a melody of running water in the back garden where we now could enjoy the sun beyond the hour when the house shades the terrace.

He forbade the American terms, front and back yards,

although Kevin O said, with its gravel the front of our place did resemble a yard—a prison yard. But he's seen to it, and the front garden is now a place of slate walkways winding between patches of flowering shrubs that Kevin promises will grow into protective buffers against the gales in no time. One must remember, however, that he is Irish with the Irish sense of time. We're not counting our hedges just yet. Before us is always the reminder of the fence post the very Irish Mr. O'Regan installed to support the gate in the lower pasture. Tim's reaction, when I commented about it being nearly two feet higher than the other posts and painted blue, was that before we knew it the bottom would rot in the ground and it would sink down. "Sure, in ten years, wouldn't they all look the same?"

Kevin O expressed a desire to see goldfish in his ponds and handed Ava a scrap of paper on which he'd listed some sources and names of stockists in Cork City. But that's seventy-five miles away; our whines rang dully against the steely barrier of the made-up O'Mahoney mind. Whose garden do we think this is?

The man works much harder and in far worse climatic conditions than many a serious farmer; naturally he is paid for his labor and talent, but he and the mad Jill, his companion of many years, have quickly become an integral part of our existence here and we're found together as often at a pub or restaurant as in the garden. They're both great fun and entirely wicked. He never hesitates to take advantage of my ignorance, most recently during instruction in the Latin names of plants, until I finally twigged he was throwing in titles such as "Scarlet Syphilis" and "Pale Blue Pudendum." And he has got to stop sneaking in those godawful plastic plants and feather dusters to see how long it will be before we notice them. On the other hand, because of Kevin O'Mahoney, now I can add wild strawberries to the breakfast müesli. It is blessed to forgive.

Ava declared she would sleep in the pigsty until I did something about the five o'clock crow. In English, that meant she planned spending nights in the guest room downstairs until I convinced a hooded crow we did not require five o'clock wake-up calls that blasted us every morning for the past week.

Ava wouldn't hear the crow in the guest room at the other end of the house, which had flowered fabric walls and lots of porcine folk art (because a neighbor told us this was the room where they once kept the pigs). I knew the dawn crier was a hooded crow because directly following his ear-splitting eye-opener he rapped at one window or another until, stark naked, I would sneak up and scream obscenities, thus defeating Ava's purpose because I could hear her giggling in the pig room.

I have a feeling that it's simply a matter of the crow liking the taste of the window putty, but Kevin O suggested that I confront the bird and shout, "NEVERMORE!" and Jill insisted it was the spirit of the recently departed Mr. O'Sullivan whose boyhood home this was, and she advised that I approach quietly, calling his name and explaining that we mean no harm to the old homestead. I'd rather holler, "NEVERMORE!"

Let Ava hide her head in the pigsty. I have a way with birds. Ever since we settled in the country the birds have seemed attracted to me. I was rewarded when a little brown wren hopped alongside as I did the rare bit of weeding, and a robin investigated my shoe while I waited for Ava to finish rummaging through a roadside antique shop. A wagtail followed me from room to room, peering in each window until, entranced, I came outside where I was eventually allowed to feed him by hand. All of it happened over a course of time naturally but in no case, except once when we deliberately courted a family of magpies—inciting the wrath of Kevin O'Mahoney in the doing, have I tried to entice the birds in any way. In fact, after the wren attempted visiting me in my chair while I was holding Phyllis-Doris, I began to fear for its safety.

Our Mr. O'Mahoney might care little for cows or mink or human animals, but he is knowledgeable about and devoted to most of the other local fauna, and much too kindhearted to carry out his threat to cut off the magpies' beaks with his secateurs because they messed around his compost pile (that Ava indelicately called the dung heap), and chased the songbirds away.

I didn't mention that there still seemed to be a lot of birdsong in the air, but I unwisely questioned the identity of the Irish robins because they are so much smaller than those in America.

"Indeed, though one hears that everything is bigger in the States," he retorted with slow, clipped precision, "such is not the case with robins. American robins, in point of fact, aren't robins at all . . . they're thrushes."

Since Kevin O worked his enchantment, Ava said she intends to drift about the place of an evening, trailing something sheer in pale lavender, but we all know that the first loose pebble would send her straight into the foxglove.

~ ~ ~

After sitting on display all weekend outside the pub which is the village bus stop, the king-sized mattress we ordered custom-made from Cork's Institute for the Blind arrived. Delivery, we'd assumed, would be to our door—not left in town for speculation as to American kinkiness; when the publican alerted us of delivery of a mattress, he said it in the form of a question, and this being Ireland, we should know better than to assume anything.

The builders returned in a large van with which the driver offered to pick up our new bed and deliver it when he collected the men at the end of the day, and I needn't face anyone gathered at the pub at the time. The mattress is here, the men departed with their usual comments of seeing us tomorrow, Please God, and my wife and our houseguest decided to lie on the thing to take the evening sun for a while longer before the two women and I attempted bringing it in from the front garden.

I have always encouraged our friends to visit, but some seasons we had known little respite from houseguests and they began earlier this year. It seemed I would be holed up in the studio for solitude as much as work.

In this respect I am blessed to have found a woman as special as Ava, whose verve for life is exquisite and without whom

I would most surely founder. From the very beginning, she has supported my need to be alone often (although I might be doing nothing of creative value at the time) and has never taken it personally.

~ ~ ~

I was considering curtaining off the front studio window because I found far too much of my solitary time was unproductive. Whole days escaped before I realized I'd done nothing more than share my thoughts with the sea. There is an Irish country saying that when one buys a hoe, it must first be checked to be sure it's the right height for leaning on. I'd been leaning on my hoe for too long periods at a time and half believed what so many other writers and artists have said: the country is enervating; the land itself mesmerizes; there is a bit of the nether world about Ireland. At least to me. It draws and captures and holds hypnotically.

For years I had a recurring dream; pleasant, but the kind one knew was a dream while it was happening. Recently I was startled to realize I hadn't had it for a long time, possibly not since we moved to Ireland. I believed I knew why. I had come to the source—that spot of slightly askew perspective, of too vivid color and somewhat hesitant motion—of a dream I've had since childhood. I'm still dreaming it, only I'm not asleep. It's not frightening but it is unsettling. So, to me, is Ireland.

~ ~ ~

The front studio window directly overlooks the boreen, where I see Ava practice her pivoting. Even though I've explained to her that my ability to execute this complete about-face turn while remaining in place without lifting the left foot from the ground was just part of my military training, Ava refuses to accept that I can do it without losing my balance when she cannot. I can't imagine why this is so important to her but, like George who dashed up the embankment to escape her flailing limbs, I don't want any part of it.

If only she had her dad's feet accomplis.

~ ~ ~

Ava came home in a daze. Why was this unlike other times? They swam, she said, under a waterfall, in the lake by the blue sheep. Ava was serious and seemed, by the quiet of her, to have had a somewhat metaphysical experience; a sudden recognition that she was acting out an old and recurring dream. Ava, too!

I accepted the part about swimming in the still waters of childhood dreams. I questioned the blue sheep. Ava immediately snapped that she took photographs—"you'll see, Mr. Hosehead." But I required no proof. She hadn't been her giddy self since returning from today's outing with her goddaughter, and I really did understand about the sheep. Free-roaming flocks are marked with colors, identifying ownership in the manner of branding cattle; one of my favorite sights is sheep I've seen recently with only their left horns painted scarlet. I reckon Ava's lakeside shepherd was overlavish in the opposite direction with his indigo dye brushes.

Singing "Blue ewes . . . you saw me swimming alone." (B. W. Ludden ventured that if you let those things lie unreleased, they just fester.) I left Ava to her musing and I believe "insensitive sod" came into play. Don't know why. I *said* I understood. Truly I do. In this land, one happens upon (or is guided to) places of magical circumstance far too often to simply shrug it off, and a couple of incidents I shall not forget, did indeed involve sheep.

Leaving my wife and father-in-law on location a December morning during filming of *The Purple Taxi,* I headed for home, and at the crest of Macgillacuddy's Reeks encountered probably the nearest thing to celestial grandeur I'll ever witness. In spite of snow on the mountain peaks and much on the ground, some green patches still mingled with the rusty red of dead foliage, and wet rocks looked black as obsidian. Slate gray sky, a presage of more snow, cast such unearthly light, rocks shimmered and sheep standing on them appeared incandescent, their wool a cold, white fire.

When I stepped out of the car into the glow myself, I realized I was crying. Swearing, too, because Ava couldn't share it. I heard the sheeps' bells and thought I should go back to fetch the cinematographer if only to watch him blow his dramatic Italian mind, but it was a mercurial scene and now, except for Ava, I'm glad for a memory so singularly my own.

More recently we discovered sheep of a different color, so to speak. I'm fond of the animals. But, I don't much care for the look of sheep's or goat's eyes. They're yellow, snake-like with slit irises. And I especially don't fancy them by the score, reflecting in the headlamps when I'm driving through a blind mountain tunnel on a moonless Irish night, wondering where I went wrong and how I got us into a demon-lined passageway to Hell. The sheep, we learned, pressed against the warm tunnel walls for hedonistic pleasure and not to scare the bejayus out of travelers. I'm not so sure.

~ ~ ~

Anytime but the week of the seventeenth you can begin work on the upstairs fireplace, we advised the builders. That week, and that week only, we expected houseguests. It would be the first time that Molly and Henry saw Clonlea since we discovered it together, and we were eager to show them our alterations under the best possible conditions.

Happily we'd misread their schedule and collected the Farrells on the sixteenth, gaining a few hours for them to combat jet lag; the demolition gang arrived sometime shortly after sunrise on the seventeenth. Nobody is *that* perverse. Charity insists that, for once in his nefarious existence, the contractor tried to please and the date stuck clearly in his thoughts. They knocked out the phony fireplace along with a chunk of wall in the living room, and exchanged the window for a doorway between the dining room and the green house which connected to the library and my studio.

Reducing two major sections of the house to rubble consumed most of their afternoon, but I didn't think the builders had dropped dead from the effort until the unmistakable silhouette of a hearse edging around the bend under gathering thunder clouds caused my knees to buckle. When I recognized the driver, I ran down to meet the ominous vehicle and learned that the contractor, who also built coffins and drove for funerals, used whatever conveyance was handy to the moment when he picked up his carpenters. The men had time only to wrap the open wounds in plastic before the hearse pulled up at the garden gate to take them home, but I'm sure they heard my banshee screams, warning that they'd be LYING in the hearse if they didn't come back tomorrow. But they did not return the next day. Or the whole week of the seventeenth.

We'd experienced this before when they built my studio and the library below it. The shell was completed and windows were in quickly but I had been warned that was not always an encouraging sign: once the interior was protected the builder felt free for job sites and cemeteries elsewhere, and the warning held true. I suppose they're no different from other builders. But nowhere else on this globe would the crew depart in a hearse at the end of the work day .

~ ~ ~

At last Molly and Henry could see the way we lived; a lifestyle for which they were directly responsible. We married in the sun room of their house in southern California, and because of the Farrells, we'd discovered our Nirvana on a southern tip of Ireland.

Like so many other blow-ins, as we outsiders are known, some plan in the greater scheme seemed to have directed us here. But the Farrells provided the reason when Henry wished to investigate properties and the tax benefits offered writers in the Irish Republic. Harboring no notions of an Irish village for ourselves, we had planned to settle in England, but Molly is Ava's best friend and she loved the idea of having them on this side of the world, too. We offered to introduce them to the country and help search out real estate and planned the annual Lismore stay accordingly.

Through Dellie, we had become acquainted with the manager of a hotel in beautiful County Kerry; we would use it as a starting point.

After a long, gray drive through fog and drizzle, our high spirits when we collected the Farrells at Cork airport deepened into gloom when the hotel failed to find our twice-confirmed reservations or the manager who handled them personally. Ireland had only two telephone directories: one for the Dublin area and another for the rest of the nation which, when Ava picked it up to seek other accommodations, fell open revealing the name of an inn set in bold type. Ava remembered that friends of Dellie's had recommended it should we ever be in the Irish Southwest.

Ava rang; it was the right place and solidly booked all season except for the next two days when they expected no one. Ava booked us in at once and we were warmly welcomed a few hours later by the innkeepers: two affable men of indefinite years and uncertain persuasion who, when they learned of our mission, showed us their friends John and Diana Ellison's house, Clonlea, which was for sale. The Ellisons had restored a two-hundred-year-old farmhouse and turned an outbuilding into a guest cottage situated on about five acres overlooking the sea.

That was the extent of land outsiders were allowed to buy in Ireland at the time, and the price was right; everything was so far beyond our expectations we advised them to snap it up immediately, but the Farrells could offer only tentative verbal agreement until they returned Stateside. Considering that immaterial, Ava and Molly spoke of butter churning while I silently wondered if they could really make the jump and Henry, speaking need for an "ugly break," evinced a desire to visit Detroit.

Before we all returned to London, the Farrells joined us for lunch at Lismore—their first encounter with Adele, who presided at table and audibly longed for the dead days of gracious living until I suggested she reflect upon her position a moment. She thought, and then said she would have liked to have been a nun.

Henry had promised to audition a drag act for a proposed English musical of his book *Whatever Happened to Baby Jane?*, and begged us to come along for moral support. Three hours after leaving the leprechauns, we climbed five flights of irregular stairs to enter the world of English fairies. I couldn't shake the thought that we had departed an ancient castle in Ireland in order to watch a couple of men in blonde curls and spangled dresses perform in a seedy rehearsal hall on a rainy London afternoon.

Unforeseen litigation, tying up some properties, curtailed further procedure after the Farrells returned home, and the Irish cottage sold elsewhere about the same time our bid on the English countryhouse was refused—astonishingly—in favor of a lower offer. A year later, while we houseguested with M. and H. in California, they received a letter from Diana Ellison stating that the sale had fallen through and since it had become imperative that her husband be closer to his doctor, she hoped the Farrells might be interested in buying Clonlea for five thousand pounds off the original asking price.

Henry suggested we take the place instead, so we asked for a trial lease with option to purchase at the end of a year. A relatively unknown real estate concept in Ireland or the U.K., our telephoned proposal was met skeptically, but the following morning we received a telegram: Offer Accepted—two words that would prove nearly as auspicious as those other two words Ava and I had spoken before a judge in the Farrells' sun room.

Doors kept opening—ensuring our decision was a right one. On the flight back to England, we met Bonnie Russell, who, due to her husband's transfer, was moving her family to London as we did—without a clue. Ava volunteered assistance and eventually the Russells took over our flat, saving us a month's rent left on the lease when the place would be vacant (because the removals company that brought the Ellisons from Ireland had been engaged to carry our belongings on the return trip).

Soon after our money went into escrow, John Ellison died, leaving one field solely in his name and the ensuing red tape held up settlement for Diana who lost no cash personally, but during the delay the pound fell enough in our favor to pay additional building costs. So often have Ava and I benefited from chance encounters and reaped the reward of fortunate timing, we've come to accept that little is truly coincidental: especially where Ireland is concerned.

I am reminded of a late night in L.A., the year I turned eighteen, when an old bearded gentleman sat beside me on a streetcar and matter-of-factly stated that my name began with the letter M. Wearing no monograms, I was relieved to answer negatively a few minutes later when he declared my first name to be Joseph. He just smiled, said, "It was *meant* to be," and got off at the next stop.

Mom, when she received my letter relating the incident, did for her the unthinkable—telephoned long distance. Shortly before I was born, my mother (as she had so many others) fed an itinerant who came to the back door hoping to exchange chores for food. There was never any work but no one left my mother's house hungry, and after his meal, this bearded man, blessing her obvious condition, announced that her boy child would be called Joseph. Out of the blue, recently, Charlotte wrote, asking if I'd ever heard the story. She was there at the time, remembered something our mother hadn't told me: the man's departing words were . . . "and he will be an artist."

This part of Ireland is known as the Enchanted Coast; our immediate section—probably named for phosphorus sparkling around the jetty—is the Strand of the Fairies. No matter how it cloys, we can't ignore the fact that for the first time since leaving America we slept in our own bed by the Strand of the Fairies on Midsummer's Night.

Was it really chance that we gained Clonlea rather than the house in England where we offered the owner a thousand pounds more than he wanted?

What are the odds that a hotel manager would confuse booking and a phone directory would fall open to the exact page the inn had (for the first time) advertised in large, dark type?

Why should litigation, in which we were in no way involved, twice complete to our advantage? I choose to believe a happy Fate introduced the Russells who, more than saving us moving costs when they took our flat, became good and lasting friends who share our wedding anniversary day. Considering age and social differences, it's scarcely plausible that Ava and I should even meet; yet we find that we've been led together to a place reminiscent of dreams we've each had recurring since childhood. We discovered it with Molly and Henry Farrell, and six thousand miles away, a year later, we contracted for our waking dream at their house in the very room where we married. Coincidence?

As the man said: It was meant to be.

The coast of West Cork.

PAINTING: RICHARD McKENZIE

Chapter Twelve

Kevin O

"Don't park there, it's for the hearse." Kevin O'Mahoney rushed out to welcome us for Sunday lunch at his house.

"Are you having some building done, then?"

I was about to remind Ava that they didn't work on Sunday, before realizing, myself, that anywhere else but in Ireland, her question would have been unfathomable.

Kevin and Jill's neighbor had been wavering on the threshold of death for several months but Jill was convinced he would pass over this very afternoon some time between soup and the pudding. The situation didn't seem to have changed much since last Christmas when, in deference to the sick man, they canceled their customary celebrations. "Couldn't have people wassailing in funny noses with him rapidly fading next door, could we?" Such altruism was forgotten today, or else they reckoned a few at luncheon might be managed with propriety. Jill was prepared to bring the widow over as soon as her husband died, and she warned us to sit tight or repair to other quarters depending on whether the poor woman came in through the front or back door.

The initial round of drinks hadn't reached halfway before Jill sprang to her feet and gasped, "Oh God! It's happened," and ran to the kitchen window. "Not to worry," she called back, "Just the peas boiling over." Lunch as always stretched throughout the day but we elected not to chance their neighbor's luck beyond tea time, and returned home with the certain knowledge we'd never regard a pot of peas in quite the same light again.

Weeks have passed since our Sunday lunch with Kevin and

Jill but their neighbor still has not. O'Mahoney is showing the strain.

"Another bloody awful "haciungalow" going up," Kevin O offered by way of morning salutation as I handed him a conciliatory cup of coffee. I couldn't agree more. His description is perfect. Hacienda wannabe bungalow cottages with out-of-scale Mediterranean-type balustrades and other non-ethnic architectural kitsch are blighting the land. It's saddening that so many of these bastardizations are replacing the natural stone and simple lines of dwellings in this beautiful countryside, and K. O. laid the blame directly upon a catalogue he called *Bungalow Bliss*. He said one can order construction plans from a wide selection of such buildings offered in the publication. We heard that the code requirements are going to be more stringent but as in most cases of this nature—certainly in California—it's a tad too late. On the other hand, I find the Easter egg-colored dwellings sprinkled around Ireland's coastal areas happy and fun—a bouquet of houses which usually retain the ethnic structure and add to the flavor of the country.

I suppose, since we're guests here, we shouldn't indulge our opinions, even though they are shared with many local citizens and because we've altered the face of our own Irish farmhouse so shamelessly. But we've kept its bones, tried not to lose the character and, judging from the number of tourists who stop to lean on our stone wall and photograph the lace-curtained window partially hidden behind the hydrangeas, Ava and I imagine we are taken for a typical Irish farm family.

K. O. and I created at least one erroneous impression with Americans who stopped to ask directions: he came from the garden carrying a basket of cut flowers just as I, with a dishtowel around my neck and with my broom and dust pan, answered their knock at the door. Thanking us for the information, they departed with comments about our beautiful garden and, we're certain—as soon as they were out of earshot—about the two old Irish fairies who live in it.

The irascible O'Mahoney mood did not lighten as the day

wore on, and when Kevin said that he hadn't caught a wink of sleep because Jill's son and daughter-in-law are visiting and their infant baby "shouted" all night, I made him rest for awhile in the hammock. While he was napping, Ava's former boss, Paul Hauge, rang from California. Paul does that now and again. After all these years, there are still a few quirks about Ava's filing system he hasn't decoded, and when he asked for Ava in a somewhat panicked telephone call some time back, she and Kevin O were hanging a fixture in her bathroom. Paul wouldn't know Kevin by name, so I told him Ava was in the bathroom with the gardener. Paul's next call to Ava came some time later at the end of Kevin's working day when, per custom, she had just taken out his relaxing one for the road; without thinking, I said, "Hang on, Ava is outside drinking with the gardener." Today Paul didn't ask for Ava immediately; he opened with "How is your gardener?" Oh blessed opportunity.

"Asleep in the hammock!"

~ ~ ~

"A fire is it, ye think, Mr. McKenzie?"

"I KNOW it's a fire. Behind the fuse box."

"D'ye think it could be electrical like?"

"I KNOW it's electrical."

"Maybe ye'd better turn off the power, Mr. McKenzie?"

"I've done that."

"May be a good notion to ring de electrician?"

"I've done that, too. I think the foam doused all the flames this time but they came back before; I can't be sure they're not smoldering down inside the wall. So we rang you."

"Oh, ye saw flames and put them out?"

"I THINK they're out. I can't be certain. That's why I rang the fire brigade."

"Oh, yes. Shall we ring you back?"

"No. NO!"

"Oh . . . well now, ye think it might be a good notion should we call out, Mr. McKenzie?"

"I think it's wise, yes."

"Well if ye think so, Mr. McKenzie, we'll be calling out."

"Thank you very much.

Instead of her usual practice of greeting me with a cup of coffee, Ava had said she heard a sort of snap and rumble and it looked like smoke was coming out of George sitting in the bedroom window, until she realized it emanated from the floor boards below, and she thought I should investigate.

When the electrician came, he assured us we had acted quickly enough although he was amazed that I was able to put out a fire in such an antiquated system, and he advised us to install new wiring because it's only through kind providence this hasn't happened before. The firemen were very good about my apologies, saying that they needed this sort of practice anyway. But the electrician, lifting his toolbox unwisely, set his bad back into such agonizing spasms, he required painkillers and an ice pack, and after ringing for a replacement, we sent him home with a bag of frozen peas Ava affixed to his lumbar area. No further word. Apparently he didn't black out and plough into the O'Donovan herd usually on its way to pasture at that time after milking.

"Have a nap," she said. "Do you good," she said when I allowed that I felt exhausted, and it must've been a full five minutes before the sound of glass shattering against kitchen tiles jolted me upright on the living room sofa where I'd settled next to Phyllis-Doris who hissed and glared at me.

Forty minutes later, having cleared the remains of the olive oil bottle and—by way of three paper towel rolls—blotted up its quart capacity contents, I sank into pacifying cushions in front of the telly. Nearly evening, sleep would have been unwise anyway.

At first Ava had insisted on helping, but years of experience assured expediency if she and the cats kept away until after the job was done. Once accomplished, however, to insure my comfort the grateful light of my life decided I had not enough light in my life, and in attempting to exchange a burned out bulb from the table lamp with that of a wall lamp, she smashed the bulb and pulled the fixture out of the wall. Only an hour since she had advised forty winks. Now, not only am I uncertain of sleep the whole of the night, we are once again in need of the electrician.

~ ~ ~

Although he is unlike any other Irishman of our acquaintance—or, indeed, anyone else—Kevin O echoes his fellow countrymen in that he will embroider most truths for the better telling. Though I want to believe that Kevin and Jill's zoologist friend nestled a weak, infant bat in the warmth of her cleavage until it gained strength, I still shall salt lightly his story that the *boys* at the inn served the bat's medicine on a silver spoon when the woman brought the little brute with her for dinner. But as devotees of the newspaper ourselves, we had little cause to doubt that the two advertisements K. O. swears he saw in the West Cork newspaper this week are anything but gospel. According to O'Mahoney, an enterprising farmer had offered a "cock lifter at under market value" while an estate agent wished to sell "an exceptionally fine house with vagina creepers all over its west side."

Add to that a couple of statements by our local councilman that have titillated newspapers nationwide. The T. D. (Teac Dail: member of parliament) has appeared on our doorstep to solicit our support during the past few elections and even though we go through the "we would if we could but we're not allowed to vote" routine each time, he still departs with "Count on ye on the day." And if it were possible, he could.

Any man who would publicly declare that a certain political situation should be "compared to an octopus spreading its testicles across the country" would get my vote even if he hadn't compounded it by objecting to the proposal of constructing a Venice-like marina in the area on the grounds that after the season is over, "Who would be responsible for feeding the gondolas?"

~ ~ ~

Meeting the cat's arbitrary lavatory selections as a part of the natural world to be indulged philosophically, Kevin O'Mahoney will pull out a urine-drowned plantlet with only marginal despair. He isn't much for dogs. "Dogs DIG in gardens. Dogs do not nicely cover their droppings." And even though he cares for the birds and smaller animal life, Kevin O "WILL NOT ABIDE COWS!"

We're not happy when Mary Monica's or other free stock wanders our way, turning the boreen into an obstacle course and ripping out the honeysuckle which extends from our garden out over the front wall, but other than occasional loss of control when I'm given to screeching after the beasts, we don't let them upset us to the extremes they do Kevin O. He carries a personal vendetta against all bovinity.

We certainly empathized with his frustration when Kevin discovered that Timmy's cows escaped and fouled and trampled the products of hard labor, but the heifers simply climbed over a mound at the back of the field which I'd suggested should be fenced in. As usual, my idea was ignored. From the beginning we offered K. O. complete carte blanche and any notions from me or Ava, no matter how practical, passed unheeded.

Surpassing expectations beyond our wildest hope, K. O. wrought a tiny Eden from the gravel and bogland. But, for reasons kept to himself, Kevin seemed to hold Mr. O'Regan as his personal serpent in the spud patch, and his attempts to wrest control of the little plot of potatoes and carrots that we share with Timmy make us laugh almost as much as the outrageous things Kevin O spouts while unwinding over a vodka tonic at the end of his work day.

Even more than having Tim's kids digging potatoes in our garden, Kevin loathes the sight of the three O'Regan heifers grazing the small northern pasture. Lodged there each year, just long enough for a grass growing respite in the upper field, the young cows normally caused no stirring of the O'Mahoney bowels, but when we asked if some trees and foliage might be possible in a near section of that land for garden shelter against prevailing gales, Kevin O jumped at the chance and set about creating what he called, "The Forest," a grove of trees guaranteed to attain majestic presence, if not exactly in our life span.

Ignoring my whining for something at least visible (I said

we Californians plant fully matured palm trees), K. O. set out tender little tree shoots. We installed a wire fence for this purpose and to separate the field at haying time or when the heifers are temporarily quartered there, and Mr. Perverse chose to plant his babies close enough to the fence within easy reach of an outstretched tongue shortly before Timmy brought his calves to the lower compound. Even though Ava and I worried about the saplings' proximity to the fence, we kept silence as Kevin O damned O'Regan and all his descendants when Tim's heifers stretched over the fence and chomped the baby tree tops. To appease him, though nothing could, we enclosed the spaces between the barbed wire with extra screening of chicken wire fencing, and escaped to London for the weekend. We returned to find a note Kevin left in the greenhouse, screaming in heavy black pencil that cows had "BURST IN" and "DESTROYED" the garden. "This WILL NOT DO!" He added that he was forced to go home and "TAKE TO MY BED," and hinted that he might never darken our boreen again.

Through the years, Ava and I have hardened to the tirades, written and verbal; artistic temperament goes with the territory. No matter how often K. O. flies over the top, he is still a pussycat. But even in that knowledge, we investigated the grounds with trepidation until, as expected, we found damage but not the havoc described.

"I realize how he exaggerates," Jill opened when Ava rang to initiate the familiar ritual of placation, "but is the garden completely destroyed?"

"Not quite beyond salvage." Assuring Jill's peace of mind by careful inflection, Ava requested that she convey the proper mea culpas, and though we had no intention of altering our arrangement with Mr. O'Regan, Ava agreed that cows can indeed be destructive. She sent our apologies and sincerest condolences, and promised to welcome Kevvy Wevvy's lovely leprechaun face when ever he felt recovered from his ordeal.

Kevin appeared the following Monday. We three resumed the accustomed, if more subdued, conversation with coffee and, to maintain the required atmosphere of penitence, Ava and I stayed indoors away from the line of fire. It wasn't until late in the afternoon that Ava called me to the bedroom window overlooking the garden where Kevin was oddly prodding the loose soil with his heel. After he left for the day, we discovered that the grounds we found relatively undisturbed before, were now indented with holes remarkably similar to cow tracks.

~ ~ ~

Danny, our retired postmaster, lives in the village but he sometimes likes to walk his greyhounds on our boreen in the evenings, and I was talking with him over the front garden wall when O'Mahoney, joining us for a moment on his way home for the day, threatened to install rubber sharks and plaster gnomes fishing from the banks if "these McKenzies" didn't get on with stocking the ponds with the goldfish he had "so NICELY requested MONTHS ago."

The odd combination of greyhounds and goldfish and mythical beings trickled through my memory like the little waterfall in our ponds, and I told Ava for once I agreed with Kevin O. We should get some goldfish as soon as possible. And perhaps a greyhound, too.

~ ~ ~

My wife didn't want my company on the trip to Cork City—said I impede her progress. Not true. But I had no desire to select and deal with goldfish on a seventy-mile drive in any case

Choosing the fish (three) proved uneventful; goldfish being pretty much clones, selecting them was the least of Ava's worries; keeping them thriving was something else altogether. Had I been along, I think I would have suggested that the fish be acquired last rather than at the very beginning of the day before she attended to other errands, but Ava went to the fish store first and carried her prizes around in a plastic bag which leaked, and water seriously depleted before she noticed it at the butcher's shop. The butcher provided a couple more bags as extra protection, added water and offered to keep the creatures safely swimming—their container suspended from a hook behind his counter—while the missus completed her rounds.

On the drive home, Ava remembered she was meant to give the fish fresh air every so often, a simple task. Open bag. Let in dollop of oxygen. Secure bag with wire twister provided. Nothing easier. Except when the bag is dropped on the roadside and the fish wriggle out while you're frantically trying to save the water.

Incredibly, the goldfish survived and seem content investigating the many crannies and hollows, slipping beneath the beautiful cerise water lilies Kevin O'Mahoney planted in his ponds.

Dellie decided that traveling was too strenuous now. She wouldn't return to Lismore again and suggested we sell her old Mercedes, keep the money. We kept the car instead. It's a classic year. We can't buy a new car in today's market for what we'd get, and no matter how impractical it might seem for country boreens, it was free and it was obvious that we would soon need another vehicle. The old VW station wagon required rejuvenation or parts replacement on a weekly basis now, and it was seldom with us anyway these days while Tyler is home, and the Ryans borrowed it often.

I can't tell a spanner from a sparkplug and live in fear of finding myself on a mountain road at dark with suddenly no power, as happened recently when Ty was with me. Intelligence, born of ignorance, bade me turn off the lights and the motor surged again. We crept across the pass, using lights as little as possible. When we finally reached the lighted village, I saw how terrified my son had been. He said something about the difference between forty years of experience and his own and I saw no reason to disillusion the lad's faith in his father.

Ava and I came up to collect the Mercedes from Con Willoughby and found the storm that left us undamaged last month had hit County Waterford with a vengeance, leaving a trail of debris through Lismore's gardens. Great beech trees which parade the castle's long entrance drive will probably have to come down and even the ancient yews felt the force. Their interlaced branches forming the arch withstood centuries, but the wind must have turned cyclonic at this point and many branches we thought protected blew away, allowing more light into the avenue than I'd seen before.

When I went into the village for the morning paper, Miss Willoughby, Con's sister at the newsagents, recalling her fright, described it as the "Black Night of the Terrible Winds," but apparently the wind unleashed other thoughts in Mrs. Cooney. I saw her smoking her pipe in her usual place on the bridge this afternoon, wearing a canary yellow mini-skirt

There are two approaches to our boreen from the main road; the effect is equally stunning from either one and, as always, when I returned from the village I gasped at the first sight of our headland from the crest of the hill. I love the dodge-em adventure of driving these back roads and silently cursing the blow-ins who don't know all the places to pull in as a matter of courtesy as well as necessity when meeting another vehicle. Maddening as it can be in the summer when the tourists make you crazy if you're trying to drive through the village, it can also be a testing experience at normal times. Parking is not allowed where there is a yellow line and *positively* not allowed when it's a double yellow line. As the Sarge said, "One line means no parking at all. Two means no parking a'tall, a'tall."

A single yellow line runs along most of the street and double yellow ones a good bit beyond that. Few people acknowledge them or bother with the parking lot at the bottom of the village, a two-minute walk from everything, and with cars parked on both sides of the main street, sometimes a tractor, a milk lorry and a horse-drawn caravan trying to manage the three-block stretch at the same time can cause, as they say here, a fierce banjax.

Thank God Moira Collins came out of her house while

everyone else was just standing around enjoying the tie-up when I was in town. Moira interceded and directed traffic when we were all caught in a banjax situation because some ee-jit hadn't the sense to simply reverse a foot, giving me room to turn down a side road to ease the flow behind me. We've become amazingly adept at maneuvering around the boreens, but getting our big automobile through town often requires prayer and guidance.

Those times we're to be gone more than a few days, we leave Dellie's grand old Mercedes in care of a service garage some twenty miles away. When we're home we pray we have no breakdowns, because the gifted young mechanic who owns the garage gets intense anxiety attacks if he travels in a motorcar for more than ten minutes at a go, and must rest for awhile to overcome hyperventilation.

He is a sweet, accommodating guy who really loves his work but we hesitate to ring him when our venerable vehicle refuses to go beyond the jetty in case it might be only a minor problem, reparable within the hour. If the mechanic must come to McKenzie, it could well be a long day's journey into night.

With that in mind, when Jill suffered a sudden attack of arthritis so severe it became impossible to drive her little Renault with its tight gearshift, we bought it from her. The old VW never quite recovered after a small boy driving a tractor hit it broadside. No one was hurt and the damage was repaired, but with Tyler away, we decided to give it outright to the Ryans who borrowed it most of the time anyway.

That is Ava's reasoning. I decided we should have other conveyance than the red Volkswagen Estate because the man who owns the fish factory drives the exact duplicate, even to the year, and my concern deepened when my wife wrote his license number instead of ours on a legal document. Ava said the number stuck in her mind because she always saw it when she bought fish.

Jill's car is blue.

~ ~ ~

I retreated to the quiet order of my hidey-hole while preparations are afoot for our party next week. Ostensibly the occasion is a birthday celebration for five friends whom we refused to let ignore the fact they are turning forty this year. But it's really about time we said a general "thank you" to all the others who've been so welcoming and helpful and accepting of our strange ways, and we've hired a large marquee, as they call tents here, to be set up in the lower pasture.

Mrs. Mac and Mr. O'Mahoney agitate with activity. Kevin manicures the gardens and my wife cooks for a multitude excluding Phyllis-Doris, George and me. The cats have choice whether or not to ignore their canned food but I am strongly advised to keep my paws out of everything. This has been so for three weeks and looks to continue as she shows no signs of succor or solace whenever I approach the kitchen. Ava feeds our freezer the stuff of kings. I am directed to the sandwich loaf.

The big yellow-and-white striped marquee adds a new dimension to the field, but Ava said Darleen would look pretty silly running the lance when I suggested that we might have a jousting tournament. It's fabulous seeing the tent out there. I couldn't be happier that they wanted to put it up a few days in advance. I feel like a kid again; we used to help raise the tent in exchange for free admission when the circus came to town.

Arranging a function of this nature is probably routine in Cork City; rural County Cork offers more challenge. We borrowed tables from the parish hall and benches from the primary school, the dance floor was thick plywood nailed over pallets (raft-like constructions for holding heavy milk containers) we borrowed from the dangerous creamery.

Fifteen-year-old Liam Mulvaney's group has been booked for its first pro gig, interchanging sets with the electrician who does discos for charity. I think Ava wanted the disco as an excuse to get electricity in the shed Timmy built onto our little barn at our suggestion (so he could store a little winter's hay without covering all our tools, sunchairs, barbecue, drying onions, and paint brushes). Apparently Tim thought the shed was too good for the hay, which he threw in the garage this year and which made finding the cat food supply something of a quest each morning. Fortunately, the Mercedes stays in the professional garage when we're away and the Renault mostly at the Ryan's who've already Ryanized the VW we gave them.

Ava is happy to have the old fridge working in the shed, and we told Liam's dad, Pat Mulvaney, he could use the extra space for storing his wines. I don't know how Tim will resolve the hay problem; just now he is more interested in working out parking arrangements in the pasture. Love the dichotomy: Mr. O'Regan seeks the best way for dealing with automobiles in the hayfield and prefers to keep his hay in the garage.

~ ~ ~

Frankie Ross, Ava's closest friend here, was one of the five people whose birthday we were celebrating. About a month ago Frankie contacted a woman photographer, newly arrived in the area, in hope of hiring her to record the big night. Kevin O warned against it. He said she had six fingers and practiced witchcraft. She didn't get back to Frankie with a definite acceptance and we assumed she wasn't interested, but around midnight she rang to see what time she was expected for the party. She sounded mad as hell when I told her we weren't actually involved but understood that Mrs. Ross had engaged someone else. Frankie was staying with us but had already gone out to the cottage to bed, and as I made the rounds, shutting the house for the night, I noticed there was a full moon. And an ominous green glow inside the marquee. I called Ava. She said it was the moon. I pointed out that it emanated from within.

"You left the lights on." She remembered we hadn't yet set out the battery lamps for the tables.

"There are *no* lights out there?"

"Uh uh." We decided to disturb Frankie.

"It's the moon," she said.

The three of us crept down the garden to the field, the blackthorn walking stick raised in front of me and the ladies crowding a little too closely behind me. The entire inside of the tent showed an eerie, unnatural light. I felt the end had come when we peered around the flap and there was my vampire, green and waiting. He turned around into the light as it changed to red and we frightened the electrician as much as he had us. The light shifted to blue. Martin had come out to test the lights for his discotheque and see how much flex he would need to extend from the marquee to the shed. Before I could stop her, Ava told him we thought he was the witch taking revenge.

~ ~ ~

In the fire of enthusiasm, I don't think she fully grasped the extent of cooking required for a hundred country appetites, but Ava delivered with full marks and she did it without help. People began dancing before we could completely dismantle the buffet tables lining the back of the floor, and before they blurred into a palpitating mass I caught sight of the fey Declan in a heavily embroidered mandarin's jacket of scarlet satin, attempting the tango with half of a lesbian couple while his stately ex-model wife, dressed in floor-length black with no back and scant top, "Rocked Around the Clock" with the postman.

Ava and I didn't sit down for a glass of wine until we bade the last celebrant safe journey down the boreen shortly before the last lamp batteries sputtered and the dawn chorus struck up. We came out of the marquee to see the estuary pink like our eyes in the sunrise and realized that the men were coming to strike the tent in three hours. It was needed for Maureen O'Hara's golf tournament, and we still had to pack up all the debris in rubbish bags beforehand or court the wrath of Kevin O. The last clear vision I had of O'Mahoney, though, he was weaving around the tables, carrying a single sweetpea and singing, "As I walk down Piccadilly with a poppy or a lily in my medieval hand."

I don't expect we'll see him for a few days.

Chapter Thirteen

McKenzie's Gap

We went to Greece to celebrate our tenth wedding anniversary. I spent a lot of time in and around this port traveling with the Sixth Fleet just after the war, when Europe was still licking its wounds and civilian visitors from other countries were few. I didn't want to see the Parthenon again; not under present conditions—roped off, burdened by tourists, but it was a first for Ava and she hoped to share the experience with me. I was sorry I went. I probably wasn't great company. I shall never forget the first time I visited the monument; so incredibly beautiful, columns lustrous in moonlight as I walked between them entranced and alone. Sadly now, I'll also remember rudeness and buses and clamor. Ava didn't have the comparison but her own memories will probably concentrate on the poppies she photographed growing through the cracks, scarlet—iridescent against the white marble.

Aboard ship, salt air worked marvels. I smiled at other passengers. And my bride was in usual form. On our anniversary day we dined well, felt exotic, glamorous, and, after a bit of dancing, took champagne outside to an empty place on deck. Just before midnight we poured the last of the champagne, entwined arms, lifted our glasses in tribute to us, drank, and tossed them overboard, the gesture bringing tears to my eyes when Ava threw hers with such spirit it caught me smack on the temple.

~ ~ ~

"The dishes are sitting in the basin of milk under the sink

because I'm mending the cracks. I think you're supposed to use milk. What else could it be?"

Click!

I think I preferred to hear Greek first thing in the morning.

Never mind. It's still good to be back because finally, after all those months, we can use the upstairs living quarters and dining room. We now have a working fireplace upstairs, too, and can sit on the sofa in front of it instead of having all the furniture scrunched into a corner as we'd grown used to over the months when the workmen showed up here only periodically.

Unimportant as they obviously thought the hearth was, the builders paid loving attention when changing the dining room window into a doorway. They unveiled the plastic covering with reverence befitting Rodin and we were pressed to find words conveying awe for the craftsmanship and tactful regret that the wonderfully knife-edged plaster walls cried out against the rest, rounded off-kilter from years of wear and settling. If they were bothered it didn't show as the men merrily whacked, sanded and sang. The doorway seems now to have always been there. Ava leaves it open constantly.

"Shall you have yet another martini?" she offered with the sweetness of an autumn morning. There is no need for that tone—this is only my first martini and I am concerned about the future of Darleen. Although Darleen has long since joined the working cows in the O'Regan's more distant fields, she still runs up to lick our legs or have her ears scratched and strolls the pasture with us when we visit her. I don't like to think about the time when she will no longer be able to pull her weight with the producing herd, but if we bought her and retired her to our fields she would always try to rejoin the others, and Tim needs our extra bit of land for a few calves every year anyway. I won't think about it now. And I will have yet another martini.

We turned the tack room into a kitchen. The pump had already been removed closer to the well near the vegetable garden. If it hummed in the night now only the cows would notice. The new well is very good; I no longer worry the machine will burn out searching for water. We will build the kitchen in wood to combat damp mold and added glassed-in front porches and a greenhouse beyond the kitchen to ensure warmth. Doors will open inward. We need no longer chance dislocated elbow sockets should we be called outside in gale-force winds. As it is now, even with the lighter winds, opening the front door from inside could be risky and nearly impossible from the outside if arms are laden with groceries and such. The present small kitchen shall serve as a pantry. I made drawings of the way we feel it should look at end result and Sean, boy architect, didn't laugh once. Now, it's to get the job done. But we've fooled them this time. With inside work, the hold-ups due to weather won't hold as excuses, and we've planned to have it all done while we're visiting Fred in the winter.

Fred has a new woman friend—Robyn Smith, a jockey nearly fifty years his junior. It's serious. Ava and I would like to see him married again. We've always hoped for that, and the age difference doesn't bother us, but this will alter family relationships, I feel, because Robyn seems a more driven sort of personality then the rest of us and I can't see it evolving into the relaxed pattern that the Fondas developed with Henry's marvelous and much younger wife, Shirlee. Hope I'm mistaken. I don't think so. Whatever, if it is at all possible for our life to be easier than it is now—just knowing Fred is taken care of, will do it. Nothing will ever snap the bond between F. A. and his daughter, and I suppose having a pretty, young companion in the house after all these years pumps iron to his ego, but it's a syndrome among older guys that I, personally, have never understood.

I still have doubts from time to time regarding the almost fifteen-year gap between Ava and me; I am not an insecure type, she hasn't given me even a moment's doubt that she happily assumes I'll be around to gripe and grouch for more decades than I probably want to, but considering the usual chronology of things, one wonders how she'll really feel when I'm even more crotchety and bewildered and she still wants to gambol across the moors. Shortly before we were married, dear old Walter Brennan said the greatest wish he could give us would be to have even half as happy a marriage as he did. We say the same for Fred.

~ ~ ~

More often than not when I find Ava in a peculiar situation—which is more often than not—I tend to sneak away lest I become ensnared myself. But when I saw her hurling large white objects off the jetty, the voice of restraint hadn't a hope. Phyllis-Doris, George, and I meandered to investigate. We were met with not a lovely scene. Ebbing and bobbing around the pier's cement steps were about a dozen plucked, cleaned, pasty, revolting chickens.

"Chicken of the Sea, I see," I said, lifting a stilling hand against any attempted explanation and, dangling legs above the water, settled with the cats to wait for it anyway.

Mike and Peggy Ryan run a Mom-and-Pop-type little restaurant a couple of miles west; quarters are tight, and they've been lodging an extra freezer in our garage. Apparently an electric point fused sometime along the way and Mike fixed it without first checking inside the freezer, but then Mike Ryan, who professes to be an automobile mechanic, uses a table fork instead of a key to turn his ignition, and his efforts go haywire with such regularity, Kevin O coined the phrase "It's been Ryanized" when something doesn't work.

The Ryans are of ambiguous pursuits, and altogether bananas. Ava discovered the freezer's contents of partially refrozen fowls, ice cream bars and bread rolls when she investigated the unpleasant odors coming from the garage. Aware that the Ryans could appear anytime well into next month to deal with the problem, Ava carted the stinking carcasses down to the jetty, filled their cavities with stones so they would sink and tossed them into the bay for fish food. Only the chickens inverted and lost their weights upon hitting the water and—still covered with bread crumbs and ice cream—bobbed around the jetty steps, driving the cats crazy trying to snag them with their claws.

Given that a young stallion fell off the cliffs out by the tower last month and startled fishermen on the jetty when he calmly swam in from deep sea, I reckon that chickens ebbing with the inlet tides won't cause much wonderment.

There was no graduation service for Tyler's class. He was a schoolboy one day, pleased to be through but left wanting some way to mark the occasion. Irish school is tougher than in the States; the kids work hard and deserve some ritual recognition besides a good grade as a reward. Ty didn't languish gloomily, though. He was helping at the inn for awhile. Said he was their "dashing barman."

"How did your shoes get so cracked, son?"

"I fell into quicksand on the mountain last week. Did you know, Dad, some people call it 'quickmud'?"

"My God, Ty, why didn't you tell me? How did you get out?"

"Don was with me. I got cold walking around with nothing on while my clothes dried but it was fun. You can see for miles up there.

"Tyler . . . You were right not to tell me."

Dashing, huh?

Kevin rang. He wanted to go to school. He didn't ask us to pay tuition at this date. He did want a loan. We have nothing but admiration for Kev, who, under his own initiative, worked to overcome his problems and to learn a profession and who now, in his little free time, counseled young people caught by drink and drugs. We shall help gladly and it won't be a loan. Now that he has learned so much—proved his ability as a chef by working with some of the best—it's been suggested by his current employer (owner of the fashionable Michael's in Santa Monica) that he attend the Restaurant School in Philadelphia to polish his craft and learn intricacies of the actual business end: bookkeeping, outfitting, hiring; everything geared towards eventually running his own place. His English school headmistress told us when the time was right, Kevin would return to school. The time is right. He should be away from southern California for a while anyway. The last girlfriend he talked about was not only a back-up singer for Tina Turner, she mud-wrestled on Saturday nights.

~ ~ ~

Hi Dad:

Happy Birthday!.

Well, this is a milestone year for us all,

You're 50, I'm 21 and Tyler is 18.

I want to take this opportunity to say how much I appreciate everything you've done for me and all your love and support that has always been here through the years and Ava, too. When I get to be 50 years old, I'll probably look just like you and that's okay with me.

Love You,
K.

Cyril, our postman, delivered my birthday card from Kevin and one from Fiji, along with the crab claws Ava requested, and left with our lawn mower. He sharpens our lawn mower's blades from time to time just out of friendliness, but many of us purchase crab claws from the postman. He prepares the claws differently than anyone else, and is reputed to be a sensational dancer, but it was his predecessor, Danny (now retired), who first made us aware of the Irish "difference"—a story he still laughs at about himself.

Before we put a mail drop-slot into the tack room, if there was no one home, post was left in the small wooden box the Ellisons had attached somewhat precariously to the outside wall next to the front door. If we were home but didn't get downstairs in time, Dan would often deliver letters to the top of the stairs in the living room. Doors were seldom locked and the postman was nothing if not obliging. While we were at Lismore for a couple of days, a large poster in a tube arrived for us and we came home to find the tube serving as a center pole for a tent of plastic wrap secured by twine around the postbox.

"Let me know when ye'll be away next time," Danny suggested on his rounds the following morning. "I'll keep the post. Didn't I have to go in and get string and paper from your kitchen?" I guess he didn't want to chance our missing anything important if he just left it inside on the dry kitchen table. Leaving a message at Danny's house the next time we visited Dellie was really no trouble. That is where we got our petrol.

But that was early on before Ava herself took to giving the sort of Irish directions I heard her impart to an English couple who stopped us on the road the other day.

"You go west at the first turning after the house that used to be painted pink."

At least she didn't say "wesht." Not long ago while listening to Tim O'Regan's yarns, our American houseguest looked at me in astonishment whenever I nodded or commented in agreement with Timmy. Our friend was surprised I spoke Irish, even more surprised to learn *that* was English—West Cork version. *Wesht* Cork. Letters T and TH are commonly transposed, Thursday becoming Tursday and water—wather, except in the cases of this and that which are more often dis and dat.

Ava, I believe, shall be banned from my working quarters. Her visits, even with thoughtful intentions of providing a late-morning coffee respite, tend to muddle. When I begged her opinion of a freshly painted effect she allowed that she couldn't really tell because she had to take her clothes off. I hadn't requested that she pose. Or anything.

Wearing the same clothes, she returned with the information that the phone call was from Roddy McDowall, who wouldn't be coming over to visit when he finishes work on

The Thief of Baghdad in London because he fell off his magic carpet and sprained an ankle.

Now, work finished for the day, cleaned of brushes and body, and intending to relax, I heard my wife talking to my son in the kitchen.

"I know you won't understand this, but it really isn't bad. Sort of like pig's breath," Ava explained to Tyler who I had no doubt understood perfectly. The little hand points towards martini time . . . Whew!

A classmate from Chalet Gloria—or maybe just an Austrian kid he met while attending Chalet Gloria—invited Tyler to Kenya. Seemed his father was the Austrian consul or perhaps an attaché in Africa—it wasn't clear, but the invitation was legitimate and we agreed, providing Tyler found an economically sound yet structurally secure means of transport.

It was a terrific opportunity, educational, too. And if there were any problem, we were assured by Betty and Jock Leslie-Melville, Tyler may call them for advice and/or assistance, but Ava said only if he promised not to play with Daisy, their pet giraffe. Tyler in Africa?!! I won't think about that now. Maybe never.

Dick De Neut's telephone call woke us early this morning with the sad news that Allen is in hospital, victim of a stroke. Neither of us spoke much all day. God, I feel helpless. We can't call Betty at the Carmel Hospital where she has been with him constantly, and if we could, the last thing she needs to deal with now is the trans-Atlantic telephone system. We'll rely on Dick to keep us posted.

Nothing had changed but I wrote to Betty. If there ever was a time to believe in omens, this had been a day of them.

A Celtic superstition I've heard in variations since we came to Ireland is that of a bird pecking at the window, signifying death. The morning crow never worried me in that respect, but I was shaken this afternoon when, investigating a sound at the front door, I found a magpie on the step—pecking at a glass door panel. Seeing me didn't seem to startle the bird who simply backed a short distance away, stopped and studied me.

One is for sorrow, I thought, and with that, he flew to a rainbow ending in our lower pasture. The Luddens and us and rainbows. Suddenly I felt lighter. I'm enough Celt to trust intuition and was totally convinced moments later when something made me glance at the mirror across the room. If one sat in a certain chair—the one I was sitting in—this mirror reflects the long rectangular front window and seems like an ever-changing picture. Since we discovered a magnificent and rather magical mirror in a dark, eerie corner at Lismore, Betty and I have had a thing about mirrors, too. Reflected in the glass today were black clouds on the horizon and every one etched in silver. Clutching at straws? Why not?

"Richard, come look," she sounded from the living room, "The swan's egg has exploded all over the chest of many drawers!" Now I *know* everything will be all right.

Allen surfaced—Thank God, without brain damage. Betty brought him home to Los Angeles, weak, his voice slightly altered but all his faculties in tact, and we laughed with him over the phone. He says without a doubt it was Betty's vigilance and unceasing reassurance that reached and sustained him.

Hammers tap again as carpenters shorten our dining area in order to gain us heat and provide a little room to keep the ironing and all the other junk such a space is certain to entice. These are the same carpenters who will transform the tack room into a spiffy new kitchen while we are away this winter and who should *not be* here until we *are* away this winter. The whole idea of requesting work during our absence was to avoid living amidst this mess again.

Work on the new kitchen, though, must wait, since the existing one will be rendered useless, and with my son the vacuum in residence, we can't afford to eat out for thirty days. Wonder what he'll eat in Africa? Like his brother's, Ty's is an inquisitive, insatiable appetite, but he'd keep trim enough if he must stalk his supper through the bush. Tyler wasn't headed for the Dark Continent immediately but he would be out of the house, working for his keep at the inn for a while after we leave.

Perhaps we should take friends' advice and invest in a boat. We could keep it in the garage and there wouldn't be room for the Ryan's freezer. Peggy rang to say she'd told a friend he could store something in the freezer; if I saw a stranger enter the garage he wasn't there to heist the Mercedes.

Ava and the car were away when the fellow and a woman I took to be his missus arrived, but I went out, all friendly anyway, to assure him he was expected. Peering in every direction, including through me, he signaled her to pass some large fish from the boot. No words were spoken but the fish seemed heavy, so I stepped in to assist and soon found myself relaying fish from the woman up to her husband waiting beside the freezer in the garage. Nothing was said during the procedure or when they furtively drove away, and it didn't sink in until I was well back in the house that the fish were salmon and the salmon season ended last week.

I opened a tin of tuna to account for the smell on my hands in case the law descended.

Ty and I drove an hour out of our way to give American kids a lift to Kenmare because they could not have made it on foot across the mountain path before dark. On the return trip, something popped. I stopped and another couple of hikers came running up for a lift. Barely had their accents sounded before I snarled, "This is a German car. What's wrong with it?" They were a young Austrian couple sent by God to reward us for the earlier unselfishness. The girl, small and fragile looking, was a mechanic. Our fan belt was shot but she thought she could temporarily repair it until we were closer to real help. Better still, she could replace it with a pair of ladies' tights.

In either event, it would do only until we found a garage. No one had tights (nicer word than pantyhose, that) but whatever she did held until, singing her praises, we pulled into the first garage sighted on the downside of the ridge. They didn't have the right-sized belt. Nor did they have tights. Nor did they want any part of us for asking such a thing. The hour approached closing time; we edged on to Bantry, found another garage. Same answer. Right. Tights it had to be.

Tyler, having suffered embarrassment from macho mechanics in two garages, at this point lapsed into German with our passengers, leaving the old man to seek the elusive garment, and I ran through Bantry town in serious prayer that somewhere there was a ladies' clothing shop still open. I found one. Closed—but just. Sales girls, still inside, opened for me. Probably to save the door panel. I didn't explain the reasons for the request or why size and color were unimportant and I can't explain why, when they brought me a navy blue pair, size large, and I paid, I was compelled to add that I rather fancied chestnut brown instead.

They worked. We got home with gratitude, gave the travelers dinner and a bed for the night. The shop girls can't possibly know me but I'm still pleased we're going to America soon. They'll have months to forget. On the other hand, in California my request probably wouldn't have seemed odd at all.

"Richard! Remind me to tell the blind not to look for our chair. It isn't there after all."

Click! We will soon be off to California. Guess I can keep a grip until then.

~ ~ ~

The last person Ava and I expected to see sitting at a bar in Beverly Hills was Paddy Maloney from Cork. We met Paddy and his legendary group, The Chieftains, in Dublin when they made the soundtrack for *The Purple Taxi*, and we were happy to run into him again, but we left Ireland only last week and didn't think we'd be carrying on with the Irish quite so soon again. Coming as it did, on the heels of the dinner with F. A. and Hermes Pan we'd had earlier this evening, I've a suspicion that my midnight swim with the world's most widely acclaimed exponents of classical Irish music might have been a tad overly enthusiastic.

Though dining at Chasen's has long since ceased being a novel experience, sometimes there is still an excitement tugging from the years I read about its glamorous patrons; I felt it this evening when the room, as always, reacted with a noticeable pause when Astaire entered.

Hermes. Ava. F. A. Me. In that order, we occupied one of the big red banquettes; the adjoining one was empty except for a single man seated at the far end directly opposite my view, obviously waiting for guests. His wine, opened and untouched, remained in the cooler stand at the end nearest Hermes. Stefanie Powers came over to say hello to us and nodded to the fellow at the next table who caught Fred's attention then and raised his glass.

"Who is that guy?"

"That is Frank Sinatra, Fred."

"God—you can't take me ANYwhere!"

He returned Sinatra's salute, causing Ava and Hermes to turn and smile before Hermes filled their glasses a second time. A beat later—nearly choking when she realized we hadn't ordered yet, Ava laughed.

"Pan! That's FRANK'S wine!"

F. A. put his head on the table. Frank's party arrived, his

daughter Tina chatted to us over the banquettes for a minute, while Fred ordered the usual old-fashioneds for us, their own wine for his daughter and good friend.

Nothing was ever mentioned.

With Fred at the track in 1980: Father-in-law's horse just lost.

"Trust me, Mac, the filly absolutely cannot fail. I was up all night studying the form. Trust me. Please."

Why do I always fall for it? With that delivery, why do I even consider his theories? But I do, and each time I value Matthau's advice over my own instincts, I go home the loser. Today's gullibility is the more ignominious. I failed to back the horse Ava suggested (which she didn't bet herself because she thought I had, which shouldn't be my fault but apparently was).

"Got you again, huh?" my love snorted, eyeing the crumpled evidence in my palm and the finger pointed accusingly at Walter. "Suppose you realize those were some odds?" I did. And another hot five bucks down the drain, too.

Jennifer Grant (with her dad at Hollywood Park), flipping her hand in a flash of youthful enthusiasm, lost her ring over the balcony onto the lower level where people were lunching, and that good fellow, Dick Kahn, one of our favorite folk, took her down to search, even going through used dishes in the busboy's trays. Lunchers stared up at them while Walter, Cary, Fred, and Ava regarded the questionable action and I, determined to worm back into Ava's graces, held a beady eye and, catching a gleam of silver, called down, suggesting that Dick ask the man at the nearest table to raise his left foot. They recovered her ring—Jennifer effulgent in appreciation—while the little woman, overlooking my smug smirk, pecked my cheek and whispered she knew I could do it. And Cary Grant said I should be an astronaut.

Not a bad day.

All in all—worth five dollars.

We were visiting my brother and sister-in-law in northern California when we received word from Jack Russell in London: not to worry, but Tyler is in hospital there for further observation. He had been staying with the Russells in our former flat and they were sure he is okay, but as he had just returned from Africa, they weren't ruling out possibilities of malaria. We're on our way home.

Ty seems fine. The brief virus proved not to be the feared malaria or even the Green Monkey Disease that, due to a high fatality rate, closed some Nairobi hospitals during his visit (and which he neglected to tell the London medics or he would be in isolation still). They never determined exactly what he had, but following a week of close observation in isolation, after his fever and headaches abated, he was released with a clean bill of health. Being England, it was the only bill. What such treatment would have cost in the States. The Royal Free Hospital apparently means just that. We'd best send them a donation if our son is ever allowed from the hearth again.

Ava and I worry and project doom; when will we learn that our sons always cope? Tyler had spent the last three months in Austria, Germany, Africa, and London, with an unscheduled eighteen-hour stopover in a Moscow hotel, and he had just accepted an invitation to spend the month of July at a villa overlooking the Italian seacoast. He planned to ferry to Wales, bus to London, boat-train to the Continent, meet friends and drive to Milan, then train to . . . no, I mustn't think about it. I still haven't sufficiently recovered from hearing about his night in Russia, or that he was able to chase down the rickety Nairobi taxi cab in which he had left his passport, all his money, and addresses.

Tyler *would* manage to fly via Aeroflot when Russo-American relations were at their lowest, and I only agreed to that because he promised to speak German during the flight, and Moscow, according to his ticket, was to be little more than a pit stop, no one disembarking unless that was their destination. With nobody the wiser, there should be no incidents. Tyler mentioned that he'd been removed along with the others traveling on to Africa and given a temporary visa (which was then taken away with his U. S. passport) with the same casual attitude he had neglected telling the English doctors about the Green Monkey Disease.

Tyler fell in love with Africa and wanted to remain and try to find employment there, but Betty Leslie-Melville advised him that the only way foreigners can work in Africa is through the big hotels, so now he has decided he would like to study hotel management at a German school his Grandmother suggested. Of all things Tyler is unsuited for, this just might top the list. But we will discuss it.

Although they followed my sketches exactly, the new kitchen isn't quite as imagined. As I saw it, the doors would be on the cupboards, not neatly stacked in the little room next to the ironing board. They told us it was a one-man job. Some days they told us that man was out sick; others, that he would be out to us after lunch, and our last begging call was met with shocked wonderment.

"If he's not wit ye—sure now—where is he? And in a glorious maneuver, they put the blame squarely on us because he is their best man and we are to have nothing less. The Irish, bless them. You sure as hell can't beat them.

Finally, Mama was back in the kitchen. Cupboard doors were hung yesterday. The will-o-the-wisp carpenter did the job in half the morning, but it was a two-day stint for the three of us just to sort out and put everything away. We shall stain the walls ourselves. Ava is usually not allowed near things that can be spilled, tipped or dropped, but she insisted I promised when I married her that she could stain the kitchen cabinets.

"Expecting an aggression attack, are we?" I retrieved the kitchen knife Ava had been using when need arose to hit the village and which, unaware, she still gripped along with her shopping basket. Like Hansel and Gretel's breadcrumbs, the trail of objects Ava often drops on her travels shall, I trust, always mark her path safely home. I don't worry.

Maybe I should.

I refused to believe a sudden fierce wind was strong enough to blow her shoe off, even though Ava stubbornly held to that reason for returning from town with her left shoe in the shopping basket. She does have a habit of slipping out of her shoes, but I couldn't understand how she managed five different pairs discovered around the kitchen in a single day. And though bras were sometimes dislodged from beneath sofa cushions following a relaxed evening viewing television, I am still awaiting an acceptable explanation how her long-missing, favorite brassiere happened into a pocket of my seldom-worn topcoat, to be withdrawn for public scrutiny one busy morning on Cork City's Patrick Street.

A friend observed, nicely, that my wife was just this side of eccentric. But, in her way, Ava holds a steady course, and if she is at all eccentric, it's because of her childlike lack of guile. She is constantly making me laugh, but I never forget this woman also mightily guards the state of my well-being and I suspect we are not as different from each other as I pretend to think, though I'd never come home with one shoe in a basket.

Ava.

~ ~ ~

Seemed as if we had hardly unpacked when F. A. phoned, asking Ava if she would accompany him to his step-granddaughter's wedding in Santa Barbara. Although she became a bride herself only recently, Fred said Robyn didn't like weddings, and wouldn't go. Fred felt he had to attend. Those things are such an ordeal for F. A. on his own, and though Pete's daughter isn't a family favorite, Ava thought that even with the expense and traveling six thousand miles each way, she must do it for her dad.

Never mind that I'd just read Steven King's *Salem's Lot* and was scared to look out the library window after dark in case one of hell's fiends was looking in. She wouldn't be away long but, before she left, Ava sneakily hung a large garlic over the window seat to thwart entry of any batfolk and which I discovered minutes after our neighbor did when she came to use the telephone. If I'd kept my stupid trap shut and not felt the need to explain, everything would have been fine, but I'd already begun spouting about my wife's sense of humor and garlic's power against vampires when the woman's expression made it clear she had never heard of such things, and further attempts at explanation were met with obvious dismay.

Since we have one of the few telephones within miles, we assured our neighbors not to hesitate about using ours. The price of the call is always left by the telephone and most of them feel free enough to come in without making a big deal over it, and we love to watch American visitors shifting uneasily in their chairs when we haven't reacted to the obvious fact that someone has entered the house and is talking on the telephone downstairs. By now everybody must know about the vampires in our library. I wonder if they'll continue to come. Hope so. I like finding the odd ten-penny piece next to the telephone now and again.

The little alcove in which I write has a clear view of the front drive where I see Ava brandishing a yardstick and striding towards the car. Attempting all doors, finding them locked, she returns to the house—one assumes, for the key. Back, having opened the boot, she seems to be measuring the interior. She nods and shivers. The temperature has dropped considerably. Less than a quarter hour ago, Ava was making tablecloths; now she joins me in the alcove. We do not exchange comment while she stares out the window, clucks her tongue, and I continue writing.

She brightens, advises I should not expect her home before

seven at least, and genuflects. It breaks my silence. I ask if she is okay. She assures she is—that it was just her leg going funny. Ava hasn't stepped outdoors since and is presently cursing at her curtain hems, which might explain her perusal of the alcove (if not what happened to the tablecloths), why she measured the car, or where she intended to go until seven o'clock

"Did you get the weather report about any gale warnings?"

"You know I never listen to the radio weather because it only tells us about 'the better laters.' " It must be difficult for her with Tyler away and only us earthlings to talk to, but it's good to have her home.

Tyler returned from Italy, suntanned and vocal, while the postcard giving us his address arrived here three days after he did. Not that that came as a surprise or would've made any difference because, for the last two weeks, he had been sleeping on beaches in Monte Carlo and Cannes and visiting his grandmother in Frankfurt before going to Paris, where he met a lad from Virginia at the train station whom, naturally, he brought home for a few days.

I had but to pick up my pen when Tyler entered with the pronouncement that Mats' cousin's girlfriend's mother in Sweden speaks seven languages, is expert in karate, and drinks petrol. He left the room immediately. Good thinking. Wonder how long he has been storing that information? And why me? He will be twenty next month, but I doubt it will change anything. Although I had hoped he might attend college with an eye towards journalism, we agreed to the hotel management training which will begin soon, and although the dogmatic Germans will surely try, I can't see them bringing Tyler to heel. Heel-clicking maybe. He'd probably like that. My son has always tended to use phrases Queen Victoria might have thought catchy.

A brochure proclaiming in German on several sheets of paper exactly what he should bring to school arrived in today's post just a week after Ty departed for Garmisch-Partenkirchen and Hotelberuffachschule-Dr. Leopold, with one suitcase and their letter stating he could pick up everything he needed once installed. Kevin O'Mahoney translated for us. Among other things students were required to have:

One small pillow (horsehair)—HORSEHAIR?
One small basket for dirty laundry to be sent home—to IRELAND?
Four table napkins
Two cases for table napkins (usually embroidered, says Kevin O)
Dressing gown
Umbrella and raincoat (rubber)
Climbing boots (waterproof with profile soles)
Slippers (leather, for constant use in school—shoes must leave NO MARK on floors)
Non-slip slippers for shower room
Apron (leather)
Skin cream or oil
One tin of Vaseline
And under no circumstances, colored electric lights.

Albert Finney said Chalet Gloria must be a brothel. What would he think about Dr. Leopold's? What do we think? What does Tyler think?

We await our son's first call home.

An architect from Dublin purchased the ruin of a Norman tower which stands on the western tip where the O'Regan's land fingers out into the Atlantic, pointing directly towards America. Two nights ago was the housewarming hooley. I would have recorded this yesterday but yesterday may not have come around a'tall, a'tall. I didn't.

The party was to thank those who took part in making the edifice habitable and even that depended upon loose interpretation, but there are now floors for the first time in centuries; a stove for warmth and cooking, and a loo. The owners didn't want electricity, and water supply is served by rainfall caught in a large container at the open-air landing at the top of the tower. Our garage was used to house building supplies last winter, which merited our inclusion on the guest list and, I fear, resulted in the decimation of a major portion of my gray cells.

We were invited for four-thirty in the afternoon, or as they say here, half-four, but we thought it wiser to wait until at least half-six before we pulled on the wellies (essential for the trek), and packed a basket of wine, the traditional bread and salt and a few useful house gifts that Ava always takes to housewarmings. We intended to stay just long enough to see the first lamp lighted, have a bite, and go home before the dark made bog-hopping too adventuresome.

Swelled by his building achievements and already serious booze intake, a jubilant Timmy O'Regan knocked my sensible glass of white wine away with one of his ham-sized hands, and thrust a tumblerful of whiskey at my face with the other. By the time the oil lamps came on with much ceremony and speech-making, and the buffet was served, we were consumed by the romance of it all—that we were the first people eating here since the Normans, and I proceeded to drown any hope of reasonable behavior.

We left at midnight when the accordion player arrived, strapped his instrument onto his back and, clinging onto a rope attached to the wall for assistance, climbed the tiny steep stairs to the open roofed tower to begin the dancing. On the way home we avoided the bogs after all. As I seemed incapable of self-navigation, my wife, little Nora O'Regan, and the equally small daughter of the new laird of the castle propelled me up the less familiar path over O'Regan farmland, assistance I thought patronizing until, in an attempt to clear the stone walls in a single bound, I found myself face down in the muck, convinced I'd been done irreparable mischief. I was informed by my wife in superior manner that cunning persuasion was needed before I believed I would walk again; Ava said I told the three of them that I had resolved to lie in the dung, passively awaiting the Banshee's scream of warning that the end was near.

Yesterday I wished I'd held to my convictions. We heard that the party went on until after breakfast, and though I don't know how the others fared with the location and precarious conditions, my bruised head and conscience and an enormous hangover were the only mishaps.

Nora said they'd named the site of my shame McKenzie's Gap.

Chapter Fourteen

Markings

Now that Fred is married, we always stay at the wonderful, small Hotel L'Ermitage in Beverly Hills during our California time. All accommodations in the hotel are suites with large living rooms and ample kitchens; we can entertain freely or stay quietly in. Fred likes to come here every morning after going for his mail and we dine together several times a week. He doesn't like to drive at night so I pick him up in front of his house and sometimes Hermes, too, and then it's like having dinner with the two men from the Muppet Show. Last week, after they made such a display of "helping" each other out of the car, and in the lift Pan did a time step while Fred suspended himself up on the brass railing inside and kicked his feet in the air, I told them to behave themselves; this was a nice hotel and we had reputations to consider if they hadn't. People are used to celebrities in L'Ermitage but when the door opened on me shaking my finger at Fred Astaire and Hermes Pan nudging each other like schoolboys, the faces of departing diners waiting for the lift were something to behold.

Fred signed to do a film in the East sometime early winter and unfortunately Dellie isn't well again. He doesn't want to be away just now, but Ava is here to be with her aunt if needed, and Fred doesn't cope easily with illness ever since Ava's mother was dying of cancer and he lived at the hospital with her.

~ ~ ~

Kevin called us from school; he was enthusiastic and top of his class, which he said was a nice, new experience, and he had met a girl "like Tomo." We gathered she is Japanese. Whatever, she'll be an improvement over a date he once told me about.

I made him stop before he said more than I cared to hear when I learned that the girl was a transsexual and, to the annoyance of the others transfixed at the dinner table, I interrupted as he was about to explain just how he had discovered there had been surgery. Some things a father should not know. I must say, my boys are never dull.

We lost Dellie. Fred spent Christmas with her, they had four happy days together for which we are grateful because it was the last time they saw each other. It was no secret that Adele never reconciled to his marriage and rather gave up after that, not fighting back with the spirit she dealt other recent bouts of illness and an especially painful attack of glaucoma. *People* magazine printed that both Robyn and F. A. had been with Dellie for the holiday, and possibly such had been implied during their interview, but Fred went alone to be with his sister in Arizona, which was the best present he could give. They were just brother and sister again; closer than most, I imagine, given all that they had experienced together. Shortly afterwards he was called East for the picture, earlier than expected, and Ava began spending more time in Arizona. Before two massive strokes rendered her speechless, Dellie told Ava one last naughty story.

In Arizona, after suffering her opinionated needling, and because he knew Dellie wouldn't restrain her tongue regarding his marriage for very long, F. A. struck a deal one evening: he would play a game of Scrabble with her only if she vowed not to say another word about Robyn. Adele's idea of words suitable to the Scrabble board differed from most players, as Fred well understood when he made the stipulation, but she agreed to behave herself and the game went smoothly until Fred noticed the letters she was placing out. C - U - N -

"Dellie!" Fred yelled. "YOU PROMISED!"

"What did *he* know?" Dellie demanded of Ava. "I could have been spelling *any*thing! Like cunnilingus." Ava told me she had to fight back tears, the wicked glint in her aunt's eyes was still there!

Ava kept her father apprised, trying not to say too much, and Fred stayed in touch, but the poor man was terribly distraught, working under such tough conditions in the cold weather and knowing that he'd probably never see his sister again. When Adele could no longer speak Ava brought some of her aunt's favorite perfume, rubbed it on her wrists, and, knowing then Ava was with her, Dellie kissed her hand and slipped off into a coma, her last sense the scent of expensive perfume.

Aunt Dellie at Lismore Castle in the 1970s.

I am ready to go east; not to Saratoga where Ava has joined her father on location, but to some place in Bucks County, Pennsylvania, where I've never been, and where we've rented a house for the time Fred will be shooting in upstate New York. He is very down in spirit, naturally, and not well physically either. Apparently they're shooting around him until he overcomes a severe cold which probably came from his first day's working outside in heavy snow. Ava felt he shouldn't be alone, especially now, and her presence has indeed made a difference. The producer asked that she stay, which is fine so long as I don't have to be there the entire time as well. I have work to do. The house we've rented is situated in a little village on the Delaware River; it belongs to a friend of Ava's in New York who uses it as a summer retreat, and Kevin, who knows the region, will meet me at Philadelphia airport. We'll hire a car and drive there where he will remain with me for the weekend. They will. He is bringing his lady. I am no longer startled by the many coincidences Ava and I have encountered along the way, but this quirky turn of events that sent Kevin to a school in Philadelphia and me to a country house only forty-five minutes away astonishes me.

~ ~ ~

The children returned to school leaving me alone and somewhat at odds with the day as I mulled most recent events over too many cups of coffee. It was snowing lightly as I wrote, making this village even more like it must have been when it was born before the time of the American Revolution, and I was slightly bemused with the thought that the Delaware River is just across the road. A cardinal bird investigated holly berries almost on the window sill, and everything was idyllic except my girl wasn't with me. She would love it so. Ava's absence accounted for most of my abstractedness, and I knew I'd feel less disoriented after she telephoned, but it was more than that. It was Kevin, too. He is in top shape, but there was a difference this time. I believe this is the girl he will marry.

He said they hadn't discussed it but I assured him he was a fool if he let her get away, and in watching them together, I could see there was small chance of that. All-American Carol is of half-Japanese, half-Armenian heritage, very bright, musically talented and diminutive with a sunny smile and sometimes a downright bawdy laugh. She is beautiful, and I told her I expected her to join our family because then there might be hope of breeding the McKenzie noses down to something more acceptable. The difference with Kevin was not so much change in himself but in the way he treated me—often displaying a touching, almost tender affection. I think, subconsciously, Kevin realized he was close to beginning a family of his own with all the maturity and responsibilities such a step required, and suddenly he regarded Old Dad in another light. Old Dad, with a tinge of melancholy, heard the march of time, too.

~ ~ ~

I went up to Saratoga to be with Ava and F. A. for a few days, to see the picture wrapped, and to touch base with cast members, Patricia Neal and Doug Fairbanks who we used to see in London. My curiosity was piqued, too. It's a ghost story I read a while back during one of our times in the States, and I told Fred then that if they ever made a movie of the book, he would be sought for one of the parts; one of the characters described him to the letter. F. A. rang us in Ireland and asked Ava for the name of the book we'd talked about. She gave it to him and handed the phone to me. "Allllright, you smart-ass. I just signed to do that part." I HAD to watch him shoot at least a couple of scenes just so I could gloat. Ava read the musings I jotted in my journal after the kids went back to school. She suspected the part about being lonely without her; said I was afraid to be alone because I'm wary of vampires. But that is sensible caution—and only slightly true. I see I must be more careful where I leave my notebook.

Fred flew home and I brought Ava back to Pennsylvania so we could have some quiet time together in this peaceful place. She has undergone so much in these past months, Ava badly needs that, and there is more ahead when we return to Los Angeles. Molly is very ill, too.

~ ~ ~

This is not a happy time.

Molly died of cancer. The funeral was on Ava's birthday and Molly was her best friend. Before we moved from Beverly Hills, Molly, Ava, and Marni held congress every Saturday afternoon, usually at our place, and today Marni served at Communion—an act so improbable it relieved the situation enough for Ava to get through the service.

Rough spoken, irreverent and funny, Marni has forsaken television producing to pursue the priesthood of the Episcopal Church, and though she can't yet officiate as a minister, she did speak to the congregation. Infusing some of the lightness that Molly's merry spirit called for, she managed away the somber farewells our friend would have hated, and we were no longer doubtful regarding Marni's astounding about-face.

~ ~ ~

Ava helped Henry with the finalizing and clearing away as much as she could. Henry was grateful for Ava because Molly would have approved of her, more than anyone else, going through her things, and she even found Molly's will after Henry had searched everywhere without results. Found it in minutes after Henry called for assistance from the only person he knew who thought like his wife. Ava walked in, said "All right, Mol, where the HELL did you put it?" She doesn't know why; there was no audible message or anything to indicate it, but Ava next asked Henry to look in a broken drawer of the kitchen table and discovered the will. "You know Molly," she said later, "She just wanted to be asked."

This trip brought about so many changes. We lost Dellie; now Molly. Betty said there is little hope for Allen either. Cancer. My brother, Lewis, died without warning last month. Next week I must fly to northern California to see my oldest brother, Wes, for the last time. Cancer. But my brothers were of the age one is automatically prepared and—in truth—I don't feel much about them. I never really knew them. All we had in common was blood and memories of a terrific woman. Age and outlook separated us; there was never the feeling of bonding I have for Mike and Charlotte even though there are several years between us as well. Sweet Rayme is gone, too. Cancer.

The news of Allen's terminal condition hit me more than

my own brother's similar state, but Allen is simply much dearer to us. He can't see many people. We've had a few brief moments—the last time without Betty. Assuring her he felt fine, he lied about his back not hurting and made her go to the studio. And he looked fine. That's the image we'll take home with us. They have no illusions. Betty told us not to prolong our stay—there is nothing we can do. It's better we go now.

Sense of one's mortality is magnified. We discuss it. I tell Ava and the boys that I intend to torment them for years to come, but should it happen otherwise—have no regrets. I am given everything because of them and when it's time to give it back—well, they'll still have it, won't they? Everything that makes my life the lovely thing it is must continue.

~ ~ ~

The old gent jigs in the bar, the pint unshaken aloft in his left hand.

"That's how my dad danced," I whisper.

"That's not how *mine* danced," she volleys.

We're home. But this time I think we've somehow returned to the other side of the looking glass; local papers tell of a tong war between Chinese factions in Cork and Dublin and a woman rabbi bought the haunted remains of the old manor house on the hill behind us. We traded Rodeo Drive for a boreen in Catholic Irish farmland and our neighbor is a rabbi?

~ ~ ~

Getting up while it was still dark and trudging through snow to his duties were not, I'm sure, what Tyler had in mind as part of his school training, but it's good for him. He didn't actually gripe about it. He couldn't. This was his choice.

Although Ava insists he is still only nine years old, Ty is no longer a little boy and this experience should make it painfully clear that very soon he shall be a man—independent and on his own.

So why don't I believe that?

~ ~ ~

Dear Ty,

BORNEO?!

No, we don't mind if—as you put it—you make certain alterations in career plans once you've completed current training. You know that we've never held that the hospitality business was really your metier, and we challenge the merits of the school, particularly since they sent us additional information in German about sundry articles needed. Requirements being: a school bag containing red and blue pencils and five green pens and one 30 cm ruler and that only white is allowed on the tennis court unless the weather is cold in which case a blue and white sweatsuit is acceptable. Dress must not be extravagantly elegant or slovenly and "du" is verboten. Be that as it may, if they've taught you the intricacies of the touring trade in deepest Malaysia, we've underestimated them entirely. Shall we be more informed when next we hear from you? PLEASE?

Actually, son, providing Momndad with information is what this letter is mainly about. We applaud your industry in working through the school holidays but when we believe you are staying with your friends in Vienna, it isn't prudent to take a job in—as you put it —"an obscure airport restaurant in Lower Bavaria" without alerting the folks. Imagine our panic if there had been an emergency and we couldn't locate you.

Now I'm not sure I've got this right. You did mean that the brother of the woman who owns the restaurant wants to train you to lead groups into the jungles of Borneo? Surely I'm mistaken.

On the home front: Ava modeled in a fashion show at the Courtyard during the village festival. The ladies showed a variety of clothes including wellies from Mick's shop, and every time your mother made her turn through the restaurant and into the pub, the commentator seemed compelled to announce, "There goes Mrs. McKenzie into the bar again." This is all for now except the news that Donnachadh is giving up medical school to become a ballet dancer and is working in a mortuary to pay for his training.

Please keep us posted. I don't want unexpected word from Timbuktu. Ava sends all love. I add mine,

Dad

Dear Son,

Perhaps you should have waited for a time we could discuss your projected new venture in person. I'm not certain I shall recover from seeing such information in black and white. The pamphlet you sent does little to calm or convince and one gets the impression copies were never made. Are you sure other young men are being canvased as well?

Just how—exactly—does one gain training required to become a guide to villages of the Dyak and since, according to the prospectus, the Dyaks are only a generation removed from head-hunting and/or cannibalism, why would you want to be such a courier? I can understand the Dyaks' point of view in the matter but couriers into the steaming jungles of Southeast Asia (or wherever it is) should also be couriers returning out of the steaming jungles. We read, too, that to attain the Dyaks' sites requires eleven days traveling, half on foot, which would indicate like time on the return trip providing, of course, there is a return trip. And what bunch of idiots are you meant to be leading anyway?

I won't ask what can you be thinking of: I've learned better than that, but I do ask that you think on it again. About the brother of your boss at the obscure airport: why was he soliciting couriers for Borneo in Lower Bavaria?

We'll speak of this again after you've completed schooling which you must do regardless if you choose to continue in the hotel business or not. Maybe by then Ava and I shall have regained composure.

Love,
Dad and Ava

Kevin rang to say he heads the school council, has been working after school at one of Philadelphia's best eateries, and it's still very much on with Carol. I believe we've seen the last of the mud-wrestlers in Kevin's life.

We told him we'd give him a trip back to Ireland for his twenty-first birthday but he decided to wait until now to accept it. He is bringing Carol over in the summer.

Kevin and Carol arrived in England the week of the royal wedding with London one big block party, and as guests of Malcolm and Veronica took part in all carryings-on of the Kennedy household where the only vestige of sanity is in Veronica's kitchen. The excitement and pleasure of showing the city to his girl for the first time and staying with old family friends instead of a hotel heightened Kevin's homecoming. London really was more home to him than Ireland. His time here was anxious. Marking "paid" to his childhood—at least through his eyes, he wasn't at Clonlea long enough to send out roots other than by extension of us. But Kevin lived, went to school and worked in England during some very formative years, and he said he felt home again when they touched down at Heathrow.

I know what he meant. How terrible I felt that first year he was back in Los Angeles—so scared and uncertain, when he told me he had been riding on a bus one rainy afternoon, for a minute thought he was in London, and the unhappy jolt that came with the realization he wasn't. I wanted to hand him a plane ticket on the spot. Even more so later when we said goodbye on our way back to Ireland and I saw the pain in his eyes when he hugged us. We all knew it had to be but I'll never forget it. I was never more wretched or more loved my boy. It's easier to deal with kids when they're rotten. The killer is when they're being brave and trying not to show it.

Tyler met Kevin and Carol in London; they flew home together. Ty's school, it seems, is once again on break. This time for six weeks. Hmmmm.

Tyler is Tyler. Kevin is happy, ambitious, and very much a man now. A man engaged to be married, but they asked us not to say anything for a while. We don't question. Carol is creating a stir in these parts and Kev gets a touch paranoid when people stare at them, but he hasn't been in Ireland long enough or doesn't remember it isn't unusual in country areas and certainly to be expected when he is with his fiancée who is—to understate—exotic. He doesn't realize that he, himself, sends out a message, something that attracts people, often causing them to turn and wonder. It's a definite vibration and he has always had it. I'm convinced that one day Kevin will be very successful. Even famous.

"Can I please borrow some whiskey?" pleaded Miss Nora O'Regan at the garden gate. Nora said some fool American cousin had arrived with a load of relations and no notice and Ma was beside herself. We could see a fair-sized bus parked up at their farm. What a terrible surprise. Kitty is a welcoming woman but she doesn't like to be caught off guard without a bit of drink in the house.

Even though she personally hates it—and it IS the curse of this nation—liquor is the first thing she feels she must offer company—and the prime reason we try to visit with the good Mrs. O'Regan away from her own parlor. She is a dear woman. We couldn't live here without such friends, but if for any reason we do have to call at their farm, no matter our protests or Kitty's sworn word we needn't drink, I am given a tumbler glass full of whiskey and am expected to swill it down. Time of day notwithstanding. Ava is allowed off with a small sweet sherry which is almost as difficult because she dislikes anything sweet (except me).

One year I waited until the morning of our departure for California before I delivered the O'Regan Christmas parcels and that was on my way into town for petrol before breakfast—not even coffee. Gotcha this time, I thought. And came home with eyes spinning like pinwheels. It's an insult to refuse Kitty's hospitality. She told me so.

Rarely can we get Kitty to sit still long enough to have a cup of tea in the safety of our own house, but after her cousins left, she came down to see to the calves, and since I was by myself, she felt it was all right to have a chat; no one would know that she wasn't dressed for calling in. We say somebody "rings" when it's a telephone call because, in Ireland, "to call "means doing so in person. We were just the two of us relaxed over tea, when Kitty told me that her cousins from Brooklyn had invited them over for a holiday, expenses paid.

"You're taking them up on it, of course."

"Ah, no. I couldn't be comfortable visiting the gentry."

I've never been paid a higher compliment.

Kevin stopped drinking four years ago. Now he doesn't smoke either. As a surprise, Ava prepared a picnic supper of four small lobsters with accouterments to mark the achievements and sent Kevin, Carol, and Phyllis-Doris out to enjoy it as they should, just the two of them—three of them—in the heather on our point above the sea this radiant evening.

I sit by the upstairs window with a little white wine (martinis are only a sometime thing now) and I count my blessings. My extraordinary mate. My men-children. Now this lovely addition, Carol, returning from their picnic with a garland of daisies crowning that long black hair. And I am complete.

~ ~ ~

Nearly sending Phyllis-Doris into permanent mental retreat when they first arrived, Kevin pounced and with much cooing and stroking pressed her to his chest. Now she wallows in the attention, follows him everywhere, complaining about the rest of us. A spark of recognition may have kindled into flame but I think she still ponders whence came this happy fellow. And seeing her again is wonderful for Kev; another tangible sign of welcome home.

I sometimes forget that we got the kittens before we married and what an integral part they've been of our lives together ever since. How discerning of Ava to suggest that we acquire pets then so she would not be the only newcomer to our close little group. Another area for the boys' affections as well as her own, in case it appeared there might be thoughts of competition for Dad.

A few months before our marriage, we took a house together because we didn't want to lose it by waiting. There were three bedrooms, one of which I shared with Kevin until our wedding made it possible to join my wife in the master bedroom several rooms away in the front part of the house. Prudish perhaps, I believed it the best way to solve the arrangement then. I still do. The move in with my new roommate was convoyed by playful punching and knowing glances from my sons—Kevin anyway—and probably my father-in-law as well. But decorum stayed unsullied.

Apart from little Gloria, in that respect I was brought up liberally because Mom had little choice. She tried. But there weren't enough rooms to separate the sexes always. Especially where Lewis was concerned. Before he found God, my brother found girls—on the road or in bars, etc., and often brought them home for a few days. My mother didn't approve but she would never turn anyone from her door who might be in need, and Lewie's girls were usually troubled and TROUBLE.

I didn't care one way or the other then, but I didn't know what my own outlook would be that not-so-distant day when my kids might bring girlfriends home to spend the night. As it turns out, I feel I'm fairly easy, go with the times and keep an open mind, but there are degrees.

Kevin and Carol stayed in the cottage.

Rebutting my observation that we were most likely the only folk in West Cork with brown sweet peas, Kevin O said it's nothing compared with the color theme he sees for the garden next spring. "Shroud grays with a hint of old liver. Something beyond commonplace to quicken hearts of strollers in the boreen."

O'Mahoney may have been joking but his sweet peas are as close to being brown as they can get while still alive, and they aren't actually in the garden where we might overlook them; they're growing in the solarium window trough along with an oversized snapdragon the hue of dog's sick.

Everything else is pretty though. And it's a confusion of color outside. So much of the bog and savage turf had been transformed since he left, Tyler was speechless at first sight of the garden—later telling its creator that he wept when he saw it. Not being aware of Ty's vernacular, K. O. said he was impressed by the boy's phrase in this day and age. If anything impresses Mr. O'Mahoney, it is usually mixed with tonic and poured over ice, but he was also, quite obviously, touched and pleased. Maybe now he will abandon this search for other floral shades of gloom and continue along the lines of the miracle he has already provided us.

Sightseeing other villages, the kids encountered acquaintances from Philly on a bicycle tour of the country. Kevin invited them to Clonlea if they got this far south. They did and Ava asked them to stay for lunch.

A curious blending of personalities. Breaking bread with us this hot Irish summer day was a nurse, an AWOL monk from Brooklyn, and a mannish artist who paints her dreams.

Chapter Fifteen

This and That

The hour was right but it wasn't the five o'clock crow knocking this morning that saved me from one of my more inventive dreams. Throwing on jeans I went down stairs to find two very wet men pounding on the front door.

"What is a gentleman like you doing in a godforsaken place like this?" were the first words after I asked them in, and spoken in one of the most beautiful voices I'd ever heard. I provided towels, donned a gentlemanly sweatshirt, and while I made coffee they explained they'd come from Cardiff, were blown off course, lost something I didn't understand in the engine, and had been fighting the storm all night, and finally just drifted in to our jetty where they had tied up.

They saw telephone wires leading up to our cottage and knew there was life of sorts; the men were most apologetic about disturbing us but felt they had no alternative. I assured them they had done the right thing and that I would drive them to the village garage for anything they needed, but this is not an early-rising community in general; nothing would be open for a few hours, and in the meantime they were free to telephone whoever might be worrying about them

We have two telephones: one upstairs next to the bed; one in the little library room downstairs. Whichever is dialed, the other rings as the numbers are selected. The Welshman dialed, my sleepy wife answered. We've gone automatic but he thought he had the operator and spoke, Ava yawned that it was a wrong number, and hung up. After they repeated the foolishness a second time, I took the phone and asked her not to answer anymore. Some ten minutes later it penetrated that I was not in bed and she had spoken with me on the telephone at an odd hour of the morning.

"Oh, please don't get up," Ava greeted them brightly, tying her robe as she peered over the banister at her husband serving coffee and toast to—now three—scruffy, damp strangers shuffling in their chairs around her dining table at sunrise. May she never change.

The third man who turned out to be the son-in-law of the skipper, on his maiden—and possibly last—voyage, had stayed on the boat in case other trouble lay ahead at the farmhouse. He also remained when I drove the others to the garage, and was happily accepting the vegetables my wife was loading upon him at our return. Ava offered them baths and made beds for their much-needed rest, but after repairing their engine, the men elected to go on up the coast to the intended destination where their wives, who had flown over from Wales the day before, were anxiously waiting. Friends from America so often ask what we do for interest way out here. Oh, this and that.

We've come to know many travelers. Sometimes meeting in the village, but mostly on our own doorstep. The house sits at the end of a road just wide enough for a car—beyond that it's only a footpath, and the garden walls have been tilted more than once by those who ignored my sign advising of the cul-de-sac and found it difficult to reverse. But some maps wrongly indicate that the road continues out to the historical edifice and consequently we have a lot of confused tourists knocking at the door for information. We usually loan them wellies, warn of the muckier patches, and direct them to the footpath which runs from the end of the boreen between our fields down to a rocky cove and further on, though not so visibly, across Timmy's land to the tower.

Maureen O'Hara quite sternly corrected my term of

Wellington boots. She said they're "gumboots." But "gumboots" hasn't the ring of "Wellington Station—as we've been dubbed in reference to the selection of wellies lined on the back porch for the use of houseguests and the occasional stranger. We've never lost a pair of boots and we've met a lot of nice people. Many have called in again on return trips to Ireland, and some have become cherished friends with whom we've exchanged visits on the Continent.

The maddest encounter occurred our second year living here when I took water to the heifers and found an attractive young English woman scratching Darleen's ears through the fence. She turned out to be the daughter of the man who owned the country house we'd fallen in love with the year we came to England on our extended honeymoon, the place we'd tried unsuccessfully to buy before we left London. The thought of living in that house changed our lives forever, and we met the girl who grew up in it stroking the ear of a cow on our little farm in Eire.

Then there are the kids. Although we've never had to push chairs together forming cribs as Mom so often did, Ava and I have made sleeping accommodations from pretty odd combinations when young bodies accumulated beyond the sum total beds. How like my mother is the girl I married. Generous. Forgetful. Strong, too. Loopy as all get out. And the doors that neither woman ever shut behind them quite often were open to kids in want.

Married at thirteen, Mom had two children before she was sixteen and took in others who needed care. Though I didn't arrive for another half decade, by age thirty-five my feisty bantam hen mother fledged eleven kids, and until I started school, she still laundered by way of a washboard, using homemade lye soap.

Given my upbringing, an ebb and flow of spotty faces around the place might be expected. But apart from Kevin and Tyler, Ava had no prior conditioning. She just cares. Better, she acts upon the moment without purpose or motive, and young people sense it. In some non-verbal intuitive way, Ava sometimes seems more related to my sons than I do; her deep understanding is all the more extraordinary *because* she is not related, a trifle totally ignored by the three of them.

Many of the boys' friends have become family members by extension and still ask to come for a few days even though Kevin and Tyler are no longer home. One summer Ty forgot he'd invited fourteen Austrian teenagers who didn't speak English to end their tour of Ireland with us, and he was working some distance away in another town when they arrived in small groups throughout the week. That was the time we had two Australian teenagers who had taken jobs in the village, staying for the entire season. Many of the kids returned with wives, then children, and if the years have seen perhaps too many young Europeans sheltered against wet Irish nights in the guest cottage, my compassionate wife is almost completely to blame.

The broom I'd just set down was gone when I reached back for it. Ghostly interference in cleaning the kitchen seemed unlikely until I caught a glimpse of my resident poltergeist walking towards the car, juggling her handbag and shopping basket so as not to drop the broom from under her arm. When she came to tell me she was away to town, Ava apparently tripped over the broom which she caught without stopping and—preoccupied—kept going. It reads very odd behavior. It *is* very odd behavior. But Ava's mind and motion whirl in so many directions at once, she isn't impeded by falling objects; she includes them. She was more bemused than baffled when I caught up with her and demanded my broom back straightaway.

Maybe it's me. A similar crazy happened recently when I left a rag mop drying on the stone wall, and it was gone for days before I discovered it woven into the barbed wire fence—one of Tim's temporary post replacements which are never temporary. I've often thought to submit Timmy's gates for a sculpture exhibition. They're certain to fetch profit and critical acclaim. Though old bed frames and springs seem most popular as a fundamental base, bald tires come into play along with broken lobster traps, pump handles, and odd lengths of hose. Barrel hoops are also favored. All are buttressed, wedged and bound together in a flair of hairy binder twine used for baling hay.

Farmer O'Regan's gates.

~ ~ ~

Seldom have I witnessed such flurry as employed by the Sarge who all but popped a wheelie, leapt from his motorcycle and approached our garden gate with the dispatch of a bull rhino. A bumble bee in its trousers can incite speedy action from the law. Fortunately I was close enough to whip the front door open in time to save the hinges; he managed to dislodge the intruder without painful incident and my friend regained dignified control somewhat faster than I did. Catching my glance at Ava's camera on the table next to where he stood in official uniform and helmet, with his pants dropped around the ankles of his boots, Dave growled, "Jaysus, boyo. Try it and ye'll see police brutality for sure!"

I missed another photographic opportunity tonight after I dashed upstairs in answer to Ava's screeches and stopped short of the bedroom door when I realized all the noise and hopping about involved a rodent. Ava had gone to bed to read while I watched television, and just before turning out her light, she told me she noticed a thin tail protruding from the louvered slats of her closet door. Her intention had been to quietly release the mouse out the window, with me being none the wiser. Ava thought mice were helpless if picked up by their tails and that's how she always dealt with them before. But when this one twisted and nipped her arm, she dropped it, the mouse ran up her leg under her nightdress—and Ava proved her blood by inventive movements even her dad might find tricky—before it ran down into a hole in the closet's skirting board.

I wish I weren't such a coward. It would've been more entertaining than the newscast I'd just seen. Though gladly embracing the legend of Ireland's little people, I found it a tad too fey when, along with fog patches and predicted gale winds on the weather chart, they indicated areas of dew.

Without question, Chris makes the best smoked salmon we've ever tasted and we like to promote as much custom for him as possible. That, I thought, was the reason Ava usually talked the distaff side of visiting couples into taking some smoked salmon away with them when they left. Since his property is difficult to locate and accessible only at certain tides and, as usual, I hadn't a clue how to find it, Ava always chauffeured the ladies to Christopher's smoke house and brought them back laden with sides of salmon and happy smiles. In country Ireland, nothing within a hundred-mile radius is truly private and, although he lives some distance away on the outskirts of another village, it is common knowledge that shortly after he opted for the simple life and they settled in the area, Mrs. Chris walked, leaving him with an infant and four other children. Until only a few months ago, I thought my wife's enthusiastic fishmongering on their father's behalf was Ava's way of insuring the little ones' welfare, but when a tall, lean stranger of strong jaw and turquoise eyes, with a shock of blonde hair unruly across a noble brow, spoke to her as we were going into our favorite restaurant, I had to rethink the concept. The elusive Christopher brings to mind a rather scruffy version of Michael York. I more clearly understand Ava's concern for the kiddies now.

The salmon man has managed to care for his family and build a thriving business, and though no one knows what he uses to make the taste so special, everybody swears by it. Achieving it, however, presented a challenge—how to order the several sides of smoked salmon we wanted to take to the States as a contribution to Kevin and Carol's wedding reception and for Christmas gifts—when the smoker resided in difficult terrain and was not on the telephone. The Irish say "on the phone" (when they mean have a phone), a term we use habitually now and which is met usually with wary confusion in America when we inquire if someone is on the phone and we're speaking with the person on a busy street corner, or some such, at the time.

Known locally as "Mary from the Dairy," Chris's niece worked at the dairy farm making cheese, so Ava went there first to gain the particulars of ordering her uncle's salmon. Mary advised that Ava give her written requirements to one of his children when they catch the school bus at the stop by the bank on their way home in the late afternoon; they might forget if she met the morning arrival. Unsure that she would recognize Mary's cousins amidst all the other children, Ava decided it best to just try to track the man down, and this time I elected to go along.

Hidden in the trees above a small harbor, Chris's place is positioned at the end of a rocky path, and the only sign of civilized occupancy was a shiny new postbox against which a weathered, white-bearded fisherman type leaned.

"Foin dee."

"Fine Day," we returned the standard polite greeting and, stepping out of the car, Ava approached the friendly old gent.

"Have you seen Chris about?"

"No, Missus."

"I could leave a message. Is that his postbox?"

"Whisht . . . Don't hold much with postboxes, Missus."

"If Chris isn't too far away, would you know where I could find him?"

Following a brief period of silent lip-chewing, our informant brightened into a gummy smile.

"Ye might go to the gap and look under the bridge, Missus."

Incredibly, Ava nodded her head in comprehension.

"If he isn't met under the bridge, Missus, call out and yer man should come from between the stones." Ending the conversation with a touch to his cap, and leaving us with the impression that we'd been lightly had, the old boy called back, "If all else fails, Missus—ye can always leave a note in the postbox."

On that note, Chris himself appeared promised to have the required salmon in time for our departure next week and told us not to worry about collecting them: he would have his kids drop them off for us at the market when they come into town on the school bus.

Since his supermarket is the only place open early enough to coincide with the arrival of the schoolbus, Tom, the owner, kindly agreed to relieve the children of their cargo and refrigerate the half dozen sides of salmon until the Collins sisters could collect them for us later in the day. They had asked us to stop for a drink on our way out to dinner, and with packing for the trips, it seemed the easiest solution. By now, we should know that there is never an easy solution to anything in Ireland. Moira and Deirdre Collins live in comfortable chaos at the top of the village, and the last time we paid them a call, we'd been invited to bring our visiting Franciscan monk friend over for a meal or—as Moira puts it, "The night you came to lunch." Dressed in his regulation brown robe and sandals, it was Brother Angelo and not Ava who tripped over their doorstep when we finally left just at bar closing time and caused the comment from someone leaving the nearby pub. "JAYSUS!" I seen it all. Dere's a drunk monk comin' out da Collins Girls."

Spinsters only by definition, these are two sharp ladies so fast off the mark with a quip they'd even give B. W. Ludden a run. It is rumored that one of the Collins girls is a retired spy, but if that is so, I think it must be the other sister, a nun living in an African order, who they wickedly refer to only as the Bride of Christ.

Tom had offered to drop our salmon off with them on his way home from work, but the Collinses didn't have the sides when we got to their house, and he still hadn't arrived when we had to leave if we were to keep our dinner booking on time. "But the salmon is already smoked," we heard Moira say when she rang his home to see if he forgot about us, and Tom's wife informed her that her husband had gone for fire brigade drill and wasn't expected home before eleven o'clock. Organizing a change of game plan, the ladies insisted that we return after dinner and wait for delivery of the fish. Even with a day's leeway before our departure, Deirdre thought the five-mile drive into town in the morning unnecessary and she quite fancied a late nightcap anyway: we were to come back after dinner and she would hear no argument.

The sisters were doing us a favor; we could hardly return empty-handed, and since the shops were closed we were forced to purchase a bottle of wine at restaurant mark-up to take to them, and because the Sarge dropped in for a social call after we got there, we had shifted more than half the hooch before Tom arrived, tired and thirsty from playing with fire. Moira uncorked another bottle. I've spent the whole of the day moving at tortoise pace and offering thanks that we aren't departing until tomorrow. Christopher notwithstanding—next time we'll buy the smoked salmon they sell at the airport.

Next time we won't take smoked salmon back to the States at all!

Misty Ireland was crystal clear when we flew out, but L.A. was socked in with such dense fog our plane was diverted to Las Vegas, where we sat for four hours without being allowed to disembark because there was no Customs availability, and six sides of frozen smoked salmon do not do well in the desert climate. Finally ending up in San Francisco along with all the other diverted flights from around the globe, we were herded onto a bus with a fledgling driver who drove us in the wrong direction nearly into Bay Meadows racetrack before he located the partially finished Aer Lingus-owned hotel, operating with a skeleton staff and no one to help with the luggage. We men passengers unloaded, carried bags for ourselves and a group of old ladies from a New Zealand flight who had somehow got on the coaches for the Irish travelers, and after seeing Ava safely to our room in the new wing of the hotel, which was under construction and miles away from the registration desk, I compounded jet fatigue searching for our remaining bags until I remembered I'd left them in a different section of the lobby. The smell of defrosted salmon should have led me to them in the first place.

Chris hermetically sealed his fish but some residue from his fingers remained on the outside of their plastic covering to linger as a reminder of the auld sod, and once again I marveled at woman's intuition; it's amazing how my wife knew to pack the fish in my bag instead of hers.

The airlines wanted to bus us down to L.A. next morning, but since there had been no breakfast or even coffee available at the hotel, Ava and I decided to stay in San Francisco for a couple of days to overcome the trials of the journey and refreeze the salmon. F. A. told her when she phoned to advise him of our delay, that he'd tried to meet our plane and they let him wait half the day before informing him that we'd been sent to San Francisco, and Ava decided he should have a couple of sides of Irish smoked salmon as compensation. Since the fish had been defrosted and refrozen, I was reminded of the iffy mushroom she once offered me. Won't kill Fred just to taste it, I suppose.

~ ~ ~

Dear Son,

Now that you are about to begin the most important adventure of your life, perhaps a few remarks from the Old Man might be welcome.

Through the years we've had our differences—some quite strong ones—and there are sure to be others, but you are and always will be very special to me. I want you to know that now even though I realize the day you hold your own firstborn child, you will understand it without question.

Nothing—no one—can ever match the feeling of wonder and joy that hit like a thunderbolt when I first saw you. You were angry and red and had too much hair even then. You were my son and I was so proud. I haven't changed.

Once, in Ireland, I drove over the hill and—suddenly—there you were cycling down the lane. Fresh faced and laughing, the hair I thought too long blowing in the wind. Seventeen years later and still the thunderbolt. I stopped the car and, not dry-eyed, watched you ride out of sight.

I have no doubt you shall be as fine a husband and father as you have grown to be a man, and I would hope that you learned from your father's mistakes, but it doesn't work that way, and you'll have a set of your own to pass on to his grandchildren one day.

You know that Ava and I wish you both the very best that life has to offer always. You also know that we love you dearly but I thought you just might want to have that in writing.

Happiness,
Dad

Even though it will be a very small affair for only the immediate family, we excused F. A. from attending the ceremony tomorrow because these functions are difficult enough for him without the extra burden of a drive out to Pasadena for the wedding at Carol's grandparents' friends' house, but he came by to offer his congratulations to them here at the hotel this morning. Tyler, who is working in an American military hotel in Germany, can't take the time off from a new job to be with us either.

Fred with Kevin and Carol just before their wedding in California, 1982.

"You've traveled with Turkish gypsies, skinny-dipped in Barcelona, and you don't know how to check into a hotel in Pasadena?!"

"I've never been in a hotel without you, Dad."

Kevin was about to leave with his new bride and he took me to a quiet corner to ask about registering, tipping, room service—hotel information his brother would have happily offered had he been able to get away from Munich for the occasion. My blue-eyed boy gave me a wonderful present. Kev had just completed his vows of marriage but I was still Dad; he didn't feel too grown-up to ask such simple advice and he asked knowing that I wouldn't laugh. He didn't know how close were tears.

Ava, of course, had been mopping her face since early morning when she read the date on the newspaper at breakfast and the dam broke. I hadn't given much speculation to my son's wedding, but considering the silly ceremony Ava and I had, I can't imagine why I thought Kevin's would be conventional. Carol's grandmother's friend, a Shakespeare buff, built a stage on one end of the living room for such readings, and today a huge spread of sushi and sashimi covered tables at the other end of the room. Kevin and Carol were joined in holy matrimony by a minister wearing turquoise jewelry on a raised stage in a stranger's living room in South Pasadena while the rest of us lounged in overstuffed chairs, with the groom's mother dabbing her eye and scratching the ears of a large German shepherd.

Transsexuals and mud wrestlers were not present.

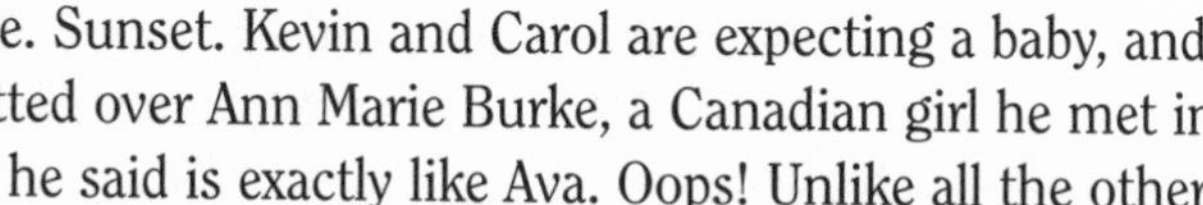

Sunrise. Sunset. Kevin and Carol are expecting a baby, and Tyler is besotted over Ann Marie Burke, a Canadian girl he met in Munich who he said is exactly like Ava. Oops! Unlike all the others he has been interested in, he told us Ann is not of Nordic heritage. Suddenly Ty decided that he was too old to be "bumming around Europe" and elected to be closer to his brother in the States. Read: Ann went back to finish school in America.

When he was a little boy, Tyler said if the Olympic games were ever held in Los Angeles, he wanted to be there. Now they are, and he is working for them. Because of his European background and his fluency in German and some knowledge of Swedish and Norwegian, his first job in America is a managerial position in the catering department for the Olympic games. Ty has made points by being able to call upon his brother's resources and expertise during the many emergencies, and the pay is terrific. It's limited employment of course, but it gives him a good start in the old hometown which he left at age eleven. Some lucky star, kid.

~ ~ ~

"It's a girl!" Kevin's voice was faint, partly due to the connection. In spite of a long, difficult labor, finally resolved by Caesarean section, our daughter-in-law and granddaughter are fine.

"How do you feel about being a grandfather, Mister Dad?"

I feel great about being a grandfather. I'm not so sure about the Mister Dad. I'll take it in the chirpy way Kevin sounded when he rang. I hope I don't appear that way to him. Still, it has a better ring than the day I heard Tyler asking Ava, "Where's the Grouch?"

~ ~ ~

We rang the hospital where Carol was entertaining her husband, her brother Marc, her brother-in-law (still dressed in official Olympic garb, including straw boater hat, we were told) and her daughter—Morgan. I asked Uncle McKenzie what he thought about his niece.

"My knees? Why should I think about my knees?

"Your NIECE. Morgan. Your brother's daughter, you dolt. Put Kevin back on the phone. RIGHT NOW!"

Am I ready for the next generation?

~ ~ ~

"YEEECH!" Ava rubbed her shoulder; otherwise didn't shift her position on the couch while we watched TV.

"What's wrong, sweetheart?

"I think I wrenched my shoulder."

"Impossible. You've been a sofa spud all evening."

"No, silly. This morning when I tried to throw the duck fat over the wall without getting out of the car."

So much for my thoughts that becoming a grandmother might have made a difference.

~ ~ ~

In spite of our eagerness to see the baby, we thought Kevin and Carol should have a chance to adjust into parenthood, and we waited until the usual time for our annual trip to see Fred and the kids. Morgan was three months old when we were introduced this afternoon, and another thunderbolt struck when my firstborn placed his firstborn in my arms.

Morgan McKenzie. My Scots–Irish–Native American–German–Japanese–Armenian granddaughter with the Celtic name and the lovely Oriental face. I can't wait for her to see Ireland. And Ireland to see her.

"They don't break," Michi laughed, offering Morgan to her terrified paternal grandmother. "They do if you drop them." Carol didn't quite shout, racing to intercept her mother's pass. Small children invariably attach to Ava and she is good with them; inventive, informative, and fun. With infants, she is uneasy; with Ava with infants, we are all uneasy. But Ava will be terrific company for Morgan when she reaches an age of sturdy confidence on her own two feet and might give granny a pointer or two.

Tyler suffered some anxieties and withdrawal pains after the full hours and the financial gains of the Olympics job ended, but he soon found work with a flaky television production company, the sort of work I suspect he has always wanted, and his Annie is moving to California to be near him. We have yet to meet her but I've a feeling the lady is going to be around for more than awhile.

I hadn't realized it had been so long since we've all been in America together. I'm ready to go home to Clonlea and pretend those two hulking men are still my little boys, and Kevin and Carol are pinching pennies towards opening a restaurant of their own, preferably somewhere in the Pacific Northwest, but this trip has given us all a renewed sense of family.

The message on the restaurant's card was brought to me by the maitre d':

Sir—you are such a gentleman. I'll ask my husband to take lessons . . .

A Fan . . .

Don Cook gave us dinner with Sammy and Altovise Davis and Elizabeth Taylor . . . breathtaking again. Sam wasn't at the table when the note arrived, convincing us all it was a set-up, but when he returned, he swore he had nothing to do with it. Although our waiter singled out a woman seated a few seats behind me as the perpetrator, I still wasn't convinced until she and her (younger) male companion smiled when I turned around to look just as they prepared to leave. Swell, I thought, she picked the snow-topped geezer as a means of approaching the stars, but I thanked her for the pretty compliment when she hesitated in passing our table. She smiled again, nodded to the others, and departed.

Who'd believe that while dining at a posh restaurant with Sammy Davis and Elizabeth Taylor *I* got the fan letter? Fred looks great and we've seen a lot of each other but he was somewhat upset that he hadn't been invited for dinner with Elizabeth. F. A. said he would have been there like a shot. We didn't remind him that everyone naturally assumed that he was otherwise engaged. It's high time we went home and set the cabbages.

Chapter Sixteen

P.-D.

As she has done since our first season here, Ava helped judge the children's fancy dress parade which always opens the village festival week. She made one of the costumes herself and gave the little girl a prize for it. That's okay; all the kids win something. It's just that I think changing the most topical category to most tropical because the child wore a hula skirt and a lei is questionable. Ava thinks I'm miffed because she didn't use my suggestion of a shamrock garland so I could make a tura lura lei, but she'll be sorry comes the day when someone else cashes in on the idea.

My favorite part of festival week is the terrier race. All terriers are eligible—big Kerry blues compete with tiny Yorkies. A pelt on a long rope attached to a winch is hand cranked up the main street. The dogs chase it but mainly follow their owners who run ahead to give them the idea. Everyone lines the street, cheering and exciting the animals even more, but I've never seen the dogs fight. Some of the owners get a little testy but the dogs have a wonderful time. So much for this week's activities, except maybe yesterday when Rex Reed passed through town and I gave him an omelet for lunch. Rex missed Angela who is in America. He missed Ava who was shopping in Cork. He missed the terrier race. And a little later in the week I wouldn't have been here to answer his call either. Ava enrolled in a Thai cookery course in Bangkok.

~ ~ ~

"I want to see China. Maybe Siam. To faraway places I roam."

The treacle tune so appealed to my mother, she asked that I

sing it at her funeral. Rarely leaving the neighborhood, she still had her dreams. But when Mom died, I couldn't sing and, unaware of her request, the others would have misunderstood had I tried. Now—an hour out of Bangkok, approaching the most far of the faraway places I've roamed—I wish I had. The words are long forgotten but how clearly that lady stays with me.

Southeast Asia. The profusion of orchids is nearly overpowering and muffled noise from mad water traffic rises from the river far below. A magnificent lacquered screen complements the silk-covered walls of our accommodations. Nothing is familiar, yet I am reminded of the wallpaper of my tiny bedroom in Grandma's cabin when I was a boy. It was just rough wallboard, numbered at the seams, but it was the same odd shade of rose as the fabric behind the screen.

Ava returned from cooking class, demanded at once to know exactly how I'd managed three hours without her, and snatched my notebook. Ava said that now that she thought about it, the bamboo print in the bedroom was like the one the Astaires had in their entry hall. ENTRY HALL!? It was probably larger than my cabin bedroom, too.

Bangkok yawned, stretched in preparation for the frenetic daily commerce, and a few boats already trickled activity on the water, but it wasn't full light yet and the height and situation of our balcony protected my nakedness when I first came out to seek the source of chanting which, like our Irish crow, had called me awake on the dot of five each morning. When I finally placed the sound, it came from a building quite close, though considerably below us and framed by the window, the tangerine robes of the monks almost pulsated in the mist of already rising humidity.

So far Ava has slept through the morning ritual but she must share this experience with me before we leave Thailand. Perhaps she won't care to stand naked. I hope she does. She will never forget the pure exoticness of being unhampered by clothing while that gong-like prayer fills the morning air and washes over her.

~ ~ ~

We sailed on a cruise after Thailand. Ava got monkey hair in her lens and monkeys in her hair in Bali where—shades of Dorothy Lamour—I was required to wear a sarong to view the Elephant God.

We beat Tyler to Borneo and tickled the nose of a friendly water buffalo by the roadside, and my personal favorite moment happened at two a.m. in Hong Kong when I joined a group around a street artist. I was the only non-Asian and he so remarkable a portraitist—I felt greatly oversized and under-skilled.

Bless Ava for her understanding. For encouraging me to indulge my loner temperament when I need to explore and experience a place on my own. In spite of those loopy idiosyncrasies that amuse me so, my lady is the wisest in our family. I didn't get to be the elephant trainer of my seven-year-old dreams, but I got to Africa, where they live. I wanted to be an artist and study in Greenwich Village. I hoped to be a part of Hollywood. To know Paris. To travel anywhere and everywhere. To live by the sea. As a boy, I designed a farm I imagined with little walkways dividing the gardens. I wanted a beautiful wife and children. I wanted it all. Dear God—I got it all.

~ ~ ~

We detoured to California on our way home to check in with F. A. and organize a few plans for Tyler and Ann's wedding next spring.

Frail and thin, Fred still drives down to collect his mail and see us every morning. We've had him to dinner at the hotel and he took us to The Bistro a couple of times, but eating seems to have become a chore. Judging from a few comments, he isn't always allowed to order what he likes. That isn't the case with us but he still eats too little.

He loves Italian cooking. We badgered Hermes Pan, the Greek, into making lasagna for us at his house—one of our happiest times this visit. Ty and Ann joined us, fortunately, because Hermes accidentally hit the lock button on the doorknob and locked himself out of the bathroom, giving Fred and the kids a before-dinner project. We couldn't find an implement small enough to release the snig in the doorknob. One learned about such things if one had small children—the hard way. But I'd come away without my specs, and dancers' tool chests aren't like real people's.

Before the kids arrived, however, I had quietly suggested to wife and father-in-law that a corkscrew might work. Ava and Fred ignored me. Ava retired from the game when Ann and Tyler joined us. I offered the corkscrew. Ann and Tyler and Fred ignored me.

Fred, Tyler, and Ann trying to unlock Hermes Pan's bathroom door.

Seeing them all trying to peer through the keyhole simultaneously reminded me of another time when we still stayed at Fred's house and I came in the front door to find Ava, her dad, and Jo, the housekeeper, kneeling as if confused in which direction lay

Mecca; the three of them in a half-circle, heads touching the baseboard in the marble entry hall. Listening to a cricket, they said.

Fred, Ava, and Jo, the housekeeper, listening to a cricket in Fred's hallway.

Fred and the kids fooled with the door until our host insisted they come to table, and one of them came up with the idea that a corkscrew should do the trick. We sat down before the food got cold, and Mr. Pan relaxed in the knowledge that he could brush his teeth after dinner. The activity piqued Fred's appetite to such lengths he cleaned his plate, and Pan's ineptitude occupied most of his conversation when we drove him home. They love it when the other does something dumb.

~ ~ ~

We were about to turn off the boreen by the church onto the main road; I asked her to check for approaching traffic from the left, I would see to the right. "Noth-ing," sang the Avabird, giving me cause to praise providence for the exceptional peripheral vision allowing me to brake in time to avoid the van barreling towards us from the left. "I meant," she whispered, "Don't go." One of these days, Alice! I don't know, maybe it was safer to drive in Beverly Hills.

~ ~ ~

PHYLLIS-DORIS
1970–1987

Beneath a white and polished stone, P.-D. curls up on her favorite knoll for the final nap. Weathering a cold winter easily, she was never in want of comfort or companionship; while we were away, Frankie lived at Clonlea until work on her own house was completed. Amazingly fit, P.-D. still jumped up on the roof by the bedroom window as she had always done, and managing the ladder to the warm loft she shared with George in the garage was no problem at all.

They were seldom alone. Our marvelous young vet, Tim O'Leary, checked in regularly, sometimes injected a little extra vitality into the old girl and Kevin O didn't go to the Continent as usual, consequently was around the place more than he normally is when there is little gardening to do. The O'Regans resumed daily feeding after Frankie left, and the builders adding a bedroom onto the cottage provided diverting annoyance. About a fortnight before we were expected home, they noticed our little black cat moving unsteadily, acting peculiarly (which to us, would not usually indicate anything amiss), and rang the vet who responded at once. A hemorrhaging brain sent Phyllis-Doris deep and forever into the haze, and Tim mercifully spared further suffering for her or any of us. Frankie waited until the last day before telephoning us; cushioning our return to Clonlea where small, dim, and dusky P.-D. has been a fixture from the onset—for as long as we've been married.

Often uncertain we weren't interlopers into her world which—considering she so often seemed on another plane—I suppose we were, Phyllis-Doris remained on firm earth where Kevin O was concerned. They chatted together and shared his lunch—cheese sandwiches her particular favorite and, thanks to the O'Mahoney, I fear more than her memory will linger. Kevin selected the headstone from our beach, buffed it and, in his fine script, carved her name, the years of birth and passing. K. O. said there shall come those to study it and speculate for whom it marks. " The poor colleen. Only seventeen and for what horror laid to rest in unconsecrated soil?" On nights of the gibbous moon, it may be whispered, she might be seen staring hopelessly at the estuary."

Tim O'Leary called in last night, said he missed her. So do we. So do we. Good-bye little cat. We always suspected you were the stuff of legends.

~ ~ ~

One of the first things we do after returning from California is to seek and drape ourselves over Darleen. We never told Timmy we named her Darleen, of course, but he knew she has become our pet and said she is the "best beast" he ever had. I don't know what marks their difference from the black and white Holstein breed of cattle in America, but thanks to Mr. O'Regan, I can now impress city slickers by distinguishing a Friesian cow of finer stock from the rest of the meadow sisterhood. "Notice the tapering muzzle," I'll point out, hoping for correct terminology. "The delicate pinkness of the nostrils. Direct your attention to the extra long legs and fine, thin tail. She'll be a milker, that'un."

Ava with Wanda and Darleen (right).

~ ~ ~

Agonizing that she hadn't taken her camera because she passed a wandering cow heading for the open door of the church out on the main road, Ava ignored my obvious "Holy Cow!", and I was struck by the incongruity that, for a California beach boy and a famous movie star's daughter, a large part of our daily conversation is directed toward the bovine.

Overlooking my wife's protestations that she knew it was a mistake to mention it—that I've always been odd on Sunday afternoons, I breezed out into the sunshine singing, "How Can I Ignore the Bull Next Door?" Given our backgrounds, such an association *is* strange. Not up to any serious efforts today, I began a somewhat giddy consideration of the cows that languish through a goodly portion of our weekly routines in rural Ireland. There are worse ways to observe the Sabbath.

On mornings fine enough to take my coffee or crayons outside, I love hearing the wheezing, snorting cough of the O'Driscoll's bull carrying up from their pasture, which is situated somewhat lower than our miniature apple orchard and hidden by a row of elm trees. Ava said he probably feels the same about me.

The fact that he is rather slight might account for his disposition but, I suspect that, as bulls go, his almost mauve coloring indicates a more sensitive persuasion. He certainly seems agreeable whenever I've seen young O'Driscoll leading him from field to field. Of the three farmlands in our immediate area, I think the O'Driscolls are the only ones still without electricity and I rejoice in the sight of the old man himself, who—to protect them—wears brilliant green plastic feed sacks over trousers that are probably older than his married daughter. Unlike his son, he is of Mickey Rooney stature, and every time I see those bandy legs reflecting in the evening light when he cuts over the fields, my mom's favorite peppery little bantam rooster crows across the years.

"Young" O'Driscoll must be approaching middle age but we've heard that he has little interest other than his land. He resembles his gentle bull: solidly built, not fat; his normally ruddy, handsome features are plum colored from long hours in the sun and winds, and he is extremely strong. We've seen him pound fence posts into this rocky ground using a huge stone instead of a sledgehammer and yet he moves with a beefy grace, ploughing his acreage, usually late into the evening, as he and his old white horse turn furrows in the time-honored manner. Quite often Ava and I will be sitting up on the hill when he is working late, and though we don't really know him, he always raises his hand to us as he rounds the end of the nearest furrow, and I am guilty with the thought that such a sight brings us peace of spirit and soothing while, no doubt, he counts the rows until the time he can quit for his tea.

Tyler was named for a song called "Tyler My Boy," a tale of an Irish lad who lived by the sea, written by Billy Barnes for his own son, and though we didn't know him at the time, Billy Barnes became a friend. Nearly a quarter of a century later, I walked by the sea in Ireland with the man responsible for my son's name. The very sophisticated Mr. Barnes had never been to Ireland, rarely left Los Angeles. One forgets how menacing and big cows appear to city folk and he took some calming down during our walk when a herd of cattle blocked our path. Despite my promises that they would part like the Red Sea if we kept going, Billy gripped my arm and walked with his eyes shut until I assured him they were passed and made him turn around to see the boy of about seven years driving them.

Disrupting my concentration upon cows, Ava joined me in the garden to inquire if I should like a refreshment and, with no discernible pause for breath, requested that I save the tubes from finished rolls of loo paper because she intends to start her runner beans in them next spring, and I was informed that she had sent away for a two-kilo box of extract of lion dung pellets to put in the vegetable garden because they'll keep the cats from peeing in the newly seeded patches and we won't have to cover them with netting anymore. Thanking her, I agreed that some iced coffee would be welcome, and that she had some nerve to say *I* was strange on Sundays.

~ ~ ~

Ava often takes a basket of lettuces for our restaurateur friends when we dine out, and although they aren't open for lunch, we dropped in with some extra produce this afternoon because we had to be in the village anyway, and just inside the door of the darkened room we discovered the vicar. Nearly hidden behind a long wooden table, he was stretched out on a bench, his hands resting upon his chest in pious attitude. Viewed in that position, the severity of his head-covering combined with the neatly arranged draping of his cassock implied the lying in state of some noble worthy, and with my wife breathing down the back of my neck, still clutching her basket, I bent over his black form to check for signs of life; I retreated so quickly when he suddenly opened his eyes, I jolted Ava and she knocked the veggies all over the table.

If I'd awakened to find strange faces hovering and string-beans and beetroot strewn around me, I'd be a hell of a lot more ruffled than our vicar, who merely sat up and yawned, "Forgive me for not responding immediately. My mind was running very intently along religious lines and on the infirm whom I've been visiting. Since mother went away I feel especially devoted to our aged ones and do what little bit I can."

Although we're sure he meant it, I don't know what that had to do with his being asleep in an empty restaurant in the middle of the day. He was probably just grabbing forty winks between benevolent missions, but for a moment there, Ava and I feared he might have gone to seek his mother.

~ ~ ~

Ava can gut a fish so quickly, I'm thinking of entering her in the fish-cleaning contest at the next village festival. I once knew how to prepare my day's catch, but that was so long ago and so foreign to present interests I wouldn't know how to begin, and as I watched my wife dispatching the large pollock on the stones by the back porch, I was convinced there is no need for me to recapture the knack anyway. I've never actually asked Ava how she learned but I imagine it was from someone at the fish factory. The only thing the three fishermen in the yellow wellies taught her in the pub a few seasons back was how to play the spoons, and I know she didn't learn how to clean fish from Phil at Phil's Phish Market in Beverly Hills.

We used to wait on the jetty for the seventeen-year-old Connie O'Mahoney to bring in his catch. This evening, when he came by to drop a fish off for us, Connie had his two little sons in tow: replicas of their dad, their gold and copper curls dazzling in the sunlight.

Our village is not a quaint place. For such a small population and simple way of life, these are warm, intelligent people with a more cosmopolitan outlook (and more welcoming of outsiders) than one might expect, and by virtue of their Irishness, of course, they are wonderfully articulate. We've never seen another community to match it and we are beholden to the karma that led us here and allows us to be a part of it.

They would regard my saying so as typical Yankee codswallop, but Larry is the best doctor, in the truest all-around sense of the title, we've ever come across, and though we have no line of comparison, Sergeant Dave, I expect, is an equally savvy lawman. On the other hand, I've never met another cop with a knack for the art of taxidermy. Ava often reports the sites of otherwise undamaged roadkills to Dave, and he has been known to return from holiday with his suitcase full of frozen dead birds. And it was at the Sarge's housewarming party where Larry tried to prevent Jimmy, the harbormaster, from choking on his dentures when he went outside to be sick. Larry knew the man was not used to much drink; the fact that Jimmy's fine teeth are all his own made the doc no less determined to have them out, to prevent him choking on them. He was only convinced that they were genuine when Jimmy's desperate threat ripped through the night air. "If you don't keep your fekkin' hand out of my mouth, I'll bite off your other fekkin' fingers!" Boy! Do I NOT miss Beverly Hills.

~ ~ ~

Even if we were so inclined, we couldn't be members of the vicar's flock because the townland out here is a different parish, so we can't answer with any authority the questions asked about him when people hear we come from this village. We learned that the man is a wealth of contradictions. Scholarly to the point that his little notes are dated in Latin or maybe ancient Greek, he is also an ardent sports fan and coaches some of the teams, and, according to Deirdre Collins, he is a lovely dancer and wears soft patent leather dancing shoes for those occasions.

He loves to stir things up and rabble rouse during his services; sometimes calling for prayers against the insurance companies or, like Dellie, whatever firm he is annoyed with at the time, and yet he makes certain to publicly compliment anyone he believes deserving. Last week we met another vicar at lunch and because our local vicar seems to be a thorny problem in church circles at the moment, he became the main topic. There were lots of stories but my favorite stemmed from a recent exchange when our lunch companion said he had been sent here by their hierarchy to interview the renegade. As well as church matters, they discussed the apparent need for a Mrs. Vicar in the future and it turned out that since his mother died, the matter had indeed been given serious thought. Ava and I went bananas when we heard that our man looked for "three" qualities in such a woman. She must have the "brains of Minerva, the body of Aphrodite, and soul of the Virgin Mary." The last requirement clearly precluded the second, so they rapidly changed the subject to his recently reported break-in at the rectory. Nothing was taken (with all that stuff piled around how could he tell?) and when it was suggested that nothing was even disturbed, he refused to be swayed from his conviction that the point of entry was through a skylight heavy with cobwebs untouched since his mother's departure. The reverend ventured, "I never said they were human."

Chapter Seventeen

Weddings

When Hurd Hatfield rang to invite us to a prenuptial party for a San Francisco socialite and her South African fiancé, neither of whom he and we knew, Ava felt we couldn't refuse. Not only was it an opportunity to see our longtime friends, the Tony Duquettes, who were flying over from California, but Hatfield planned for dinner to be at little tables scattered around his grounds and it was assumed that Ava would bring along enough cloths to cover them. We were, of course, also expected to arrive early enough to help set up.

"Did I ever tell you that the German fisherman I brought to your house the first time we met married Bette Midler?" Hurd asked when we pulled up and refused to get out of the car unless he assured us his dog was safely tethered or muzzled. Ava asked where he wanted her tablecloths? Hurd said he forgot that he no longer had those little tables. Ava went in search of Tony and Beagle Duquette. I picked up a broom and attacked the entry hall.

Had the Duquettes realized how far Hurd's romantic description of his dream house was from reality they would not have recommended it as the ideal setting for a wedding party, and when he saw H. H.'s dark manor, set designer Tony Duquette felt duty bound to transform the place into something a bit more celebratory of young dreamers who've traveled from distant lands in order to seal their love in magical Ireland. Tony knew he didn't have time for jet lag.

Typically, Hurd didn't seem to mind that Tony wanted a large armoire repositioned in a different room and, until he remembered me, almost volunteered to assist with shifting it himself. But when Tony moved a small piece of china to a less visible spot, it became another matter entirely, and he pointedly returned it to its former pride of place.

“HATFIELD. You can’t WANT that thing on view. Take it to the kitchen where it belongs.” Grinning, Tony handed the pot to Hurd again who grasped it in both his hands either for protection or to demonstrate firmness of intent and, grimly, set it down almost too forcefully for fragile pottery.

“It is rare Chinese Export that should be seen and appreciated.”

“It’s an ugly teapot.”

“White thorn!” Ava’s exclamation turned all attention towards the doorway, where her entrance was preceded by the twisted branch of white flowers she shook at her host.

“Hurd, you must know not to ever EVER bring white thorn into the house. It’s fierce bad luck!” My wife’s superstitious warning smacked so much of Timmy O’Regan, I was surprised that, in her dither, she didn’t say “’tis” as well.

Obediently, Hurd followed Ava into the sitting room where, to foreign eyes, bowers and bowers of white thorn perfectly accentuated the occasion for which they were brought in, and before I joined them Tony snatched up the offending teapot, stashed it deeply back on a low shelf out of harm’s way. To my knowledge, Hurd never thought of it again. He had similarly decorated most of the other rooms.

“Are you sure you don’t mean it’s peacock feathers that are bad luck in the house, Ava?” Hurd wrung his hands. “I must ask Tony if they still have that dreadful peacock they used to let come in after luncheon. It was always tamale pie.”

Knowing when to quit, Ava acquiesced that perhaps she had overreacted to the superstition, and though he was clearly torn between the flowers’ beauty and ominous reputation, Hurd opted for the effect. The displays stayed put and Hatfield returned to his game with Duquette, vying to see which one could undo the other’s efforts in the shortest amount of time.

The presence of thorn in the house worried some of the local people enough to remark about it later, but the bridal party remained unaware that the flower sprays everywhere forebode an unhappy future, and the party turned out a right hooley for sure.

Hurd's insistence that the Duquettes stay with him rather than at the comfortable, large country guest house nearby, where many of the rest of us had booked, demonstrates his cockeyed outlook. Neither his house nor his crazed Dalmatian dog, Uhlan, are welcoming of outsiders. Uhlan the Terrible, dotty as he is spotty, ate a portion of the sofa bed in our guest cottage and all the W pages from our telephone directory some time back when Hurd brought him down for a weekend visit. I *assume* it was Uhlan.

With Ava, Hurd Hatfield, and his dog, Uhlan, at Hurd's house, 1989.

Hurd regards his menacing pet with adulation, and, probably because they never cease, he turns a deaf ear to the steady murmuring growls and snarls that threaten anything that moves within the silly animal's visual scope. H. H. seems to be equally unaware that, although his house is indeed large, he will see the end of several years before it is restored to the stage where it can accommodate the number of guests his natural hospitality envisions.

For the present, two bedrooms and one full bathroom, with

a downstairs loo off the kitchen, are not suitable amenities for two gentlemen and three ladies of advanced years, especially since the somewhat invalid Mrs. Duquette, of necessity, was accompanied by her maid companion, a stout Mexican woman who spoke no English.

Hurd's friend Maggie, over from Connecticut, shared sleeping arrangements with Uhlan and Hurd in the attic that she preferred not to think about, and we learned from Beagle that the nice Mexican lady's proportions far surpassed those of the slim chaise lounge Hurd provided for her bed. Due to crippling travel fatigue and time disorientation, it seems no one rested easily except the host and his psychotic dog.

It was a beautiful night for a party. One might think Hurd held casting calls. The boys in the band providing dance music in the large foyer after dinner, and the lovely raven-haired girl plucking her harp strings and singing in a soft pure voice before dinner were more John Ford than Dorian Gray. And Hurd Hatfield was at his best. Our contributions turned out to be invaluable after all. To complete the illusion of a cinematic tableaux, formally clad Yanks, Irish, and South Africans arranged themselves in picnic groups over Ava's gingham tablecloths spread around the grass, where they enjoyed the meal catered in from a Cork hotel, and partook of champagne while the catering staff, I'd say—took more than par.

One waiter was in training for the ballet and, as Dottie Parker so kindly used to say about some of our neighbors, "You practically had to stand on his ankles to prevent him floating away." We learned of the young man's calling when he preferred to grande jetté over the picnickers after collecting their finished plates and executed an arabesque while refilling their glasses. Cut of a different jib altogether, the other waiter, a massive bloke of ginger hair and like complexion, had already too much drink taken halfway through dinner and—leaving his colleague to plié and pirouette through serving of the pudding—established more or less permanent lodging in the downstairs loo.

At one point, by which time the musicians were equally

oiled, a sister or cousin of the bridegroom attempted to partner the budding Nureyev when, lowering his classical standards, he bopped across the dance area, balancing a tray of empty glasses precariously aloft, until I took the tray from his hands, continued with it to the kitchen, and left the dancing fools to pas de deux their toes off. He never left the floor after that, and deigning the waiter's jacket he immediately removed and slung behind the bandstand, I assumed clean-up patrol and completed his appointed rounds, pleased that the fancy dress-shirt studs Ava gave me last Christmas sparkled so brightly against the glasses.

The tough little band leader egged him into performing a rapidly fiddled old country reel, which he attempted with interpretive ballet movements, and our former waiter's star turn ended ignominiously when, whirling out of control, he crashed to the floor at the feet of a dazed Hurd Hatfield who had the haunted look of a man convinced that his entire world was collapsing around him, too, and didn't quite understand how it happened.

The Mexican lady, who hadn't understood anything, watched with an almost beatific expression, stayed until the bitter end when I delivered my last tray of empties. We all stepped over the immense pointy-toed, two-toned cowboy boots of the ginger-haired waiter passed flat-out in the doorway, and our mixed and slurred accents mingled to greet the dawn of the happy wedding day. Ava and I weren't invited to the service, but shortly afterwards Terri Sampson rang from northern California to tell us our names had been listed in the *San Francisco Chronicle*'s society column along with some of the other guests at the Hatfield party. The society page. If they only knew.

After we got it, Dellie's Mercedes was much sought for weddings, and we came as part of the package. Ava decorated; I drove the bridal carriage to the church and the happy couple on to the reception. I drew the line at livery. This was after all free service, an act of good will.

Her old car doing country weddings—Dellie would've

Waiting (in car) with Timmy O'Regan to drive his daughter, Marie, to the church, late 1980s.

loved it. It dressed up nicely; the double-tone shades of white and pale gray appropriately endorsed the occasion and agreed with any mixture of flowers and ribbons.

In the middle of a benevolent summer, Marie O'Regan's wedding day dawned gray, but not soft enough to wilt the yards of white satin ribbon Ava attached to the hood ornament and otherwise festooned around the chassis. Flowers from our garden stayed fresh in the little vials Ava tied over the door handles to good effect, if hindering entry. Balloons left over from our party flitted from the antennae, and transmission fluid flowed from the gear box or wherever it isn't supposed to.

Mechanical things elude me. I find them hectoring, but even so, a real person should have grasped the significance of residue on his garage floor. Ava found it alarming but she kept suspicions to herself when we wound up the boreens to the farm to collect the O'Regans, père et fille. She mentally noted to have Mike Ryan check the motor at the church as quickly and as discreetly as he could.

Bringing a nostalgic lump to my throat, young Donal O'Regan requested my assistance at tying his tie, and time drew short as the bride, framed in the window, twice removed her wedding dress and put it on exactly as before, while her dad shifted his feet in the Timmy Waltz, chain smoked, leaned on the car, and talked to the two of us inside.

Donal O'Regan gets ready for his sister Marie's wedding.

Marie, until then a level-headed young woman of quiet composure, fell apart so strenuously we stopped halfway to the church to insist she take relaxing breaths and to assure that she looked perfectly beautiful; that her worries, "Jesus, Dad, do my big ears show?" were unfounded.

Just before we left for the hotel reception fifteen miles away, Ryan added another can of transmission fluid when no one was looking, and the slow drive through the village, hooting—as they say for honking—with townsfolk coming out of the shops to cheer, was accomplished easily enough. Under the circumstances, the bride and groom wouldn't have noticed the groaning motor, but on the main road the crunching noise became so violent to our ears, Ava over-compensated by speaking too loudly and too fast, and I gunned the motor with such purpose we left the entourage in our wake.

When Marie suggested we wait for the others, I couldn't admit that if we did, she and Stan might have to hitch a lift because, once stilled, I wasn't certain the car would start again. But God grinned, the engine sneezed and caught and we were pulling up to the hotel when the bridegroom asked if there was a problem with the car.

~ ~ ~

For Sean Mulvaney's wedding, they left the date off the invitations and the church had double-booked, causing a last minute change of location to another church and confusion for both sets of wedding guests when signs and directions were posted outside the first one. But our involvement was solely with transportation and a simple matter since Joann, the bride, stayed in our guest cottage the night before.

The day was gloriously sunny and Joann lovely, strolling in our garden in her wedding gown before it was time to leave. Unlike Marie O'Regan, she didn't have to lift her skirts, avoiding mud and muck to get to the car. And the Mercedes behaved.

Ava thought the road-sign warning, "Heavy Plant Crossing," might be in reference to the ambulatory killer plants from her favorite sci-fi thriller, *The Day of the Triffids*. I told her it just meant to watch out for heavy machinery moving in the area. Now, I'm not so sure about that. O'Mahoney has long nurtured teasels in our grounds. "The stately teasel," as Kevin O will have it, a tall khaki-colored plant with long thin leaves and prickly pod blossoms (for want of a better word), has spread its seed widely about the property and they are beginning to gather on the knoll like Triffids plotting attack. I think they're weeds but K. O. insists no farm should be without them—they are invaluable for carding wool. It was a set-up of course. Kevin O regards sheep as kindly as he does cows. He was just waiting for such a day when he and Ava could skip about bursting balloons left over from the pre-wedding dinner we gave the Mulvaneys, and singing "Pop goes the teasel."

Kevin O thinks I'm kidding but I would like to get rid of the plants. Every time I mention it though, they seem to turn and listen. They're taller than I am. Something must be done before it is too late and the teasel goes for Pop.

The prettiest wedding was that of Sean Norris, boy architect. Our only duty was to attend. We drove to Galway to a tiny church in the country with no village or other dwellings in sight, and fortunately went inside early just as the priest came out to light the candles and joined in harmony with a lone singer, a soprano practicing unseen in the choir loft.

Sean's strapping father sobbed from the moment he sat down and continued, increasing in velocity throughout much of the ceremony as his eldest son repeated his vows. Sean and Mary designated their chosen Scripture passages to be read from the seats, making it almost musical as readers changed without the usual awkward pauses when they approach and depart the pulpit. During benediction the soprano sang again, a sweet haunting hymn unknown to us, and Sean himself—nearly doing his dad in altogether—opened the floodgates for the rest of the congregation—still kneeling next to his bride, he began to sing as well.

Coming down the aisle surrounded by his truly beautiful daughters, Timmy O'Regan flashed his remaining teeth so proudly even my eyes brimmed. Or was it because those four stunning women were little girls when we first became neighbors? Led by Nora—the single bridesmaid; trailed by matron of honor Marie, and, unable to walk three abreast down the narrow passage, Catherine and Ann glided just slightly behind their dad, each holding his hand.

Timmy O'Regan and his daughters at their double wedding.

Our little guest cottage has been a blessing. This time one of the bridegrooms and eight of his relatives stayed there the night before the wedding. Cramped together, somehow they all managed to bathe and dress and have breakfast and were still in high spirits when we waved them away to the church in the groom's van, which advertised his exterminating business in large and explicit terms on the side.

"Like the fox—taking them all," Tim muttered outside the church after the double ceremony; a first for the village and for us. He'll be completely undone when it's Nora's turn. So will we. My introduction to Nora was the sound of her singing home the cattle. I remember the three of us cavorting on the bales at the end of a day of haying, and Ava dressing her as Stan Laurel for the childrens' costume parade.

Don Cook offered his garden for Tyler and Ann's nuptials. Tyler's godmother, the Reverend Marni, will tie the knot. Who'd have thought? Now Annie must find courage to tell her Catholic mother that this is the service and wedding they want. We're happy to pick up the tab but Ann said her mother has always envisioned a little something at Saint Patrick's Cathedral in New York. A California poolside ceremony with an Episcopal woman priest may be a cry too far.

It seems that no time at all has passed since my first grandchild was born and my younger son only began to toy with the idea of marriage himself. But Kevin and Carol have already presented us with Morgan's little sister, Kirby, and opened a restaurant in Seattle. Reviews for both the baby and the restaurant are glowing, and after seeing my newest grandchild, I'm certain that one day Kirby will have an equal following. For the time being, however, her dad's place is the one attracting public attention. Though Carol feels she shouldn't make the trip so soon, Kevin will make a lightning appearance and promised to organize the catering for his brother's wedding.

Pressed for suggestions about wedding gifts, Tyler allowed they are pretty well established with household stuff from when he was microwaving for Jesus. I forgot he worked as production assistant or something on a religious cable TV cooking show for a while and they gave him much of the kitchen equipment from the set when it finished. He said they really need cash. We agreed to relay the information but felt many people would rather give something memorable. He said they could use a humidifier.

Ava assumed control, more firmly stressed inquiries as to needs. Flatware perhaps? Place settings? Ty thought a self-making omelet pan would be nice. They have a set of dishes. Thinking she struck a nerve—a set can be added to—Ava urged description of the china. Tyler said they bought it at seven-thirty in the morning.

Through the years, Tyler has managed to leave his wallet on top of a London taxi; his driver's license, alien ID card and billfold on an Irish mountain top; his traveler's checks, passport and cash amidst the throngs of Munich during Oktoberfest—and all the aforementioned in an African cab at dawn. And Ann lost the pants to his wedding suit on a sidewalk somewhere between the clothing shop and her car in Westwood. Each time, he recovered everything intact. Except the trousers. After much searching the store found a matching pair not part of a set but they cost extra and required frantic last-minute alterations. This is definitely the girl for Tyler.

"People don't much believe in miracles anymore," the Reverend Marni began the service. "But the fact that I stand before you as a priest of God is a miracle. That of all the people in this world, Tyler found a beauty who actually understands him is a miracle, too." A murmur of assent circulated the garden. Most of the guests have known each other longer than good manners allow acknowledgment. They remember Marni as a television producer from the days we all associated "rev" with kick-starting;

when the boys were little guys and Tyler talked funny. Some things never change.

Nineteen years ago two seven-year-old boys solemnly swore to be each other's best man. They remained best friends, kept in touch even after Knut Adolphson returned to his native Norway, and Knut came from Norway to keep his promise. During his speech, the best man said he knew his accent was different from his classmates and that drew him to Tyler, who really talked strangely.

I choked up at Kevin's wedding. Seeing Tyler and Ann join hands under the beautiful bower of flowers should have sent me

Tyler and Ann with Reverend Marni at their wedding in California, 1986.

spilling over when Ava took my hand, too, but less than an hour earlier I'd urged the bridegroom to scrub the green mud pack off his face and put on more than the pink jockey shorts he'd been running around in since breakfast. He looked like the Incredible Hulk in identity crisis, a difficult image to shake.

The guitarist and flutist from our hotel played before the service, and for Annie's entrance, and the last strains of "Tyler My Boy" at the end. Unseen, but heard, the gardener next door raked and rasped leaves across pavement during a part of the service; a passing helicopter momentarily drowned the words at one point; and, except when Ava waved the silver cake slicer Ann's aunt had brought over from Ireland, drawing blood from the forehead of a nearby waiter; Roddy McDowall recorded everything on video tape.

Ann's mother voiced some doubts about procedures, but our family has always been cavalier regarding protocol. At our wedding, not only did my bride put my ring on the wrong finger, some of the guests pelted us with gumdrops when they couldn't find any more rice to throw, and my best man fell in the mud while seeing us off and required a cold shower (the consequence of surreptitiously lacing his orange juice with champagne). There were no such problems for Kevin at his brother's wedding. He arranged for staff and the tables and umbrellas placed throughout the garden and oversaw the catering without giving up his place as part of the family. Even with eighty-some guests, a lot of the marvelous spread was left over, and though he didn't tell us, we learned later that Kevin took everything to one of the missions downtown before he flew back to his wife and daughters.

Publicity tour for That's Entertainment, Part II*: Fred and Ava, Gene Kelly (behind Fred), and Johnny Weissmuller (behind Ava).*

Chapter Eighteen

Fred

F. A. is noticeably failing. His inner ear balance problem is no better, weight is down, and, mainly, he is mad as hell. Hard to believe that only six months ago he drove himself to see us after he collected his mail in the mornings, and that we had dinner together five out of seven evenings.

He couldn't attend the wedding but he has made a great effort to come to the hotel while we're here, and in view of his health, we've extended our stay instead of returning to Ireland immediately after the wedding as planned.

Fred has been grousing about old age for a few years; now he is simply mad at it. Frustrated. We sat in the car when I drove him home after a visit of only about forty-five minutes and talked about growing old. He swore a lot—something he doesn't do often, never in front of his daughter or most women. I managed one laugh from him. Sort of a snort. But he seems pretty miserable and apologetic for not feeling up to coming out with us now. His concern about that made me feel terrible.

He thanked me for taking care of his little girl. I reminded him that was his request on our wedding day, but actually, she takes care of me. We spoke about Ava. He patted my leg, said sometimes he wished his wife were as adult as mine. "Are you sure you mean Ava?" He snorted again. I told him we appreciated the fact that there was someone around to make sure he took care of himself. He said he appreciated my telling him so.

For exercise, after I dropped him off, F. A. selected the terrazzo front walk of his house rather than the back lawn. He slipped and conked his noggin. His doctor assured us it was only a bruise That was two days ago.

This morning he rang, asked me to bring him down for a

visit. When I got there he was already outside as always, waiting in glorious Technicolor. He wore a nifty cravat instead of a tie. The tie in place of a belt. Yellow shirt. Beige trousers. A pink sweater matched pink socks. He wore my favorite brown suede shoes with the chains and a sport coat of Donegal tweed. Even a little jewelry. Going public without his hair for the first time in years to my knowledge, a jaunty hat concealed the bald and bruised.

I always drive down into the garage when I bring Fred to L'Ermitage. Other people are seldom there and we can take the lift straight up to our floor so he needn't walk through the busy lobby. Ava was talking to one of the attendants when we arrived and she was visibly surprised at the look of him when her dad emerged from the passenger seat. The men at the car-hire desk reacted, too. In better form than anyone has seen him lately, Fred seemed pleased when they complimented his jazzy threads. It's nearly Easter and Ava told him he looked like an Easter egg. I noticed tears. She was so happy.

We had a few laughs, he gave it his best, but after awhile, the strain of being out began to show and he said it was approaching his lunch time. "I have to go eat ugly soup." F. A. is on a prescribed weight-gaining diet and I suppose the soups are full of things more nutritious than visually appealing.

"I know I have to eat all that stuff," he said on the way home, "But when I'm finished, why do I still have to have five grapes?"

He was serious. I couldn't laugh. And I don't know the answer. As always, he thanked me profusely, a little apologetically, and I tried to lighten it saying that I wanted to go out anyway. Planned to go for a long walk.

"WALK!!" he repeated, recoiling at the thought as if I'd confided a desire to run amok on Rodeo Drive with a chainsaw. "You want to walk?" Then—softly, "Richard, I hate this. I refuse to be a happy old man. But I'm okay. I know you've stayed longer than you should. Tell Ava it's all right to go. I want her to."

I walked for a long time. Wondered what to tell my wife. Thought about my own feelings. Even though he looked great today, F. A. can't last for long. Ava knows that. Now that I've written it, I've confirmed what I've been thinking all afternoon. I don't want him to linger. He is my friend. I love him. But he is Fred Astaire. Fred Astaire must not be an infirm old man. I think Ava feels that. I know Fred does.

Like many others since his marriage, we aren't invited to his house, and coming to us requires enormous effort on his part. I think he more enjoys telephone visits anyway. If we remain beyond another week or so, Fred will realize it is because of him. He has enough on his plate already. If we stay, we'll be like the five grapes.

It's good to be home. We can use a little O'Mahoney levity. I hope it's levity. Kevin O said that since we hired Bob to do the general maintenance, he is at last freed to create a pavilion in the lower field. We are indebted to Monica Mulvaney for her mistaken but inspired idea that we were in search of someone to assist in the garden when she sent Bob Walden to us. Kevin could indeed use some help, but his is a low tolerance quotient and we've not dared suggest that before. A retired navy man, Bob is dependable and quicker than mercury. He is available only a day and a half a week; this is his third week and the results are incredible.

Ava always tries to ring her dad when she thinks he will be in his bedroom and can see the telephone button light flashing. Either the apparatus is faulty or perhaps the sound has been deliberately turned off. Fred's hearing is fine but he never seems to hear the phone ringing anymore. Often, after Ava finally resorted to calling her father via the house phone, he said he had been in his room the whole time but hadn't heard the ring and wasn't in the vicinity to notice the light. Lately she relies mostly on kitchen channels to reach her father though that isn't an easy solution. English isn't readily achieved always and the staff changes with some frequency now.

Until a couple of years ago, F. A. had the same private phone number for over thirty years. We don't know why it was changed after so long, but at least Fred knew about it and we were informed of the fact then. Slightly over a month ago it was changed again, alarming information discovered when, unable to reach her dad on his own line, Ava rang the house and found that number was no longer in service. She called her brother and when he failed, too, Freddie, who lives over a hundred miles north of L.A., got in touch with the old family lawyer, who drove up to the house immediately and found Fred walking around the driveway for exercise.

Fred seemed unaware of the change. He gave his kids the information as soon as he had it himself, but after years of comfortable familiarity, it didn't occur to him so many old friends weren't alerted either. Nor did it occur to us until we ran into the Pecks at a restaurant last month and Greg asked if we had F. A.'s new number, said everyone was frantic. Especially Robert Wagner. We gave them the number which Veronique promised to circulate, and Ava rang R. J. with it the next day. We assume there'll be no other surprises.

~ ~ ~

"Don't disturb her, Dick." He hasn't called me that in years. "Just checking in. Ask Ava to give me a call tomorrow. Love to all."

The phone rang at two-fifteen. Five minutes ago. I'm still reeling. Each night since we came home, I've slept on the bedside nearest the telephone; girded for bad news, I awakened at the first ring. I expected word about F. A., not from him. He rang because he thought he had just missed someone on his personal line, thought it might be Ava. Few people have ever had that number. Possibly only Freddie, Ava, Dellie, Pan, and Bill Self. Fred rang Ava first without thinking of the time difference, and, apologizing for his confusion, he didn't want me to go downstairs to wake her because he thought my appearance at this hour would frighten her. I assured him he was right; my appearance at this hour would traumatize the cat.

He sounded so damned good, I hate waiting. Time enough tomorrow. Ava, too, has been only on the edge of real sleep these past few weeks. Fred used to get a hoot out of phoning us before the system went automatic. Irish operators could never seem to locate our village and the Americans, of course, hadn't a clue. Listening while they searched the lines, F. A. learned to direct the operators through which towns to route connections, and though they never knew who their informant was, it all got very chatty.

Now I'm wide awake. Relaxed awake. A little mental peregrination should do the trick. I'm so relieved I'm going to shift back to my accustomed side of the bed.

Say goodnight, Dick.

Thrilled by my report, Ava rang Fred as soon as the time was feasible. She agreed that his voice was stronger but she thought he was exerting for her benefit because it weakened by the end of their conversation. Still, he was upbeat and Ava is in lighter spirit than she has been since our return. Me, too.

My brother-in-law was quick to allay our fears when he telephoned, but F. A. is in hospital. No one knows where and he is under an assumed name. He has pneumonia and instructions have been given not to put anyone through. We can't even speak to his doctor. Freddie said the word was F. A. wants to spare his children hovering over his deathbed. That certainly sounds like Fred. We have no choice anyway. We've kept the news to ourselves. Bedtime is the worst; Ava starts at every sound. In the protection of the pig room she needn't worry about hearing a middle-of-the-night phone call, but I doubt that she gets much sleep.

Without realizing we're holding vigil, Dave brought Ava a blackbird's nest containing a couple of magpie eggs. Two for joy. Bless your sensitive cop heart, Sarge. And Bob discovered a hedgehog nest under the hydrangea.

Ava needed hedgehogs and birds' nests today.

~ ~ ~

She sits silently, occasionally reaches for my hand, grasps tightly, retreats where thoughts take her. I've never been so impressed with her grace and dignity. Never loved her more. No one is aware of who she is. We accepted no newspapers, hope nobody speaks about her father within our hearing. Ava must realize I am recording in my notebook. Like her, I can't concentrate on reading anything and otherwise I feel so helpless. I am here for her, but grief is so personal and in this case isn't allowed to be personal. That she sits without moving is statement enough. I think Ava is preparing mentally for what lies ahead in Los Angeles.

The travel agent had been alerted that we might need an emergency departure so arrangements were made as much as possible before the news of Fred's passing reached the general public.

We were informed immediately. I took the call from Freddie's wife, but Ava already knew when I went to her room to tell her. She heard the ring. Normally no one would telephone so early. Thank God for the time difference; the news vultures didn't receive the word until hours later, giving us a chance to get things together, and Frankie came out to field and screen calls so that we could talk to friends, evade the press and the curious. Even so I couldn't avoid a few words with reporters, and after speaking with them, some words came to mind that I wish I'd used.

They seemed surprised that I wouldn't let them speak to Ava or tell them our flight plans and that we didn't know and didn't care about the terms of the will. They were surprised, too, that we'd seen Fred so recently and that we spoke to him only last week. Through the assistance of neighbors and friends at the airport, and the furtive ploys of the travel agent, we managed to get out of Cork and London just a step ahead of the gentlemen of the press; they'll probably make up intrigue and tempest anyway. I don't know why they feel that happy relationships won't sell newspapers.

I expect they would have little interest in our real memories. My memories. Ava's are another level. But I'm going to spend the rest of the flight reminiscing, writing random thoughts about my friend. I need to.

F. A.

For such a private man, he sometimes did the most amazing public things. Ava once left her wallet on the top of the seat back of her open convertible when she pulled away from a filling station, and all the contents blew out. Fred decided the bills and cards were strewn about the railroad tracks along Santa Monica Boulevard near the station, and after dinner insisted upon searching the rubble between the ties to the great amusement of the passing parade of general public. We didn't find anything, but the wallet was later brought up to the house by a one-armed man who found the address on Ava's driver's license.

~

I remember:

The two of us sneaking into an X-rated movie and Fred's rapid departure out the door when the woman at the candy counter boomed across the lobby, "Did you see who THAT was?" Ava said she was going to steal one of his scarves and post it to him with the message, "You left this at the Pussycat Theater." I'm sorry we didn't do it.

~

He used to send letters to the editors himself if he had a gripe or even a compliment, and loved it if the fictitious names he signed appeared in print. He was a little paranoid about it though, would type the letters and mail them from different parts of town.

~

The night in response to singing on our front porch, we opened the door to find Fred and Hermes wearing shoulder-length fright wigs, headbands and dirty faces, love beads, and carrying flowers. They'd come from mingling with the latter-day hippies on

Sunset Boulevard and got away with it because that crowd was always so spaced they wouldn't have believed their eyes anyway.

~

For its come-back issue, *Liberty* magazine hoped to honor F. A. as Entertainer of the Century. At that time he was well into his seventies and had been performing professionally since he was five years old. He groused and groaned about the "intrusion," and made us attend the luncheon with him. Fred said he felt he had to accept the award because it would be rude if he didn't and they might give it to somebody else—and "that would be wrong."

~

When I first began dating Ava, I was illustrating a catalogue for the Arthur Murray dance studios, and one evening Fred came in while I was waiting for Ava in her sitting room. To make conversation, I mentioned I had to draw a couple dancing the Paso Doble and had no idea what it looked like. I was given an on-the-spot demonstration but couldn't remember anything to sketch later because I was so overwhelmed that Astaire had danced for me. Ava agreed that could be disconcerting; even she had trouble rationalizing why Fred Astaire spun around her bedroom some mornings when he came to wake her for school.

~

Because I was her escort for her twenty-first birthday party, I went up to the house early, nervous as hell in a new dinner jacket I couldn't afford, wary of the evening ahead. I wasn't new to the game but this was big-time stuff and I felt insecure regarding the reactions to the obvious difference between our ages. Fred met me at the door, made me a drink, and took me by the arm on a tour of the place where the band was setting up and waiters were finalizing touches. He kept asking questions: Did I think the dance floor extending over the lawn was too near the pool? Were the lights and tables okay? Did I think the music would disturb the neighbors?

I suddenly realized the Great International Sophisticate was as nervous as I was. Ava arrived to prove us both right, said she had whiplash from slipping outside her bedroom door, and walked strangely the rest of the otherwise splendid evening.

~

I can still see F. A. with camellias decorating the band of his Panama hat which he wore to pick the flowers outside his dining room window many mornings.

~

I can hear him discussing the soap operas with Jo. After the programs were finished, she came from the kitchen, he came from his bedroom, to meet in the marble rotunda entry hall where they would sit, facing each other on uncomfortable straight-backed Chinese Chippendale chairs and argue and speculate over the goings-on. Then he would ring Dellie in Phoenix to rehash and see if she confirmed his and his housekeeper's suspicions.

~

He wasn't a reader; this friend of kings once asked me to tell him what *Romeo and Juliet* was about, and when we found a letter to Ava's grandmother from A. A. Milne, Fred remarked that he knew him, too, said there was usually a small boy with him—his son—Christopher something,

~

He loved to putter, to fix things, and spent a lot of time in hardware shops and the dime store. When Jo complained she thought the new electric broom was pulling too much pile from the carpet, Fred cut the teeth off rendering it useless. But he was proud that he solved the immediate problem.

~

He glued rhinestone earrings from the dime store to his house slippers.

~

Ava's great-aunt on her mother's side left Fred a Rolls Royce when she died. He already had one, so when we were without a car just before our move abroad, he suggested we use the extra

Rolls, a Silver Cloud, which we accepted with some trepidation, and when it refused to go more than halfway across a four-way intersection, I had to push it the rest of the way—a sight of some hilarity to other motorists. I phoned Ava; she contacted her father, who informed the auto club and then beat them to the site of my embarrassment to point and scoff like the others. The reason for his glee escaped me until he mentioned his relief that the car malfunctioned while I was driving and not him. No matter how many standing ovations he had received in his lifetime, F. A. never quite believed the reverence in which he was held. It hadn't occurred to him that most people would push a Rolls Royce for Fred Astaire.

Then there were times he had cause: when he dropped a bottle of cough syrup at the checkout counter of the drugstore, and even though none of it splashed on her, the woman behind him yelled at him and continued yelling all the way out the door.

"I feel under house arrest." Fred would ring our room at the Connaught when we were together in London while he cut a record with Crosby. "Come talk to me." And I would find him alone in the lobby like a naughty little boy sentenced to sit in the corner.

He didn't like the lounge where he felt too approachable, but he couldn't have been more visible than in the seat he usually chose by the front door where I'd join him, and sitting side by side, we would watch people coming and going. It was a canny choice; almost everyone entering looked straight ahead, and few people would recognize Astaire out of context, sitting in a straight-backed chair just to the left of the entry way. Sometimes we were rewarded: waiting Ava's arrival for dinner, we sat in the usual spot when a sheep-like sound echoed down the corridor. As was his custom when trying for my attention, my father-in-law jabbed an elbow in my ribs. I used to come away from some movie matinees with him in serious need of surgical binding tape. The ba-aa-ing sound continued until a very old gentleman approached the dining room entrance. "Your usual table?" greeted the maitre d' escorting him in, still bleating. Fred nearly knocked me off my chair and we were out of control when Ava joined us.

~

Fred was tickled by his mother's attempts at sneaking stuff through customs, but he suspected we were cheating the government if we brought in duty-free liquor when he met our flight, and finally he asked that we not do it, said he would pay the difference.

~

Like royalty, F. A. exercised amazing bladder control, but mid-drive to the next location when we stopped to lunch in a small Irish hotel, he asked that I go with him to the men's room. A fellow was just leaving as we entered and nobody else came in, but there was a reception line of both sexes waiting in the hallway when we emerged.

Fred didn't stop; he murmured appreciation for a few compliments and the Irish didn't press for more. Used to such attentions, Fred was clearly disturbed that they'd been offered outside a public lavatory. I told him that the last time I'd peed with a movie star was at Chasen's and I stood next to Roger Moore who allowed that we could get frostbite from the ice cubes they put in the bottom of the urinals. My retort was something on the order that if Roger could get frostbite, he was a better man than I, oh, Gunga Din. It cheered Fred but I don't think he understood about the ice at Chasen's and I doubt that he ever read Kipling.

~

He loomed in the doorway while Ava and I watched *Easter Parade* yet again. Usually if he found us viewing one of his films, Fred left with some disparaging indictment of our sensibilities, or else he switched the television off and settled to speak of other things. That afternoon he seemed absorbed in the performance himself, suddenly began to cry. "I was so damned good," he wailed rubbing his eyes, and water poured between his fingers. He'd come down the hall earlier, heard the TV, and gone for a wet sponge to set us up.

~

He saved Garbo's cigarette ashes in an envelope after she called on his mother. For Pan, he said. But Hermes never received them.

~

A Sunday morning at Dublin Zoo when F. A. danced with an orangutan. Separated by glass from Fred, Ava, George Penny and me, the orang gave a performance he probably did for everyone but not, I expect, with the same results. A sort of vaudeville turn: Jump up and down, spin around, ending on the beat, arm extended, hand outstretched. Da da de da—Hey! We were the only people in the monkey compound. To the animal's and our delight, F. A. copied the routine, then the two of them repeated it together with a big finish when Fred pressed his palm flat against the window; the orang mirrored on the other side, and they moved their hands as one in a wide circle. I'm glad we were without a camera. So sweet a moment is best left a memory to call back when the heart weighs heavy.

Kidding him, Jimmy Cagney said that there were traces of the hoodlum in Astaire. That holds true for his sister. But Dellie was more on the surface, less deep than F. A., who when he tried to be racy still seemed like a nice kid testing the waters to see what he could get away with. He relished the bizarre clippings we sent him from London and he was intrigued by the underworld as he imagined it. Fred might have wished for a private image different from his public one but he couldn't quite pull it off. The adjectives applied to him were true. He was a good fellow—never a guy. F. A. bowed out at the right time. But I shall miss him terribly. Me and the world.

~ ~ ~

Though sunset begins, Ava and Betty remain on the beach, gleaning the shore of sea glass. Most of the past three days have

Fred Astaire (1899–1987). PHOTO: AVA ASTAIRE McKENZIE

been the same. Betty, bless her, invited us to join her in Carmel after the ordeal of last week; the best possible interlude before we return south for another week of touching base with old friends.

Seclusion in this lovely place is exactly what Ava needed. No phone ringing for us. Just the company of Betty and her dogs and some inquisitive otters and seals. For me, the added pleasure of familiarity—the sounds and smells of the northern California seacoast. I grew up on the other side of this bay. The ladies seem not to tire searching for the bright bits of weathered glass, and although I've foraged with them a couple of times, I would have elected to remain up here in the house, alone with my thoughts, even if Betty hadn't dismissed my treasures as "sea plastic."

We've had some laughs. With Betty it's included in the territory and we owe it to Allen and Fred.

We said goodbye to F. A. privately. In accordance with his wishes, he was buried beside Ava's mother—close to his mother and sister. Fred specified that there would not be a public funeral or a memorial service. We were told that at her press conference Robyn announced there would be a memorial later. She was unaware of his wishes I suppose. Of course he was right.

There were tributes from all over the world; those from America were the sort usually reserved for great statesmen. An organized memorial now would be anti-climactic and a public service could have easily degenerated into a circus. But those were not Fred's reasons for the privacy. He left a written statement that he had received so much in his lifetime, he felt it was more than enough.

Our boys recorded the television tributes for us but we aren't ready to hear F. A.'s voice or see him in motion. People mean well when they say how proud the programs must make the family feel and they are right, but by depicting his work and artistry, the programs show *him.* We need to adjust, to let go. Her brother said he isn't sure if he will ever see the tapes and I don't think that Ava will either. Betty told us after all the years she still finds it painful to hear or see Allen on an old show. But it is gratifying to know that someone we loved was loved by so many others who feel they have lost him, too. Their words help.

Fred once accused me of being sneakily well-dressed. I didn't know what he meant exactly, but after he said it I gave special attention to my attire when we were together. In that respect, I was struck by the appearance of we five at his graveside. Our clothes told so much about us.

Ava wore a dress of Dellie's. Simple; dark green silk shot with colors. Hermes, medium somber, with the Italian cut and flair that always marks his costume. I chose what F. A. called "the uniform": the blue blazer, gray trousers, striped tie and white shirt that he told me was always correct. Freddie was tieless but in a white shirt and tweed jacket with a spot on it he found in his father's closet. He hadn't brought a coat. Freddie didn't know how special was the one he selected: an Irish tweed F. A. purchased during the filming of *The Purple Taxi* in Dublin, and Ava and I had been with him when he chose the fabric. Robyn wore dark glasses, tailored white slacks with a rhinestone belt, an off-white blouse and running shoes.

Bill Self told us he had been at the cemetery, unseen—viewing from a distance. Bill and Hermes were Fred's closest friends. Bill perhaps more the confidant, a pal for over thirty years. Whenever possible he and F. A. played gin rummy after church on Sunday until it became too much of an effort, and I cannot believe that Fred ever knew that his contact with the Selfs had been inexplicably cut off during his last few months shortly after Bill and Peggy told Robyn that they'd run into us at the White Elephant Club in London. Some speculated that since the phone numbers were changed without informing friends and—worse—family, it seemed as if Fred were being purposely isolated.

Of all people, Bill Self should not have had to learn of Fred's death through a general newscast or to attend his funeral surreptitiously. We are heartened by his determination not to let his best friend leave without bidding him good-bye somehow, but I'm saddened that he couldn't have been with us to do so. Though Bill and Peggy Self have been our longtime friends, too, we didn't actually see each other during our visits and weren't aware of conditions at the end. But when similar objections were raised regarding Hermes' presence at the service, Ava insisted he be included, and to make certain, we drove him.

To shut out Hermes Pan was unthinkable. He had been F.A.'s associate since the beginning of the film career. He is devoted to Ava and Freddie, adored their mother, and even resembled Astaire enough to be sometimes mistaken for him. Pan is family.

Monsignor James O'Callaghan—Father Jim—co-officiated

Ava, Hermes Pan, and Baryshnikov at the American Film Institute tribute to Fred Astaire, 1981.

GLOBE PHOTO

the service with the rector from Beverly Hills' All Saints Episcopal. Although F. A. was neither Jewish or Roman Catholic, a Hebrew reading was included in the service: touchingly appropriate as indeed was the presence of Monsignor, an intimate of the Astaires for nearly as long as Pan. Father Jim spoke at Ava's mother's and Adele's services and it was he who demanded that the children be alerted.

Robyn wanted to watch the interment and since Freddie had driven her he remained, too. But the rest of us had no wish to see the least earthbound man we knew lowered into the ground. Certainly not his daughter. Hermes and Father Jim returned to the hotel with us for lunch and our own gentle wake.

Judging from Robyn's apparent and understandable disorientation, I'm amazed to hear she was able to return to work at the track the next day; probably very wise of her. Some time ago, F. A. said we were being good sports always inviting Robyn to dinner with him but to let it ride, and though I think it might have pleased him, I was relieved that she chose otherwise. Our evenings would have lost the spark and spontaneity that made them special.

After the burial, in honor of that lovely man, the four of us tried to keep conversation as light as possible, and Father Jim provided a marvelous anecdote at lunch—something so like Fred: As a young man, before entering the priesthood, Monsignor sought any employment he could find in the rough times following the depression and one job was a janitor at MGM. Taken with the charm of the Irish kid who cleaned his dressing room, F. A. invited him out for a square meal and, in a borrowed suit, Jim found himself at a famous restaurant having dinner with Fred and Phyllis Astaire, Hermes Pan, and the Alfred Vanderbilts. Monsignor O'Callaghan at seventy-odd is still handsome, at that time he must've had movie star quality. It isn't surprising that Mr. Vanderbilt laughed and asked what he really did at the studio when Jim said he was the janitor and had trouble convincing F. A. to drop his empty beer cans in the wastebasket instead of around the room.

Alfred probably still doesn't believe it, but the story is verified by H. Pan and a perfect summation of the Astaire character; Fred liked the fellow who cleaned his dressing room, reason enough to have him out with other people he liked. That attitude is my wife's greatest legacy from her dad. As they say about her in Ireland, she has no sides. What you see is what she is. Ava is the same whether she is dancing with a duke or scouring an arthritic elderly neighbor's cook stove. I've seen her do both.

She sleeps untroubled. How different this flight. We will soon be back in our garden and won't cringe everytime the telephone sounds. I expect Ava will return to the bedroom upstairs and I'll be back down in the pigsty. We found that in spite of the recent necessity for it, we really did sleep better apart. I can always visit. I'm so relieved to ramble—jotting nonsense, aware that the lady beside me can settle in now to the period of healing begun when we buckled our seat belts in the knowledge we'll be in Ireland when we remove them.

Yesterday was Independence Day. Everyone has been so great; we got through it but I would rather remember the holiday for that long ago Fourth of July morning when we delivered the calf and helped a new life begin.

If it weren't for the help and protective consideration of L'Ermitage Hotel, this difficult time would've been harder. Flowers never stopped. The hotel provided a massive arrangement waiting in our rooms when we arrived and others came from all over the country. By the time we left for Carmel, we'd run out of space for them.

Of all the tender demonstrations, the most touching came from Emil, one of the young men who doubles as porter and parking attendant. In case of waiting reporters when we arrived, we asked the driver to go directly to the hotel garage instead of unloading in front as usual, and Emil opened the door without knowing who the passengers were. Recognizing Ava, he began to cry. I went ahead to register and, at the lift, looked back to see them still standing at the car; Emil with a suitcase in each hand and his head on Ava's shoulder as she patted consolation. And I nearly lost control myself when all the staff on duty came to offer their sympathies at the check-in desk.

The get-togethers weren't really sad affairs. F. A. would have hated that. Mostly they were light-hearted salutes. He would have hated that, too. Gene gave a dinner at our hotel the night we returned from Carmel. Ava thought it not good timing but wished she'd had a camera as we said goodnight to the group. Kelly, Cyd, Tony Martin, Hermes Pan; a lot of her childhood waved from that elevator.

Leonard Gershe and Gloria Romanoff made the evening of most blithe spirit at Trader Vic's—one of Fred's favorite places, but I couldn't help thinking that the last time we were there with F. A., Randolph and Pat Scott joined us. Randy was Ava's godfather and only a few months ago we lost him, too.

It was touching that so many waiters at the restaurants F. A.

frequented made such a point of speaking their condolences, and some offered comments better unheard, but we cherish one observation consistent among them all: they said when they saw Fred out with us—he was always laughing.

Our evening with Bob Wagner—special. R. J. adored Fred. We were already seated when he arrived at the restaurant carrying a pair of clogs brought from Switzerland for one of the waiters—the sort of thing Ava does, and because he wanted a time of "just family," he came alone. R. J. went to school with Ava's half-brother, Pete, and long before F. A played his screen father, he knew him as just one of the school dads.

Having entertained F. A. often at his house, one our oldest friends, Don Cook, wanted to do something, and we are grateful for the gathering of friends he arranged in the same garden where Tyler and Ann were married.

Roddy, of course, was Roddy. An astute guy with an ability to get directly to the heart of things. Roddy is good stuff. Wicked and witty and tender and generous.

Understandably, Freddie returned to his family without further participation. Never much of a socializer, her brother didn't know these people the way Ava does nor, for that matter, do I.

F. A. knew I kept a journal, something that I hope will make an interesting pastiche for my family one day. Once at Lismore, Dellie asked if she could read what I was always scribbling and she must have mentioned it to Fred, because from time to time he would inquire how it was coming along. Although he knew it was just family stuff, mostly about life with Ava, he got the notion it was fiction. Sometimes I wonder about that myself. Just as Adele was convinced that Helen Rayburn had been in the circus because we told her Helen wasn't hurt when she tripped in our pasture because she knew how to fall, F. A. subscribed to the idea that I was writing a novel and often said he admired my ability to create plots. After repeated explanation that this is sort of a diary in which he features with the rest of the gang, but his daughter is the star character, he finally got the picture. He liked that, but he said I should still write a book. How I wish I had his faith. Fred's and Dellie's ways of looking at things were so much more inventive.

The maitre d' at The Bistro always called him "Misterfredastaire" as if it were one word. Kevin and Tyler called him "Mr. A."

So long Mr. A. Misterfredastaire.

You made me laugh too much to cry for you now.

Home. Sunday afternoon. The sun's broad smile spread across the mountain, down over a church steeple into the valley and beyond to the ocean, and someone leaned against my shoulder at the summer festival up near Goats' Path. I turned to see who would have pressed so firmly and was introduced to an unattended dapple pony making a friendly overture. How blessed we are to be a part of this now.

Antique clocks number among eclectic collectibles throughout our house and only two work with any regularity. Ava set all the permanently stilled timepieces at quarter to three, the opening lyrics to "One For My Baby." Commonly credited to Sinatra, the song was really introduced by F. A.

I don't know at what time our days have begun or ended these past few weeks but they've been quiet and peaceful and kept to ourselves. Mostly sunny days. We've barbecued in the garden, walked the meadows, worked, and tried to keep up with the mountain of correspondence, and this morning came to the aid of a young blackbird that had caught its wing in netting, trying to get at the gooseberries. Once cupped in my hands he stopped thrashing long enough for Ava to extricate the wing and flew away without a hint of appreciation.

This evening for the first time we saw an otter playing in the cove, and when we got up to leave, we noticed a small shark circling the jetty directly below where we'd been dangling our feet.

He was probably only a harmless basking shark and he couldn't reach us, but seeing a shark in so close does give an old beach boy pause.

Kevin rang to check in and tell us that Morgan requested polka-dot presents and chocolate cake for her birthday, and Kirby fell on the cake before they could light the candles, and they'd felt Grannie Ava's influence six thousand miles away.

Hidden on our little beach—seen only by her sister and, unknowingly, by Ava, Timmy's sister, the nun, tied on orange water wings and splashed in the bay.

I just came in from turning hay in the northeast field with Kitty and Timmy. I think we're back on course. As F. A. himself used to say: Another phase has been ended.

Letters of sympathy for Ava—admiration for Fred—still arrive daily. They represent a cross section from the very famous to everyday people and those who didn't know her dad at all. One lovely sentiment that Ava wished she could acknowledge came from Scotland, was addressed "To the Daughter of Fred Astaire—Ireland," and signed simply: "A Fan."

My favorite came from an elderly pharmacist we met walking on our boreen a few summers ago.

Dear Ava McKenzie:

On the strength of having met your good husband and yourself at your charming home on the point, I feel I want to sympathize with you on the death of your beloved father.

I was first enthralled by the dancing of himself and his sister in a musical comedy in London many years ago. Ever since, I associate him with a few lines of our poet, W. B. Yeats:

For the good are always merry
Save by an evil chance.
And the merry love to fiddle
And the merry love to dance.

For me, your father is the epitome of those lines. God rest his dear soul.

Nancy McCarthy

Fred and Ava in Ireland, 1950s.

Chapter Nineteen

My Astaire Way to Paradise

Named for Ava's great-uncle, Henry Bull, our new kitten, with a perfect circle marking each side, quickly became O Henry. Then, "Ohhh Henry." "Now—NO Henry!" Possibly not Henry at all. Tim, the vet, said he had never seen a female in those gray tones and the kitten certainly behaves like a male. Henry might need an "etta" but we'll stick with the name.

Henry's presence has been more therapeutic for Ava than I'd dared hope. She has been quieter than usual but now the sounds of Ava are beginning to be heard around the place again. Yelps and crashes, giggles when she drops our dinner on the floor, or more likely—and worse—when she trips up the stairs and spills my drink because a small gray paw suddenly bats at her from between the newel posts.

~ ~ ~

Rereading an old and treasured book, Ava exclaimed, "It's like reading it all over again!" Welcome back, Sweetheart.

~ ~ ~

Saturday, we planned a supper of cold vegetables, shrimp and mussels left over from lunch Ava gave Sara Giles (from *Vanity Fair* magazine), who flew from New York to interview her for a magazine piece about F. A. Before we could open the fridge door, the police sergeant appeared suffering serious dehydration. Well out of danger at midnight, he left and I reeled to bed without eating. I lost a pound. Ireland is the only country I know where a quiet evening at home with the soberest intentions can be corrupted by the law.

~ ~ ~

Ava allowed that she is getting tired of the shrews in the night. Papa done told her not to leave the window opened for Henry.

~ ~ ~

Sunday, the Collins sisters, who gave us Henry, and their sister, the nun visiting from Africa, called out to check on his progress. They were tucking into their first gins and tonics when Pat Mulvaney rang to let us know he was coming to collect some of the wine he stores in our shed and would bring a friend to help so as not to disturb us. Ava went down anyway when she heard the car because she wanted to send some vegetables to his wife. The phone rang again. I excused myself from the ladies to answer it in the bedroom, nearly dropped the receiver when I glanced out the window and saw my wife handing a head of lettuce to the Taoiseach—the Prime Minister of Ireland.

I stayed with the single glass of wine, but after watching the Prime Minister juggle lettuces and burgundy through the front gate, our guests settled back for another wee drinkie abetted by wife. With respect to the Sister sister, I kept gentlemanly tolerant, and we had the supper planned for the night before around midnight after they left. I lost another pound.

Wednesday we expected Hurd Hatfield and Maggie, his houseguest, for lunch—one-ish. At two, H. H. rang to cancel.

Thwarted by time yet again, they thought it best to press on to Kerry without delay. We can't be annoyed with Hurd as we might with someone in tune with reality. We especially forgive his vagueness now, because not long ago Ava's prediction of bad luck when Hurd brought white thorn into the house came true. Hurd forgot he'd left his electric blanket turned on and he lost some major things before the ensuing fire was contained. Without Hurd and Maggie, however, the two of us, who had Ava's splendid and beautiful meal, also consumed the wine meant for a quartet. We saved the cheese board for dinner, by which time a visiting young electrician who is working in Pat Mulvaney's pub in the village appeared to install illegal phone jacks, and the Prime Minister came for more lettuce and left with string beans from lunch that I couldn't eat because they felt rough and gave me gooseflesh like peach fuzz and dentist's tongue depressors do.

Thursday we went to Lismore to see Adele's stepson and his wife who rented the castle for a fortnight. Being there was easier than anticipated. We thought we could never go back after Dellie died, but this was family of sorts and we wanted to see Clodagh again and Con Willoughby. Our last visit had been for Adele's memorial service held in the church.

Dellie wished to be cremated, with such remains placed near her mother in the family plot, but Ava brought a few of her ashes back to Ireland. Some she spread over the graves of Dellie's children buried in the churchyard, and some she kept for our own garden in a spot known only to herself. Ava had hoped to scatter the rest in Dellie's favorite part of the castle grounds but the castle was rented then as well. She could hardly knock on the door and announce her intentions. Ava quietly gave her aunt to the breezes over Lismore Castle's garden wall. Dellie would've hated the fact that the castle is now rented to others, but how she would've laughed at sneaking over the wall.

Last night after I'd gone to bed around midnight a car stopped outside our gate, turned the motor off, and I thought someone got out. I told Ava that I'd gone upstairs without turning on the lights because I had a better view from up there, but when I did, the car was turning around, and though I could see shapes I wasn't sure if there were two people or if one was just the headrest over the passenger seat. "I'm never sure about that either," she agreed. "I always think they're nuns."

And the beat goes on. Emptying the clothes dryer like the good spouse I am, I intended to go the step further and fold her underwear neatly away, but decided just to dump it on her bed instead when I discovered in her underwear drawer a foil-wrapped triangle of cheese and a biscuit resting on a lace-bordered square of apricot-colored silk. Ava's initial reaction to my bizarre discovery was: "That's not where I keep my knickers." Then, accusingly, "I never use that drawer. They would have stayed there forever, you know." Although she apparently truly doesn't understand how it came to be there, Ava seems more concerned with the quality of the cheese, says it looks like the kind they give you on airplanes.

Given that I once found an electric blanket in my sister Charlotte's fridge, and my mother baked a dozen eggs in their carton after forgetting that she'd stashed them in the oven, I guess that cheese and biscuits in my wife's lingerie drawer should come as no surprise. Does karma select the women in one's life? I wonder.

Shortly after his wife died, Pat Mulvaney suffered a severe stroke and, though undergoing therapy, was expected to spend the rest of his years in the convalescent home. Our friend Christine is the only local physiotherapist and when Ava heard that Christine had a commitment abroad for several months, she asked to be taught the exercises Pat would require. My wife wouldn't want this recorded but I am so proud of her. Ava turned into a marine drill sergeant. She forced Pat to work every day and continued the routine after he came home until, within an amazingly short span, the man who everyone said wouldn't leave the hospital alive was behind the wheel again. That might be a double-edged achievement. Mulvaney was a menace on these roads before his stroke.

This morning, as has been my custom for several years, I awakened on the dot of six and, as usual, prepared to drift off again until a more civilized hour, but my eyes snapped open as jarringly as when a window shade escapes in the drawing and rolls itself back up. Cattle stampeding outside the bedroom tend to have that effect. When the rumbling diminished and silence resumed, I sank back into the pillows, smiling that I thought I'd heard Mary Monica's cows on the loose again and ravaging the garden where we've been weeding and setting out new plants all week. But Mary Monica's herd is no more.

After two of them failed health inspection, she was forced to give up the remaining stock as well because she seemed unable to contain them in her own fields. Playing the helpless innocent she pretended they always escaped but in fact, because her grazing land is inadequate, we all suspected she drove them out herself, and since almost all the farmers in the area are related in one way or another and regard her to be a touch dim, they endured her free-rangers until there became a very real danger of them contaminating others.

Mary Monica no longer searches for her prodigals late mornings after she is sure they've feasted enough to content themselves with her leaner pastures and, in spite of the years of griping and shouting for vengeance from higher places, I miss her.

I remember the first morning I saw her approaching through the mist, her long ginger-striped gray hair escaping from the cowl of her-full length dark cape which was blowing in the wind. A painter's dream, at first I believed her to be Asian-Indian or African but as she came closer, shockingly vivid blue eyes shone above the high cheek bones of a delicate and very, very dirty

Irish face. According to a neighbor who trained as a nurse, Mary Monica often fell asleep by an open fire and came for help one middle of the night when a live coal had fallen out and burned her leg, but she was so black from accumulated grime and coal dust, she had to be bathed before they could locate the injury. I tried painting her once. She always carried a walking stick nearly as bent and gnarled as herself, and even though I included her constant companion, a surprisingly chipper little terrier, in the piece, the end result was more doom than drama. I appeared to have captured the angel of death on canvas.

Mary Monica still lives on the hill but it's not the same. She sort of lost spirit when her cattle were taken and she could no longer play the game. Cleaned up and better groomed, she turned out to be a rather handsome old girl—and there *is* something girlish about her with those startling eyes, dainty, even features and the openness of a somewhat mentally hesitant woman who has always lived alone, albeit on one of the choicest properties here about. She is shyly sociable when met on the boreen—rarely now—but not, I'm sure, as simple as most people say, and I bet Mary Monica misses that cunning, blackened old crone who once so sweetly thanked me for helping her drive her cows when I came shrieking out the gate after them, as much as I do.

Mary Monica isn't the same so neither is the painting. I kept the background but replaced the despairing figure with a likeness of Olivia, the Ferguson's prolific sow, gazing out to sea in the setting sun. Pig pictures are highly saleable and I'm nothing if not pragmatic.

No, it wasn't Mary Monica's cattle that roused me from my bed this pure and clear morning. It was fifteen of Mr. O'Donovan's playful bullocks who had somehow overcome the O'Donovan pasture security system. He is a gentle man of strong integrity, and since we're so close to the water and situated, too, near cliffs dangerous to the frisky and untried, I considered it an act of good faith to drive his cattle back to the main coast road whence they came; but little bulls, I learned, do not accept directions happily, and fifteen little Irish bulls facing down one morning-frail, easily-cowed old Yank, is not the way I like to greet the day.

After swigging a hefty draught of delicious air and nearly wincing under the heavy-duty glory of the morning, I was pleased to have been called out so early but also noted that though only waist high—if just one of the boys decided to charge in the accustomed fashion with lowered head, I would be dealt a serious mischief; I didn't brazen authority as I would larger cows, and sidled over to the car, fortunately left outside overnight. Cattle droving in Dellie's old Mercedes . . . Yeeehah!

Nudging each other into the hedgerows and stopping to sniff out goodies, the gang took its bloody own time. Herding them home wasn't quite the snap expected with the more docile cows under like circumstance, and once there, ignoring the cattle-guard grid in the driveway, some of the delinquents maneuvered around it directly upon the lawn, her oasis in Mootown, which Mrs. O'Donovan keeps beautifully manicured and flower bordered.

Irish farm folk, at least those with whom I'm familiar, seem to sleep in longer than their counterparts elsewhere and they tend to work later to compensate. I'm a basic night owl, too, but not being able to rouse and alert at least one member of the family while trying to keep its stock from dead-heading the hydrangeas severely tests one's understanding nature. Even their rotten dogs, ordinarily out harassing passing motorists, were silent and nowhere to be seen when I elected to just return home and try to contact an O'Donovan by telephone—let the beasts do what they would. At least they were safely out of harm's way away from the cliff's edge. I had done the neighborly thing. With that in mind and in the knowledge that I'd blocked the boreen with the car in order to dissuade any silly buggers from pulling an about-face, I nearly ran into the jetty wall when I rounded the turning and confronted all the bulleens huffing and puffing at the garden gate exactly where I'd found them before.

Finally annoyed enough to get up and answer my persistent ringing, a junior O'Donovan consoled and assured me that I had not fallen victim to a cruel druid prank this morning of the summer solstice: they have over thirty calves and the balance of the herd must've returned from wandering further up the boreen, indeed towards the fearsome cliffs, while I was attempting to guide their compatriots back to home grounds. I was thanked greatly, if with some amusement and, except for one missing, all was put to rights shortly following breakfast. At lunchtime, I discovered the renegade, who, entertaining notions beyond his years, had somehow contrived to scale the wall and barbed-wire fence into the field with our own heifers. I rang the O'Donovans once again.

Ava slumbered unaware of her husband's wrangling expertise but, then, neither was I with her when she swam with a mink; the same, we think, that once came to stalk our goldfish but perhaps it was only Ava's company he sought. We've since seen him often enough, lurking near the jetty these light, late evenings when we've been there marveling as the phosphorous sparkles up through the water, and the assertiveness of his stare implies more cheek than curiosity. He certainly is gorgeous but I don't like him much. Minks enjoy sport killing to the degree that they've wiped out some of our neighbor's entire poultry population in one go without eating any, and will often tackle animals greater than themselves. They are vicious. Not to be encouraged. But Ava is thrilled that a mink swam in her little secluded inlet near our point when she did and shrugs away my concern at their proximity to each other.

Bucolic in excess, this has been quite a day, most of which, like the previous week, has been devoted to slogging in the garden, I mostly tending flowers while Ava coaxes and thins vegetables, after which she insists it is her religious need to cool and cleanse in the icy Atlantic waters—but before she quit for her lunatic plunge, six swans flew over bringing the usual tears to her eyes. Swans are quite territorial, only three live over by the estuary, and when they fly they're roof-top level when they pass the house. These were much higher, underwings and bellies radiant in the sun, and we reckon they've flown some distance with a determined location in mind. Seldomly glimpsed on the move, they are wondrous to behold, a sight we've yet to experience without a sigh of delight.

After Ava returned from frolicking with her pal, the predator, as just desserts for hours of tilling sod, we repaired to the lower garden with a glass of cool white wine to enjoy a little country night music. I love the evening birds—the swallows choreographing songs of the blackbird and skylark, but we were offered a more eclectic ensemble when the peacock called from wherever he lives, somewhere near the estuary, and was answered by a rooster. Bubba the seagull, who has been a regular boarder ever since he saw me throwing some fish scraps off the jetty and followed me home a couple of summers back, arrived to add his screams of hunger from the cottage roof which, in turn, brought response from a cuckoo: a chorale repeated until I thought to run in for a tape recorder, but was concluded before I could do so, when an oystercatcher flew over adding his kleep (with a K) warning of a crowd of street gang starlings who descended on the garage roof cursing and looking for a rumble.

Bubba the seagull at Clonlea.

Later, while I was watering the squashes, Ava called for me to come back to the terrace quickly and quietly. Unmoving, a hedgehog stood directly next to the chair leg. At first, thinking it was Henry approaching, Ava said she paid no attention to the figure at her feet, but then she remembered that Henry never moves anywhere gradually, and glanced down. By now, we should also know better than to ever go outside without a camera, and there wasn't time to get one when the animal stopped blinking at Ava's toe and ambled into the confines of the foliage, which, to my relief, explains the scuffling noises I heard coming from there yesterday. I hope. We think it is a female hedgehog with a nest hidden deep inside. George showed no interest in her whatsoever, and because of their protective thorny coats we're not concerned for the safety of the little ones, we only want to see them.

From the few encounters I've had, hedgehogs seem more curious than afraid of people, but they're nocturnal and, until now, I've not seen them active other than at nighttime. This is the longest day of the year, though, and I suppose Mama must forage by her biological clock regardless what the sun tells her, and since they're so approachable it's fortunate that they do not invite cuddling. I informed my wife, who I sensed was considering the possibilities, that hedgehogs are notoriously overburdened by fleas. Still it's nice to think that a family of them nests beneath the wild fuchsia bush in our garden.

Devoting so much time to the garden cuts into more remunerative activities in the studio and soon I'll have to forsake the soil to toil in the oil, but, as years advance, I notice that the nurturing of new and tender plants holds great appeal. It's been a long while since we've been allowed much freedom for this indulgence, but after he'd been with us enough years to become a fixed part of the surroundings, Kevin O'Mahoney departed towards rougher pastures to enhance, and fresher minds to mold. His artistic temperament and, indeed, fine talent, would brook no interference in his grounds, or independent ideas that he didn't think of first. In truth, he was bored. His remarkable achievements had matured to a point of mostly needing just maintenance; at least, that was our hope, but to my requests for even more simple ground covering and the undemanding flowering shrubs to combat weeds and lighten his workload though not his paycheck, he cast the tolerant eye heavenward, sighed, "if that's what you REALLY want," and continued to devise new out-of-the-way places in which to secret oneself and ponder fairy dells—places never used—and the only pondering I managed was why the hell did he take away large parts of grown shrubbery and wild fuschia and open a little wall to the eastern breezes from which I sought shelter in the mornings and where I'd requested even more of the same in the first place?

Mostly our ideas were based on concern for his health. Like us all, he was slowing down, the work was hard; we had enough floral beauty and shrubs, with little attention, grow to massive size quite happily on their own in this climate. But clearly Kevin O considered it a test of wills where, of course, he always emerged the victor to whom we sublimated and coddled. Finally with a surge of testosterone, when I overheard Ava pleading with him about woodruff or some such and because we'd already heard from everyone else that he intended to quit, I pointed out the little disparities in our arrangements these long years standing, that the land was listed in *our* name.

We've never sacked anyone in our lives and as I stormed into the house I heard Ava ask him to reconsider, but he left of his own volition and returned a portion of the bonus we added to his severance pay. We weren't actually upset. God knows, through the seasons, we grew hardened to his outbursts of high dudgeon eliciting histrionics worthy of the Abbey players, and never allowed them to interfere with our friendship.

We quite miss the O'Mahoney venomous diatribes regarding mankind—particularly friends and citizens who represent it locally—and his narrative expansions that surpass common blarney and cry out to be printed and bound in fine leathers. Every time we stroll the grounds or revel in a compliment about them, we bless Kevin O—give him the credit and praise deserved because underneath it all lies a kind and timid soul. We are fortunate he was an integral part of our lives for such a long time. But—oh, the calm. The enjoyment of working together in the garden now that he is not.

Happily the amiable Bob remains. Coming twice a week, he does cracker-jack handy work as well as gardening, and the place looks as if it were tended daily which, counting our efforts, I suppose it is. We no longer encounter lovely surprises, wee blossoms peeking from under steps and the like for Ava to discover, but Ava can also plant the vegetables she wants, where she wants them, now, and if our flower displays are more plebeian, I am learning. I have a painter's eye and, until I gain more knowledge, I can select what I think looks right for the time being. And it's fun. I added flowering shrubs like crazy. The wall is replaced, the fuschia allowed free growth for shelter once more.

Kevin, who constructed the ponds and terraces and installed stone steps advancing up the hill with all the skill of the Incas, reacted to my yearly pleas for some sort of rockery in the front of the house pleasantly, but said he didn't understand what I meant. Now that I no longer have to beg permission, I built the damned thing myself and it looks great. The part of the place one saw first was always the last attended and often summer was nearly through before this difficult patch met the splendor of the rest. Hardy alpine plants, requiring almost no care, dance around the stones now. The few weeds are within control and my wife is getting just a bit sick of my smugness. I also planted a baby elder tree in the very spot where Kevin had the other one that I'd cosseted into substantial size cut down. He hated that tree, said that Judas was hanged from an elder tree. So?

Bob has introduced an innovative watering system and netting barriers thwarting the birds at berry time. All is tidy, soothing the Virgo id, and—best of all—we no longer fight the seemingly futile battle against blanket moss in the ponds that O'Mahoney blamed on O'Regan, insisting that it was the result of some farming chemical that filtered down from Timmy's lands, and which we cleared up almost instantly after we sent for a solution from one of Bob's gardening weeklies that advised how to cope with the problem common to garden ponds everywhere.

It's nice these mornings—I'm enjoying breakfast outdoors to watch the fish feeding, too, and, now that the water is clearer than it's been for years, I've installed a little clay mermaid riding a fish that Kevin O'Mahoney fashioned and presented me when I admired it at his house during a Sunday lunch. Placed at the bottom of the pond, a reminder of many good times and a gifted friend, she also evokes a more disturbing memory in that the last time I watched a mermaid playing in a fishpond, I made her myself and I was eight years old.

This evening was so lovely we would have remained outside until bedtime, but when I noticed that the starlings had reassembled on some distant telephone wires, and remarked that birds gathered in that manner remind me of musical notes on a scale, and tried humming the tune I thought they composed, Ava abruptly announced that she had to start dinner and fled into the house.

In spite of her rather pointed departure, my girl kept of high humor and gave us a great dinner. No further mention was made in reference to my attempted serenade of the starlings and on an ordinary day that probably would have been the end of any fowl experience, but halfway through the meal Ava squealed, began punching my shoulder and repeating my Christian name until it penetrated that she was trying to tell me to look outside where a shellduck and nine babies paraded in single file just below the window.

They turned at the end of our house where the boreen bends and narrows down to the sea, which was, obviously, the mother's intended destination, and when she marched them back and forth a few times, we realized she was confused, and in their efforts to keep up, the ducklings were very tired.

Shellducks are marsh nesters; she must've moved them a long distance, and to prevent them waddling tiny webbed feet raw—with the odd thought that on a larger scale I'd already done this once today—I went down to drive them towards the beach. Mama commanded something at my appearance which made the kids stay very still, huddled into a turned-up corner of a soggy piece of corrugated cardboard blown onto the lane. She didn't attempt to fly, just kept walking until I was close enough to touch the little ones, and then quacked another order which sent them scurrying in pursuit with more speed than I thought possible under the circumstances (we keep the path cropped relatively short but not in terms of little ducks). Once assured the mother had them fixed on a steady course, I turned back to see Ava, grinning through tears, and holding a camera in the window, and I went in to join her and finish our supper.

Something recently provoked the thought that very soon I shall reach the end of my fifty-ninth year, and I needed a good laugh. I got two in the afternoon post. Although my elderly sweetheart who sold us milk in gin bottles has gone to claim her rewards, some things remain sacred. Didn't Kitty send fresh milk in a Power's Whiskey bottle down to us with the postman because he called at their farm first? Along with milk, Cyril delivered a questionnaire advising that I've been suggested as a candidate for inclusion in *Who's Who in the World*. But that wasn't from Kitty O'Regan. She knows better.

I shall thank them very much, explain they've made a flattering but definite error. Unless they also publish "Friends of Who's Who" I would fail to pass their qualifications to such a degree it might embarrass us all. Anyone with a substantial credit card must be listed on their computer printout. I have no illusions otherwise but it did start me thinking: how far the journey that brought me to a position where my name would even crop up. We do, indeed, consider the accomplished and the celebrated among close friends of various circumstances and nationalities. It isn't unusual now to visit private houses in foreign countries, and if we still wonder at our familiarity with some of the world's major cities and obscure villages, too, I no longer feel the same thrill that prompted my writing initially. I continue to be amazed. Intrigued by our lifestyle, I'm always curious as to what waits around the corner. Where next year or next month or tomorrow will find us. Who we'll meet. But I've come to regard serendipity as the norm.

Ava has retired as this magical day, yet in twilight, draws to a close and I'm weary, too. Not sleepy. Deeply content, with that feeling of rightness that comes from working hard in good air and sunshine, smelling the ocean and relishing the creatures around us, and I've been considering that now is the happiest note on which to quit this accounting. There have been so many endings. And beginnings. Soon another decade for me as I creep down the mountain on—I trust—a long and slow descent. Kevin and Tyler build families of their own. Ava continues to soar and carries me with her shining spirit. But there seems little reason to continue recording for family interest. The village caught up with the century. A big new school with the only planetarium in Ireland overlooks the harbor. Grocery shops have expanded. Modernized. And, sadly, old Mr. Hegarty no longer totals up my purchases on a biscuit box and tells me to pay him at a later time when there is less traffic at the check-out counter. We have a pharmacist; the telephone system has long since gone automatic; the postal vans have changed from orange to green; and the passing of Fred and even little P.-D. brought to a close a special period in our lives together. In the words of my father-in-law: it's another phase.

Men bent in some haste on insuring the lineage, Kevin and Tyler are grown up. I, grown older. But Ava, I feel, has grown the most, and now while it remains midsummer's night for just a little longer, I round off this sporadic diary on the anniversary of when we first began our dream, and close the notebook with a salute to our own first lady.

There are those who say we've got it backwards but, to my thinking, Ava's step in seven-league wellies from California's Beverly Hills to Ireland's seacoast was spot on target and somewhere along the way she came to an understanding with the soil: a comprehension of the land and its produce that kept us healthier, happier—certainly saner—than Rodeo Drive ever could.

But she never learned to pivot.

This is my valentine. Like our photo albums intended as a

memento of a family time. Purposely frivolous. I want the memories pleasant. By and large they are. We are a fortunate lot. Given our blessings, I consider it immoral not to be basically happy, nice people, and that brings me to the point I've been implying from the start. I began these observances for the future interest and, possibly, amusement of grandchildren formed in the yawn of time, but I really kept the journal because the three I hold most dear are caring individuals. Decent and special. I thought somewhere that should be written.

Thanks, Guys,
The Grouch

At home in Ireland, 1975.

Index

A

B

C

D

F

G

H

J

K

L

M

N

O

P